Essays in
Phenomenological
Theology

Essays in Phenomenological Theology

Edited by
Steven W. Laycock
and
James G. Hart

State University of New York Press

Published by
State University of New York Press, Albany

©1986 State University of New York

All rights reserved

Printed in the United States of America

For information, address State University of New York
Press, State University Plaza, Albany, N.Y., 12246

Library of Congress Cataloging-in-Publication Data
Main entry under title:

Essays in phenomenological theology.

   Includes index.
   1. Phenomenology—Congresses.   2. Theology—
Congresses.   3. Philosophical theology—Congresses.
I. Laycock, Steven William.   Hart, James G.,
1936-

B829.5.E79 1986   230   85-14674
ISBN 0-88706-164-8
ISBN 0-88706-165-6 (pbk.)

Contents

Preface

The present volume is devoted to the application of phenomenological concepts and methods to the issues typical of philosophical theology and philosophy of religion: the being and nature of God, and the divine modes of relatedness to nature, to society, and to the self. An important, though by no means exclusive, source of inspiration for this collection was the first Conference on Phenomenological Philosophical Theology, held at Indiana University, Bloomington, in the spring of 1982, coordinated by Professor James G. Hart, and sponsored by the Lilly Endowment, Inc., of Indianapolis, which sponsorship the editors acknowledge with much appreciation. The project of providing philosophers and philosophical theologians a volume of this sort has its inspiration, however, no less in the rapidly expanding *corpus* of work in phenomenological theology currently appearing. Selection of essays for the present volume was governed in large measure by the editors' intent to assemble, from significant contemporary manifestations, a broad and representative spectrum of phenomenological-theological persuasions.

Contributors

JAMES BUCHANAN, Assistant Professor of Religious Studies at the University of Montana, has published in the areas of phenomenology, comparative philosophy of religion, and Taoism, and is the author of *The Myths of Understanding: Science, Hermeneutics, and Rhetorics in the Study of Religion* (forthcoming.)

CHARLES COURTNEY, Professor of Philosophy of Religion at The Theological and Graduate Schools of Drew University, has published in the areas of French philosophy of religion and the implications of interreligious understanding. He is the translator of *The Problem of God in Philosophy of Religion*, by Henry Duméry.

JOHN N. FINDLAY is presently the Bowne Professor of Philosophy at Boston University. He has written book-length studies of Meinong, Hegel, Plato, and most recently, Kant in *Kant and the Transcendental Object*. His phenomenological ethics is entitled *Values and Intentions*. The most elaborate statement of his phenomenological philosophical theology is to be found in the two volumes of Gifford Lectures: *The Discipline of the Cave* and *The Transcendence of the Cave*, to which his *Ascent to the Absolute* is a companion piece. He is also the translator of Husserl's *Logical Investigations*.

JAMES G. HART is a member of the Religious Studies faculty at Indiana University. With John Maraldo, he is the co-author of the commentary and the co-translator of *The Piety of Thinking: Essays by Martin Heidegger*. He has published essays on the phenomenology of religion and the philosophy of mind. He is presently completing a work on an Husserlian social philosophy.

ISO KERN has spent much of the last decade in Beijing, China. He is presently writing on the Chinese Buddhist reception of Christianity in the 17th century. He has published significant essays on Husserl and is the author of *Husserl und Kant* and *Idee und Methode der Philosophie.* He is also the editor of the three volumes of *Husserliana: Zur Phänomenologie der Intersubjectivität.*

STEVEN W. LAYCOCK is a member of the philosophy faculty at The University of Hawaii at Manoa. His essays fall largely in the areas of phenomenological axiology and phenomenological theology and include work on Anselm and Hui-neng, as well as a critique of Gustav Bergmann's "The Ontology of Edmund Husserl." He is the author of *Foundations for a Phenomenological Theology* (forthcoming).

THOMAS PRUFER has taught philosophy since 1960 at The Catholic University of America in Washington, D.C. He received a doctorate in 1959 from the University of Munich on *Sein und Wort nach Thomas von Aquin* and has written on Plato, Aristotle, Augustine, Hume, Husserl, Heidegger, and Evelyn Waugh. Notable among his contributions to phenomenology are his essays, "Welt, Ich und Zeit in der Sprache," "An Outline of Some Husserlian Distinctions and Strategies, Especially in the 'Crisis'," and "Reduction and Constitution." He received the Danforth Foundation's Harbison Award for Distinguished Teaching.

ROBERT R. WILLIAMS, Professor of Philosophy at Hiram College, has published extensively in the area of Continental philosophy and is the author of *Schleiermacher the Theologian: The Construction of the Doctrine of God.* He held the post of Fulbright Senior Research professor in Tubingen, West Germany in 1981-82 and is currently completing a book-length study of Hegel's concept of Recognition and *Geist.*

STEVEN W. LAYCOCK

1. *Introduction: Toward an Overview of Phenomenological Theology*

Phenomenological theology, as it has appeared within the contemporary phenomenological movement, is an inchoate discipline, laboring to articulate its own methods and subject matter, and it would be ill-conceived to seize advantage of its nascency in order to polemicize in favor of one of the positions represented in the present volume to the detriment of others. Rather, it is my hope that the following exercise in intellectual cartography might prove of somewhat greater worth. Phenomenological theology is an uncharted philosophical terrain concealing significant autochthonous issues that deserve to be mapped. In the following few pages I shall attempt to tease out important disagreements concerning the nature and modes of relatedness of the Divine implicit in the various essays at hand. Before taking up this task, however, I feel that a few general remarks are in order concerning the philosophical techniques wielded by practitioners of phenomenological theology.

Phenomenological Theology and Its Methods

In a brief passage extracted from a conversation with Sr. Adelgundis Jaegerschmidt, OSB, Husserl articulates with precision and with ringing significance the predominant vector and context of phenomenological theology:

> The life of humans is nothing but a way to God. I try to reach this goal without theological proofs, methods, supports; namely, to arrive *at*

1

God without God. I, as it were, must eliminate God from my scientific existence in order to pave the way to God for humans who do not have, as you do, the certainty of faith through the Church. I know my procedure could be dangerous for me were I not a human deeply bound to God and a faithful Christian.[1]

This is not the voice of an apostate seeking to rejoin the fold of the faithful. Nor is it the utterance of the Psalmic 'fool' who saith in his heart, "There is no God," but who endeavors nonetheless to achieve that metanoetic transformation which would make the desert of nihilism and absurdity blossom with abundant meaningfulness. It is, rather, the candid avowal of a perpetual phenomenological 'beginner' seeking to articulate the sense of the Divine from the matrix of prearticulate experience.

The reader need not be lectured by me concerning the niceties of phenomenological methodology. Several of the papers contributed to this volume contain fine expositions of the general phenomenological procedures of *epoche*, reduction, free variation in imagination, and reconstruction. Nor is it nececessary, at the outset, to elaborate the significant results of phenomenological investigation. Husserl himself has contributed to the phenomenological enterprise rich and lucid foundational explorations of many regions and levels of experience, many specific 'phenomenologies.' And his students and followers have amplified his insights and provided original 'phenomenologies' of their own. One can say no less, then, of phenomenological theology than that it is offered in the spirit of an original phenomenological investigation of a specific 'region' of experience recoverable through recognizably phenomenological techniques and strategies. But one can say more. Phenomenological theology is the specific phenomenology *of God.* And it is perhaps evident from the passage quoted above that Husserl regarded phenomenological theology as the 'end' of philosophy, for the sake of which his own incessantly renegotiated 'beginnings' were enacted.

"Phenomenology", of course, is not merely a name for whatever Husserl himself has wrought. Certainly those who stand, wholly or primarily, within his philosophical shadow are no less to be accounted phenomenologists. And, although perhaps with somewhat less appropriateness, we may legitimately agree to deem "phenomenological" even those philosophies that were developed chronologically prior to Husserl's but nonetheless fall within a certain recognizable dimension of philosophical concern and practice continuous with that of the contemporary phenomenological movement. For example, borrowing the term from Lambert, Kant referred to his precritical work as 'phenomenology'. Fichte's thought provided phenomenological inspiration even for Husserl. And, as Williams's essay will ably attest, Hegel's magnificent conceptual edifice is profoundly phenomenological. But certainly phenomenology, or 'protophenomenology', did not begin with Kant. As Kern will teach us, there may be reason to welcome even the Buddha and the 'old master', Lao-tzu, as phenomenologists for their meditative insights regarding the nature of egological 'causality'. Augustine's writings are, in part, brilliantly phenomenological. And Plotinus's transformation of meditation into philosophical technique is no less so, as eloquently illustrated in the lovely phenomenological neoplatonic vision that Findlay shares with us, as well as in Courtney's fine exposition of Duméry's phenomenology of the One.

Phenomenology, in a sense of sufficient amplitude to embrace both Husserl's ancestors and his progeny, is specified in terms of two coordinates: its subject matter and its method, grist and mill. Phenomenology applies itself, not surprisingly, to "phenomena" (roughly, though *only* roughly: appearances), and does so through "reflection". But disagreement breaks out immediately among the practitioners of phenomenology concerning the nature of phenomena and of the reflective method. For Kant, phenomena are generated by the noumena that they occlude. For Husserl, there is nothing of the proto-etiology posited by Kant spanning noumena and phenomena. A phenomenon is rather an object (a thing-in-itself) *as it appears*. The 'thing itself' is revealed in the appearance of it. For Kant, phenomena are appearances-to a 'deduced' transcendental ego, but are not, except in the proto-etiological sense, appearances-*of* the objects they conceal. In Sartre's vision of the egoless impersonality of consciousness, phenomena, while decidedly appearances-of, are not appearances-to. And for Husserl, an appearance is necessarily endowed with both 'genitive' and 'dative' reference. For Husserl, the reflective method of phenomenology is transcendental, involving a 'suspension' of our natural doxastic positing of the world. For Heidegger, Sartre and Merleau-Ponty, our very being-in-the-world precludes the possibility of a 'complete' reduction.

While our subject/method coordinates offer little hope of unanimity among those whom we would classify as phenomenologists, they at least enable us to isolate a certain range of philosophical views as decidedly phenomenological by virtue of the following two, perhaps insufficiently nuanced, distinctions: Philosophies either take phenomena as their subject matter or they do not; and philosophies are either reflectively achieved or they are not. Thus is generated the following fourfold schema of philosophical permutations:

1. Philosophies that take phenomena as their subject matter and that are reflectively achieved.

2. Philosophies that take phenomena as their subject matter but that are not reflectively achieved.

3. Philosophies that do not take phenomena as their subject matter but that are reflectively achieved.

4. Philosophies that do not take phenomena as their subject matter and are not reflectively achieved.

Patently, philosophies falling under category (1) are phenomenological, and philosophies falling under category (4) are not. But categories (2) and (3) may well give us pause.

At the bottommost stratum of Husserl's 'archaeology' of the mind we find the 'primal presencing' brought to light in Hart's "Précis," the very wellspring and ineluctable condition of consciousness. But the capacity of reflection necessary to descend to this chthonic depth becomes problematic precisely because the living present is the very source of the reflective experience itself, the 'eye' that cannot see itself. Here reflection confronts the limit of its phenomenological utility, and in the face of certain pressing methodological questions, we are forced to rely upon the technique of 'reconstruction', extrapolating, as it were, from the vectors established by previous reflective-eidetic analysis. Yet the theory of primal presencing is assuredly integral to Husserl's phenomenology. Likewise, the transcendental ego of Husserlian phenomenology can only equivocally, and with well-nuanced reservations, be regarded as a 'phenomenon'. It is not an object but a subject, and consequently not an object-as-it appears. Yet again, the theory of transcendental egology is clearly integral to Husserlian phenomenology. Our intuitions regarding categories (2) and (3) await clarification through a more adequate delimitation of the coordinates of concern and practice.

If we revise our conception of the subject matter of phenomenology to include not only phenomena but also anything essentially connected with phenomena, and if we enlarge our conception of phenomenological method to include eidetic and conceptual techniques that, while presupposing reflection, nonetheless serve to extrapolate beyond the limits of reflective access, the schema thus generated confines phenomenological views exclusively to category (1). Setting aside Husserl's occasional discussions of reconstruction and postulation, one might claim that there simply is no philosophically significant subject matter beyond the range of an eidetically registrable essential connection with the phenomenal and no genuinely philosophical method that does not presuppose the reflective turn. Were this so, we should have succeeded in confining not only phenomenology, but all of philosophy, to category (1).

Be that as it may, it is clear that a distinctively *phenomenological* theology—in contradistinction to either a 'positive' theology, with its assumption of textual or traditional authoritarianism, or a speculative-natural theology, with its procedures of deductive and inductive derivation—seeks to discover its Subject Matter, the Divine (*theos*), in that web of intuitively articulable necessities in which phenomena are caught and seeks to do so by means of the reductive-eidetic-reconstructive techniques characteristic of phenomenology. Phenomenological theology, in Husserl's exquisite phrase, seeks to reach "God without God."

The phrase *God without God* might readily appear to be an ill-fated solecism to those whose philosophical sensibilities are moulded by speculative theology. But far from being an abandonment of philosophical concern for the issues surrounding the being and nature of God, Husserl's renunciation of the proofs and methods of (natural) 'theology' represents, rather, a rejection of the very pattern of thought that halts, uncomprehending, at this arresting phrase. Speculative theology predominantly involves the attempt to *deduce* the existence, essence, and modes of relatedness of God from principles at least as rich in implicative content as that of 'God exists'. The phenomenologist's objection to this procedure is not merely a reaction to the vaulting impiety of imagining God as 'following' from more fundamental principles and thus being led around on a 'chain' of deductive steps. The impropriety is less an offense against fastidious relgious sentiments and more a violation of rigorous phenomenological method.

While this is not the place to explore in any detail the series of nested 'reductions' evolved in Husserl's insistent attempts to get at the 'affairs themselves', it is appropriate to note here that the reduction has at least the function of ruling out, from the very inception of philosophical endeavor, the *matabasis eis allo genos*, which would otherwise be involved in the attempt to account for the transcendental in terms of the natural dimension of consciousness. And the circumvention of this 'category mistake' has the concomitant effect, little remarked, of rendering impracticable the fallacy of *petitio principii*. The reflective 'suspension' of operative theological beliefs, in what we might call the 'theological *epoche*' and its attendant disposition, the 'theological reduction', ensures that a properly phenomenological theology does not beg crucial questions concerning the theological issues under investigation. Husserl's theological path, an alternative to Jaegerschmidt's "certainty of faith through the Church," explicitly assumes that insight concerning the divine Being and Essence is achievable as the culmination of scientific advance. "God without God" is at least the God delivered to philosophical thought—delivered, that is, to the reflection characteristic of philosophy as a "strict science"—without fallacious circularity.

As useful as valid deductive procedures may be within certain contexts, it is easily seen that valid deduction, the formal function of which is merely the transmission of truth from premise to conclusion, is, from a logical point of view, generally question-begging. Barring the so-called 'paradoxes of implication' deplored by relevance logicians (e.g., the implication of any proposition by every contradiction and the implication by every proposition of any tautology), if a proposition, p, implies a second proposition, q, then p implicity 'contains' q. That is, p, is equivalent to a complex proposition of the form 'q & r & s . . . .' But ignoring irrelevant content, the implication then is, quite patently: that which holds between q (as contained implicitly in the premise) and q (as the explicated conclusion). Or more perspicuously still, the real inference is simply 'q because q', which is inescapably question-begging.

In its etymologically original sense, de-duction is, of course, a 'leading' of thought, in a disciplined manner, 'away' from a given discursively articulated perspective and, by suggestion, 'toward' another perspective lying, as it were, on this 'way' of thought. And it is not entirely fair to condemn the traditional natural-theological 'proofs' for the existence, and for certain aspects of the nature, of God as unambiguously circular. Indeed, such proofs may be conceived as strategies to induce a metanoetic shift of perspective whereby the world comes to be seen in the light of a divine agency. Yet undeniably, natural-theological proofs can be, and frequently are, formulated as formal-logical inferences and as such are culpable of *petitio principii.* If the ontological argument of Anselm, for example (a movement of thought that will receive further attention as we proceed), is understood as a valid deductive inference, 'God exists' being implicitly contained in the thesis that God is that-than-which-no-greater-can-be-thought, it amounts to little more than the question-begging inference, 'God exists because God exists.' The theological reduction, the attempt to arrive at God 'without God' (i.e., as the 'destination' of the endless march of 'strict science'), sharply undercuts the formal-deductive procedures of speculative theology. To infer theological truths is thereby to have assumed them, to pull the same rabbit out of the hat that was previously surreptitiously concealed within it. And the interest of phenomenological theology is decidedly invested in the 'rabbit', not in the 'trick'.

Even granting that the deduction of a given theological thesis, p, from a premise or conjunction of premises, q, is logically progressive, we are moved to inquire into the truth of q. If q, in turn, is deduced from r, the level of our inquiry into the truth of p is removed still another step. It quickly becomes evident that, if p is to be capable of verification, then either it, or a privileged 'link' in some deductive chain leading to it, must, in some way, be nondeductively determined to be true. Infinite chains clearly preclude verification. And finite chains, as we have seen, involve a fallacious assumption of the very thesis to be demonstrated.

Accordingly, phenomenological theology proceeds directly to the heart of the matter, attempting to dispel the mists that would shroud the pristine self-evidence of theological truth. Its task, like that of phenomenology generally, is primarily that of clarification, elucidation, and the dissolution of whatever would cloud the crystalline lucidity of eidetic registration. It has often been said that, whereas speculative philosophy attempts to explain, phenomenology seeks only to describe. And this accords well with the antideductionist methodology of phenomenology. Phenomenological description has nothing to do with the mere registration of empirical matters of fact. Nor does it involve the framing of empirical generalizations. Explanation, on one prevalent reading, is no more than the implication of a certain body of data by a given explanatory hypothesis. It has become a commonplace that, except in cases of 'perfect' induction, a given body of empirical data may be subject to an indefinite array of hypothetical accounts, each serving, as it were, as a 'perspective' upon the data to be explained. Hence, while one explanatory hypothesis may be 'better' in certain canonical respects than the next, empirical generalizations cannot pretend to the self-evidence demanded by phenomenology. And empirical *explananda*, while perhaps epistemologically more secure than their hypothetical accounts, certainly do not comprise the stuff of which philosophy, let alone philosophical theology, is made.

The Nature of God

A typical example of 'self-evident' phenomenological judgment is the thesis, extracted from noematic investigations, that color cannot exist without spatial extent. To 'see' this is not to witness a 'relation' spanning color and extension. There is no *tertium quid* inserted between the two determinations. Color and spatial spread are *immediately* united, and are intuitively 'seen' to be so in eidetic intuition. Phenomenological theology strives for the same quality of lucidity and apodicticity in its pronouncements concerning the being and essence of God.

In our example, color is a 'moment', an eidetically inseparable 'part', of extent. Whereas the cap of my pen is both physically and conceptually separable from the pen itself, being thus, in Husserl's acceptation, a 'piece' and not a 'moment' of the pen, its specific affordability, its capacity, under certain conditions, to be used as a pen is typically used is an inseparable moment of the pen *qua* pen. Precisely four modes of eidetic relatedness (not to say 'relations') may obtain between determinations *A* and *B*: (1) *A* may 'found' *B*; (2) *B* may 'found' *A*; (3) *A* and *B* may reciprocally 'found' one another; and (4), the 'null mode', neither *A* nor *B* may 'found' the other (where 'founding' is the eidetically registrable ontological dependence of one determination upon another). And all phenomenological investigation involves the descriptive registration of founding relationships among the reflectively revealed determinations of experience. Having said as much, we are now prepared to express, with somewhat greater precision, a crucial assumption concerning the Subject Matter of phenomenological theology. The 'God of the phenomenologist' may be a 'Moment' founded upon some other determination of experience (and hence, an *abstractum* in the appropriate Husserlian sense), or a

Being that itself founds other determinations of experience (a *concretum*), or again, a 'Determination' standing in the relationship of reciprocal founding with another determination, or finally, a complex Being comprising variously related 'parts.' The very possibility of phenomenological theology precludes the consideration of Deity as a mere 'piece', as a Being 'null-related' to experience. Hence, the purported truth of any doctrine according to which our *only* cognitive access to God occurs through the entirely contingent, the 'gracious', irruption of the divine Presence into human experience would thereby invalidate the project and falsify the results of phenomenological theology.

Several candidates for phenomenological-theological Subject Matter pass immediately in review. God, as we have noted, may be conceived as founded *abstractum* (Object), founding *concretum* (Subject), as a 'simple' and internally undirempted abstract/concrete determination of experience, or perhaps as a 'complex' Subject/Object embracing subject and object as 'parts'. As 'Object' God might be understood as a very special item *within* the perceptual world, much as the human-formed Zeus of the Greek imagination. Or God, at least in one of the divine hypostatic emanations, might, as Findlay urges, be conceived as a logically unique denizen of the *topos noetos*, "an object in which *all* suprapersonal Values will be present together." God as Holy Spirit is, for Findlay, "a unity of those very Values themselves, a unique, logical unity that not only places such a synthesis infinitely beyond any synthesis of instances but also opens its component excellences to infinite forms and degrees of participation." God is not an entity exemplifying value, a valuable 'Object', since "the most glorious *instance* of Values is only one among others and cannot be worshipped," but is rather the very Framework in which Values, the simultaneous exemplification of which would be impracticable or inconsistent, are set. Or God might, alternatively, be conceived as the ultimately transcendent Object of all objects, the very World itself as the ultimate teleological "pole" of all intentional activity, or again, as the Horizon of all horizons, as Being (in at least one Heideggerian sense).

Williams's impressive essay clearly warns against the snare cast by certain critics of transcendental phenomenology—notably Ricoeur—who would entangle such a God-Object theology in unwitting atheism. If God is an 'Object' and thus a 'predicate', or abstract moment, constitutive of transcendental subjectivity, then the Divine has no more reality than a 'projection', a mere objectification, the being of which is wholly dependent upon synthetic-constitutive activity. Such a Feuerbachian 'theism' is equally and indifferently an atheism. Hence, in Williams's characterization of Ricoeur's riposte, "to introduce a transcendental method into theology is like inviting an atheistic Trojan horse." The God-Object of Findlay's theology, however, is designed to circumvent the subtle atheism of which Ricoeur warns. Inasmuch as God "transcends the distinction between subject and predicate or between existence and essence," the Findlayan Unity of Values cannot Itself be said to be a 'predicate' of transcendental subjectivity. According to Williams, however, a realistic, hence a neoplatonic, God-Object fares little better. For Hegel, and for Williams following him, God as *ens realissimum*, a supremely real entity but an independently existing *entity* nonetheless, is of necessity a bloodless abstraction.

For Duméry, however, as portrayed by Courtney, "the Absolute is not an object. It is that by which there are objects." The Absolute is "transordinal, beyond determination, and . . . pure unity or pure act." Being transordinal, God cannot be set in series, even in binary, contrastive polarity. God is not 'this' as opposed to 'that'. Like Findlay's Holy Spirit, Dumery's Absolute is not 'predicate' as opposed to 'subject', or 'being' as opposed to 'essence'. And the Absolute, moreover, is not *abstract* as opposed to *concrete*, 'Object' as opposed to 'Subject'. The capacity to fall into binary contrasts is exclusively characteristic of mundane objects and finite subjects. But transcending abstraction and concretion, the Absolute of Dumery's theology is clearly not subject to the Hegelian rejection of the *ens realissimum* as an ideational will-o'-the-wisp. Kern's conception of the One furthers the logic of the Dumeryan Absolute. Though the One 'transcends' the schemata of contrast, It does not exist 'beyond' the realm of reciprocally contrasting entities. "If such a being were outside, it would exist in opposition to the transitory; it would thereby draw limitation and relativity into its own being." For Kern, the One, as manifested through its egological facet, is at least roughly congruent with the Buddhist conception of Absolute Nothingness (*sunyata*).

Ricoeur's charge of atheism is, of course, otiose against a God conceived as divine 'Subject'. As Subject, Deity might be understood as the Synthesis of all monadic conscious life, or as one universal and eternal Act of consciousness. Perhaps there is something 'divine' about the empty intending of the World-pole co-occurrent with every monadic intentional act. Or then again, perhaps the Divine lies deeper than monadic act-life. God might be conceived as the 'Primal Presencing' that is the chthonic Source of monadic intentional activity, or perhaps, following Hart, as the entelechial moment of primal presencing, "the infinite ideal of perfection and the good, immanent within the monadic universe in a way that establishes an *eros* for realization." Or again, perhaps God is to be regarded in part, as my own contribution suggests, as the Subject of all subjects, whose act-life is mediated by the universal, intersubjective community of monadic subjects.

Or finally, perhaps God lies on both sides of the subject/object divide, the absolute Subject-Object, Alpha and Omega, Beginning and End, as several of our contributors contend. In Williams's Hegelian view, for example, God is the absolute identity of identity and nonidentity, the unity of objective synthesis and subjective dispersion, a notion reminiscent, in certain respects, of Husserl's transcendental subjectivity. "God is God's own other," writes Williams; "God can maintain himself in the process of self-othering self-negation." For Hart, the divine entelechial principle accounts for "the single, absolute, intersubjective intentional life with its dual aspects of ego-pole/world-pole, constituting/constituted, reason/being, appearings of what appears and what appears, immanent being and transcendent being, and so forth." And in my own reading, God is seen not only as the Subject of all subjects but as the Object of all objects as well. God-as-Subject intends God-as-Object, through the mediation of the intersubjective community.

The foregoing considerations display the range of philosophemically variant conceptions of the nature of God as illustrated in the phenomenological-theological positions represented in the present volume. But phenemonological theology does not halt here. The various modes of relatedness in which the Divine is engaged are subject to phenomenological investigation as well. And Kern's "Trinity" of dimensions within which human life is lived, the three 'faces' of the One—*Nature, Society*, and *Self*—affords a very helpful tripartite schema for considering the 'manners' of a deific relatedness.

God and Nature

Prufer's rich essay reflects the striking Thomist insight, elaborated in Sokolowski's fine exposition *The God of Faith and Reason* (South

Bend: Notre Dame Press, 1982), that the Being answering to the Anselmian formula, "that-than-which-no-greater-can-be-thought," introduces with the act of world-creation no value exceeding the
supreme value of God prior to, or considered independently of, creation. The complex *God-plus-the-world* is not 'greater' than God alone,
else patently a being is conceivable that is 'greater' than God. It
follows, then, that the divine creative activity is atelic, a radically free
expression enacted out of the insuperable abundance of divine
greatness, which in no way enhances that greatness. God does not act
in order to achieve some greater good. For no greater good can be
achieved. Creation is, as Prufer stresses, "gratuitous." God is neither
logically nor axiologically compelled to create.

The world ('nature') can be seen, of course, either as the product
of divine creative fiat or, as it was prevalently regarded by the Greeks,
as a sempiternal and self-existent being. Creationism is thus, as it were,
a 'perspective' on the world. But perspectives are clearly underdeter-
mined by their objects, and world-perspectives are no exception. To
say that creationism is a 'world-perspective' is thus to recognize that
there is nothing about the world itself that *guarantees* its truth. Hence,
a phenomenological explication of the sense of 'world' cannot
legitimate our regarding it as 'creation'. The sense of 'creation' is not,
then, a *moment* of the sense of 'world', but a *piece*. Hence, since
phenomenology aspires foremostly to establish founding relationships,
creationism is *eo ipso* precluded from preferential phenomenological-
theological consideration. Were the reference of the sense of 'creation' to the Creator the *only* mode of conscious access of which we are
capable, then assuredly phenomenological theology would be impossible. Creationism is preserved as a possibility for
phenomenological theology either through the admission that the
eidetic interlocking of the notions of Creator and creation is strictly irrelevant to the phenomenological-theological revelation of the Divine
or through the denial of its perspectival character, and the consequent
assertion that the very being-sense of 'world' entails its createdness.

The Prufer/Sokolowski reading of the Anselmian formula
assumes, clearly, the conceptual separability of God and world. The
inference from "God is that-than-which-no-greater-can-be-thought"
to "God-plus-the-world is not greater than God alone" presupposes
that God-plus-the-world can, indeed, be *thought*. But God-plus-the-
world is a contingent amalgam. So long as creationism is understood
as a world-perspective, 'world' can be understood without reference

to a Being who creates the world *ex nihilo*. And in Prufer's phenomenological Thomist view of creation, God is essentially to be conceived independently of world. The intelligibility of 'God-plus-the-world' thus presupposes the intelligibility of their merely contingent relatedness.

Should it turn out, however, as the Prufer/Sokolowski reading seems to permit, that the disclosure of the world makes necessary reference to a divine 'pole' of unity as a condition for its manifestation, a species of 'pantheism' being thus capable of phenomenological verification and thus a necessary truth, the inference from Anselm's definition to 'God-plus-the-world is not greater than God alone' immediately loses its assumed legitimacy, the Anselmian formula falling prey to reductio ad absurdum, since 'God-plus-the-world is not greater than God alone' would then entail the evident contradiction, 'God-plus-the-world is contingent (in virtue of its meaning) and non-contingent (in virtue of our present assumption of pantheism)'. Findlay, for one, asserts that "pantheism, when it does not try to *compose* Divinity out of what streams from Divinity, is obviously an absolute aspect of truth."

But one need not appeal solely to pantheism in order to undercut the Prufer/Sokolowski inference. Should Deity turn out to be a moment, perhaps even a reciprocally founding moment, of the world, then nothing more is thought by thinking 'God-plus-the-world' than is thought by thinking 'God' alone. In this case the inference is clearly valid. But the assumption that renders it valid conflicts with the thesis that God is conceptually distinct from God-plus-the-world.

Despite their admission of the strictly phenomenological necessity of pantheism, however, Prufer and Sokolowski nevertheless insist that God as Center, or Unity, or Horizon of the World, or as the very World Itself is *not* the God of Christianity. Decisively Christian theological commitments are achieved only through acceptance of the 'Christian distinction' between God and the world. Only one term of the God/world distinction exists necessarily. The other is gratuitously contingent. And the 'field' of the distinction is no 'greater' than its necessary term. If, as Findlay urges, pantheism, or at least some species of 'panentheism', is, from a rigorously phenomenological vantage point, "an absolute aspect of truth," phenomenological theology is clearly incapable of rising to the Christian (and, one might add, Islamic and perhaps Jewish) insight. Phenomenological pantheism asserts that *both* terms of the God/world distinction are necessary, the purported contingency of the world thus assuming the focus of the dispute. For Husserlian phenomenology, the necessity of the world is a bestowal of transcendental subjectivity and ultimately of primal presencing, the world possessing no more necessity than its primordially constituting source. Prufer's phenomenological Thomism is thus compelled to reject either the necessity of primal presencing or the 'transmission' of its necessity to the world. To assume the contingency of primal presencing is, of course, to deny the very possibility of phenomenological constitution; and to suppose the contingency of the world as the unitary 'pole' of synthetic constituting activity is to entertain the merely contingent 'rationality' of the constitutive process. Constitution is either impossible or, if it is possible at all, endowed with a merely contingent capacity to achieve unity through multiplicity and is thus threatened at every moment with the dissolution of its achieved identities into an utterly disintegral manifold. Since constitution is by definition the constitution of unity, the profound foundational issue is precisely the question of whether chaos is, indeed, a genuine possibility.

Setting this thought-provoking question aside, we should note that the ontological 'proof' is not necessarily to be viewed merely as a deductive inference. As Williams points out, the movement of thought from prearticulate concept to concrete actuality is the very pattern of the Hegelian phenomenological dialectic, culminating in a "fully mediated self-transcendence." Or in Hart's exposition of Husserl's stance: "The only trace of a theological or 'ontological' proof is in the question whether the realizability of the ideal of life is necessary for a present meaningful life, and whether only an actual 'God' can secure the conditions for this meaningfulness." For Husserl, "that-than-which-no-greater-can-be-thought" is an incompletely constituted ideal, the indefinitely approximable *telos* of all conscious life. It is not that the reality of the ideal is inferred from its concept but rather that the liberation *in mente* from nihilism, and hence the apprehension of an organizing 'form' of otherwise chaotic experience, presupposes the active striving for the ideal. The 'inference', as it were, is not logical but praxiological and in principle can never terminate in its ideal 'conclusion'. The divine entelechy and *prote hyle*, the reciprocally founding moments of primal presencing, exist in a state of 'dynamic disequilibrium'. As Hart maintains, "The waking mind . . . is not free to constitute chaos," it is "irrationally driven" to constitute being rationally. The 'naturing' of nature by nature is the endlessly progressive realization of the ideal. But nature, as boundless potentiality for form-taking, cannot in principle be exhaustively 'natured'.

God and Society

While phenomenology may proceed on the basis of a certain 'methodological solipsism', it is remarkable that this does not of itself preclude the revelation of God through third-personal reflection upon Nature or through second-personal reflection upon Society. Indeed, Williams defines phenomenological theology precisely as "the explication of a *social ontology*." *Geist*, in the familiar Hegelian formulation, is "an I that is a we and a we that is an I." God, as "intersubjective-social reality," "resists reduction to the alternatives of either a first-person account of consciousness or a third-person account." At the divine Center, for Findlay, "everyone . . . will be everyone, though more centrally himself, much as God is everyone though supremely Himself." And for Hart, the divine entelechy constitutes, through the society of monadic subjects, a "godly person of a higher order," the progressively constituted, but nonetheless inescapably partial, realization of the ideal of perfect social integration.

The intersubjective *Ineinandersein* characterizing such social-theological visions is analogous to a hall of mirrors in which each reflecting surface is reflected in all, and all in each. For Findlay, this state of perfect, unimpeded intersubjective interpenetration is endowed with timeless absolute being, eternally subsistent. In the Williams/Hegel view, this social-ontological integration of monadic *partes inter partes* is implicit in the "pretheoretical grasp of Being," the explication of which is precisely phenomenological theology. For Hart, and as suggested in my own essay, the reciprocal 'mirroring' of mind within mind in forms of loving receptivity and compassionate expressive praxis is neither an eternal actuality nor a state achievable simply through the rational-dynamic enterprise of tracing out the strands of being-sense. This intersubjective hall of mirrors, denoted in one of its uses by Husserl's richly suggestive term *Gotteswelt* serves, rather, as the ultimate *telos* of all conscious activity. Writes Hart: "As essentially entelechy, the divine ego/mind is also facing the ideal pole-idea, which is itself as mediated through the infinite potentiality of the monadological *prote hyle*." Divine act-life is mediated through the 'actualization' of the community of finite monads, the 'in-forming', as it were, the 'poetic' *Auffassung*, the 'fashioning' of social 'cosmos' out of social 'chaos', thereby constituting or 'realizing' by progressive degrees, the ideal-pole of intersubjective interpenetration. My own contribution achieves a very similar vision. The actual monadic community, always incompletely integral, never existing completely *partes inter partes*, functions as an 'appearance' of the world-pole, which I understand as the *telos* of perfect 'communalization', perfect *Ineinandersein*, and mediates the always inadequate and perspectival presentation of God-as-Object to God-as-Subject. Divine progress in the direction of a fully adequate self-presentation is tantamount to human progress in the direction of intersubjective integration.

Advancing the logic of the hall of mirrors yet another step, it should be apparent that, in the ideal, this cleverly devised arrangement is 'empty'. An opacity at the center of the 'chamber' would of course be reflectively transmitted throughout. But its very opacity would occlude all or part of those 'mirrors' standing opposite one another, thus rendering incomplete the reflection of each in all and all in each. For Findlay, the 'chamber' is eternally vacuous, not subject to the intrusion of any such distorting occlusion. For Williams, opacity amounts to conceptual implicitness, a fully explicated social ontology revealing the concrete reality of *Geist*. And for Hart, and for myself, the hall of mirrors undergoes the endlessly progressive process of construction. It is not 'there' from the beginning, either eternally or implicitly, but is synthetically fashioned, as it were, piece by piece.

God and Self

Phenomenological theology has its inception in the reflective conversion of consciousness, establishing a dimension of intuitive access to prereflective act-life obliterated in the 'one-dimensional' natural life of the mind. As Husserl asserts, "The I . . . bears its God in itself,"[2] and if phenomenological theology is to be possible at all, the Divine must be accessible to the solitary philosopher through some typically phenomenological technique presupposing, and intimately connected with, reflection. Or in Williams's apt characterization, phenomenological theology is "a view that interprets God as positively related to, even given, in religious experience and that grounds transcendental method in this larger, concretely historical view of experience." Laying aside, for the moment, the issue of how a distinctively 'religious' experience is to be recognized without a prior grasp of the sense of 'God', which in turn is to be extracted by reflection upon such an experience (an apparent circularity of sense), it is clear that phenomenological-theological reflection cannot, on pain of distorting the straighforward natural life it reveals, 'compete' with prereflective consciousness. In Duméry's view, then, as sketched by Courtney, "No judgments are made as to religious truth or falsity; such judgments are religious or theological." Or as Kern maintains, "Phenomenology as such describes; it does not postulate. But on the basis of, and motivated by, its description, metaphysical postulates can be raised, so that one may speak of a phenomenologically motivated metaphysics." Strictly speaking, according to Kern, "Phenomenology is itself not theology." Theology is rather, in a sense redolent of Aristotelian signification, "genuine metaphysics."

According to Duméry and Kern, the function of phenomenological reflection is simply that of clarifying and articulating the implicit 'sense' of first-order experience. Or, as Williams asserts, "Phenomenological theology is the explication of this pretheoretical apprehension of Being." Indeed, as Husserl himself maintains, the attempt to arrive at "God without God" would be "dangerous" were the subject of reflective investigation not "deeply bound to God." Still, if it should turn out, as Anselm clearly supposed, that the Being of God is a determination to be explicated out of the concept of the divine Essence, or as the Thomist might well prefer, should the Being and Essence of God prove to be identical, phenomenological explication of the sense of first-order religious experience might indeed *pace* Duméry and Kern, deliver theological truth. Duméry apparently assumes either the heterogeneity of the divine Being and Essence, in which case explication of Essence cannot, of course, deliver Being, or, with Aquinas, the infinity of the divine Essence, in which case explication would be endless and could terminate in no ontological conclusions at all. In Hart's acceptation, 'first philosophy' (not yet metaphysics or theology) is "a study of 'God' as the idea of perfection and as the *telos* of human life in terms of its essential features—and not in terms of its actuality or existence." It is not that God-as-*telos* is a timeless eidetic structure capable of interminable analysis, an infinite 'essence'. The divine teleological 'Omega' is not an infinite form but an infinitely realizable ideal. God-as-Object is inchoate, incompletely existing, a Being-in-Becoming progressively realized by the entelechial striving of the inframonadic divine 'Alpha'.

Duméry's Absolute is arrived at through what he calls the "henological reduction," a methodological prolongation of the Chinese-box series of Husserlian reductions characterized by a 'bracketing' of multiplicity and culminating in the directedness of the mind toward the One, a divine Unity utterly devoid of the slightest shade of multiplicity. The unity characteristic of human subjectivity is a unity-in-multiplicity, or in Duméryan diction, human consciousness is a 'one-multiple'. And perhaps for this reason Courtney claims, on Duméry's behalf, that the Absolute is "beyond the grasp of the acting subject and the critical philosopher." We can, as it were, 'reach' toward the Absolute, but cannot 'grasp' it. Here phenomenological description becomes otiose. For description at least presupposes the conceptual distinguishability of the unity to be described and the aspect designated by the descriptor. But not even the distinction of unity and aspect is to be found within the One. Findlay, on the other hand, while agreeing that "all religious and mysical experience moves in this interiorizing, unitive direction," does not share the Duméryan/Kernian vision of the absolute oneness of God. The Unity at the 'center' is not absolute. "At the Center," Findlay writes, "the distinction between persons will be no more than a nuance"—but a *nuance* nonetheless! The conscious state at the Center does not involve a "blurring of content." Distinctness is maintained in a "single glance" analogous to the way "a shepherd can see the whole of his finite flock and know just how many they are, without counting them one after another." The Holy Spirit is not absolute unity but the most intimate possible integration of multiplicity.

Moreover, in vivid contrast to Duméry's position, according to which the installation of the human 'one-multiple' at the standpoint of the absolute One is flatly unthinkable, Findlay writes as if "ascent to the Absolute" were, indeed, a live possibility for human consciousness. "One," he says, apparently referring to the human subject, "will grasp a whole system of interconnected truths in the utterly luminous, but also utterly wordless and imageless, manner in which, even in this life, one grasps such trivial truths as that . . . a certain number is a product of two others." The possibility of a 'positive' phenomenological description of the Divine entails, it seems, the feasibility of assuming, at least by degrees, the divine outlook. If, indeed, to witness the Divine does not carry this entailment, then God either possesses an 'outside' at least partially impenetrable by human intentionality or does not have an 'outlook' that a human subject might (progressively) assume. A bipartite integrity of 'inside' and 'outside' aspects cannot be the absolute One. But a Being without an 'outlook' cannot, on the other hand, be endowed with the qualities of wisdom or benevolence typically attributed to God. If to see the Divine is, at least incrementally, to see divinely, God has no 'outside', being thus more genuinely unitary, but may well, as Findlay assumes, have retained a 'mind'.

Implicit in our earlier comments regarding the 'perspectival' nature of the doctrine of creationism is the general insight that perspectives cannot be verified in virtue of eidetically registrable founding relationships between the perspected object and the determination predicated in accord with the perspectival 'slant' on that object. Perspectival determinations are *pieces*, not *moments*, of the object's 'sense'. Perhaps the most sweeping challenge, not only to phenomenological theology in particular but to phenomenology generally, is, then, the deconstructive claim that there simply *are* no 'moments' of sense, an assertion equivalent to the doctrine of Nietzschean 'perspectivism' (an evident misnomer). Buchanan's iconclastic counterpoint to the project of transcendental phenomenological theology urges the following Heideggerian position with regard to the superabundant richness of life-world experience: "The method of reduction enters this density only to find that each attempt to clear away by bringing to light and bracketing results is yet another layer of historical entanglements, which must be encountered and bracketed." The reflective-eidetic strategies of phenomenological enquiry cannot, in Buchanan's view, seize upon the sense of any ultimately founding subjective *concretum*, and we are thus 'lost' in the bewildering plurality of perspectives, unable to extricate ourselves from this chaotic plurality in order to witness the 'cosmic' system of perspectives as such. Buchanan reminds us, however, that phenomenology is a distinctively linguistic enterprise, its deliverances articulated in words—words indeed that are, in his view, ineluctably metaphorical. Accordingly, that 'vocable' that would sing the full manifestation of the system of perspectives Buchanan calls the "Word." And accordingly, also, since we are incapable of traversing the 'gap' between our ineluctable 'lostness' in the density of mundane experience and the extramundane synoptic vision represented by the Word, Buchanan is prompted to assert that "words figure and refigure the gap, giving it voice in the hope that one day (the coming day) they will get it right and speak the cosmos as Self, Truth, and God." The "gap," in Buchanan's view, between the stratum of metaphorical discourse and what we might call the 'absolute presence' of the world, the 'omniscient' display of the world as presented simultaneously from every possible vantage point, is precisely *faith*—faith, that is, *in presence*, the absolute presence 'metaphysically guaranteed' by the very 'onto-theo-logical' constructions that the deconstructive enterprise is to abolish. And, though we shall clearly never stand in the noontide Presence revealed by the Word, by dwelling 'faithfully' in the tension between the theoretical iconoclasm of Derrida and the social-praxiological hermeneutics of Ricoeur, between 'transgression' and 'appropriation,' between '*ABSENT*/presence' and 'absent/*PRESENCE*, we may at least find ourselves "dancing with the darkness in the light of hope."

An 'absent presence' is, of course, a *presence* that is absent, much as a lofty star, hopelessly beyond our reach, remains indifferent in its existence and nature to the plight of its human admirers. The logic of 'presence,' however, demands a 'dative of manifestation'. Hence, though the absolute presence of the world may indeed remain ineluctably absent *to us*, it nonetheless inescapably requires a Being who enjoys this manifestation, a Being, that is, possessed of omniscience. The contrast with Husserl's view is striking. The latter characterizes as a "fundamental error" the notion of God as "the Subject of absolutely perfect knowledge, and therefore also of every possible adequate perception, [who] naturally possesses what to us finite beings is denied, the perception of things in themselves." Such a view, Husserl maintains, is "nonsensical." "It implies that there is no *essential difference* between transcendent and immanent, that in the postulated divine intuition a spatial thing is a real (*reelles*) constituent, and indeed an experience itself, a constituent of the stream of the divine consciousness and the divine experience.[3]" For Husserl, the 'absolute presence' of the world is not an 'absent presence', but no (perceptual) presence at all. It is simply 'absent', as an approximable, but ultimately unrealizable, *telos*. Omniscience is phenomenologically impossible.

Alternative perspectives are, of necessity, presentations of *the same* object in alternative ways. Hence, the impropriety of the common label for Nietzsche's view: 'perspectivism'. For Nietzscheanism and its postmodern images, the 'center' drops out. No unity is perspected, and thus, there are no genuine perspectives. Yet this second-order claim 'deconstructs' itself, sharing, in Buchanan's insightful characterization of Derrida's claim regarding all texts, the logical fate of the Epimenides paradox: "All Cretans are liars and I am a Cretan." Husserlian perspectivism (properly so called) and deconstructive 'aperspectivism' (to reverse the misnomer) cannot amount even to alternative *perspectives* on first-order experience, since this would presuppose a unitary matter of concern subject to alternative modes of consideration. For 'aperspectivism', the two 'views' (if this expression does not already import too much) are strictly incommensurable. For perspectivism, in the proper sense, aperspectivism is flatly false. But again, this third-order incommensurability thesis is itself incommensurable with, and not contradictory to, what for perspectivism is its negate: the commensurability thesis. We need not be detained by further elaboration in this direction. The Husserlian rejoinder is evident: a consistently applied deconstructivism 'deconstructs' itself and cannot, in consequence, enter into logical competition with its 'negate'. Or rather, it simply has no negate. It appears as a 'frictionless' ideality, providing no 'traction' for the implication or contradiction of any philosophical position and having no 'place' within the 'logical space' of philosophemic alternatives, being thus, as it were, a 'nonposition'. To be sure, even for Husserl the task of articulating the entire 'cosmic' system of perspectives is open-ended, offering hope of progress but not of completion. But the posibility of transcendental phenomenology relies upon something far less grandiose: the simple feasibility of making unambiguously *true* pronouncements concerning the nature of first-order experience. If first-order perceptual experience is perspectival, as Husserl maintains, it should be possible to say, correctly, that this is so. Or, should prereflective experience turn out on closer inspection to be aperspectival, it should be possible to assert unequivocally that the Husserlian pronouncement is false. For deconstructive aperspectivism, of course, such pronouncements represent mere 'perspectives' (in the strained Nietzschean sense), being thus neither true nor false. But more crucially, and fatally for Husserl, this 'Neo-Protagoreanism' cannot consistently assert even of itself that it is *true*.

Despite the profusion of more suggestive alternatives, I have chosen, in an effort to avert even the appearance of supersession among the consistently excellent contributions to this volume, to arrange the essays in a perfectly pedestrian and, I presume unobjectionable, historical sequence according to significant sources of philosophical inspiration. Kern's "Trinity" heads the list, not simply because of his long-standing interest in Confucianism, Taoism, and Buddhism, the three springs of the Chinese intellectual tradition, reflecting, respectively, a balanced apprehension of the social, natural, and egological dimensions of human life, but also because of its utility in organizing the ensuing discussion. Findlay's reflections on the Holy Spirit and Courtney's exposition of Duméry's phenomenology of transcending are unmistakably Plotinian in their lights, although their Neoplatonic inspiration is differently appropriated in each case. The evident Thomism of Prufer's "Creation, Solitude, and Publicity" appears subsequently, succeeded by Williams's Hegalian "Alternative." Hart's "Précis" and my own piece on the theology of intersubjectivity have their impetus straightforwardly in the work of Husserl himself. And Buchanan's contribution, "Rhetorics of Appropriation/Transgression," is 'post-Husserlian' in its inspiration.

It is the editors' hope that this pioneering collection, *Essays in Phenomenological Theology*, will prompt active discussion and searching critique. It is to the promotion of continuing scholarship and the advancement of reflection in this rapidly burgeoning discipline that the present volume is earnestly dedicated.

Notes

1. This passage was translated by Professor James G. Hart from: Sr. Adelgundis Jaigerschmidt, OSB, "Gespraeche mit Edmund Husserl: 1931–1936" in *Stimmen*, 199 (1981), 56. Cf. also Husserl's conversation with Edith Stein, cited in R. Dumareau, 'un témoin de la lumière: Edith Stein," in *Les Études philosophiques*, nouvelle série, 2 (1955), 238–249, quoted in Henry Duméry, *Critique et Religion: Problèmes de méthode en philosophie de la religion* (Paris: Société d'Edition d'Enseignement Supérieur, 1957), 165.

2. Edmund Husserl, *Drei Vorlesungen ueber Fichtes Menschheitsideal*, MS. F I 22, p. 25, quoted in Stephan Strasser, "History, Teleology, and God in the Philosophy of Husserl," Tymieniecka, ed., *Analecta Husserliana*, vol IX, 325–326.

3. Edmund Husserl, *Ideas: General Introduction to Pure Phenomenology*, translated by W. R. Gibson (New York: Macmillan, 1931), 123.

2. *Trinity: Theological Reflections of a Phenomenologist*

I. Why am I what I am? The Question of the Causes of My Reality

I would like to begin with the question, Through which causes is any human being what he or she is? Through *what* am I what I have become in my total bodily, psychological, and social constitution?

Traditionally three kinds of causes are offered as an answer to this question:

1. I am as I am because of *natural causes*, that is, physical, chemical, biological causes; I am as I am because of inherited genes, because of the stars, because of a particular climate, because of a certain kind of diet, and so forth.
2. I am as I am due to *social causes*, such as being raised in a certain way by my parents and at school; having a particular language; belonging to a particular culture or certain social class.
3. I am as I am *through myself*, through my own responsibility, because I have made such and such decisions, because I have acted in this way or that.

Each of these three kinds of causes urges on its own, that both the others be reduced to it alone as the sole cause; that is, it tends to absolutize: What a human being is in each instance is 'ultimately' determined through heredity and through the biological circumstances of his or her life. This would be a naturalistic absolutizing. Or: The human being is in his or her reality the ensemble of social relations.

This would be an absolutizing of the social causes. And finally, what I am is ultimately determined through my own past and present thought and action. Such a position is usually labelled "subjective idealism."

The purest and strictest form of this third position was assumed by Buddhism: *Everything* that I am, my capabilities, my social position, indeed, that I am a human being and was not born an animal or a god or a demon—indeed, that I was born at all—is nothing else than the fruits of my own past deeds, my *karma*. Consistent with this position we find the Yogacara school (or Vijnanavada) teaching that even the version of the world in which I find myself is nothing other than a world made determinate through my own prior deeds.

All three of these absolutizing reductions hold a certain fascination due to their clarity and logical simplicity. They all have a theoretical power in their consistency, that is, in their willingness to think one of the possibilities through to its conclusion. On the other hand, they are also perhaps related to a form of madness (as to the megalomania of the self, or to the hypnosis of social contagion, or to the hysteria or intoxication of an irresponsible nature) in that they attempt to absorb our existence in one direction and thereby to repress our other dimensions.

However, none of these absolutizings appears to be sufficient. For example, the I-self, the subject, seems indeed to be *universal*. It embraces the entire world as the object of its consciousness; it encompasses all human beings as its actual and possible co-subjects. I cannot speak of a nature that would not be an object of my consciusness or of Others who are not consciously present to me as my co-subjects. And yet I cannot come to know the laws of nature by reflection on my self or through the analysis of consciousness. The laws and the morphology of nature are not deducible from subjectivity. If one wants to know what comprises African fauna, it is not through reflection on oneself that one will learn this. Rather, the best and most immediate way is to travel to Africa and take a look at the fauna for oneself. As is well known, the law of gravity was not discovered through an analysis of consciousness. With all due respect for the analysis of consciousness (whose value one will hardly find me calling into question), it nevertheless seems to me that not one single law of nature has been discovered through the analysis of consciousness. This is perhaps debatable. Kant attempted to deduce the a priori laws of nature (*natura formaliter spectata*) from transcendental subjectivity; Schelling even derived electricity and magnetism from the I. But first of all, one can doubt whether these deductions were truly successful. And secondly, even if they were assumed to be valid, we would in no way be dealing with discoveries of laws of nature but, at best, with subsequent attempts at justification of laws that were determined in another way, namely, in being occupied with nature. Even such a brilliant analyst of consciousness as Husserl did not believe it possible to deduce natural laws from transcendental reflection. Phenomenologizing cannot be a substitute for natural science.

However, the matter has an analogy in the opposite direction. Nature, or natural science, as the case may be, is indeed universal. There is no subjective thinking or acting, no consciousness that is not physically, chemically and physiologically conditioned. But it still seems to me to hold analogously that, although nature conditions subjectivity, i.e., that although subjectivity *cannot be without* nature (analogous to the above-stated claim that nature *cannot be without* subjectivity), so we will never know what perception, thinking, willing, feeling, and so forth, are through physiological, electronic, or other kinds of natural scientific research. At best we can attempt to establish certain coordinations to physiological or other natural processes, after we have already gained certain notions about perception, thinking, willing, feeling and the like through either sporadic and inexpert or consistent and systematic reflection on consciousness.

Finally, something analogous seems to me to hold for sociality in its relationship to nature and subjectivity as to what holds for all relations between these three universal causalities. Sociality is also *universal*. Those realities that we know as nature and as the subject of consciousness are conditioned through our language, through social ideas and norms, through social situations. But it would still seem that social-scientific research into causes of whatever sort cannot substitute for natural science or for the analysis of consciousness. On the other hand, it does not seem that the analysis of consciousness, the analysis of the I, can succeed in deducing the alter ego, the *socius*, from the ego.

Here I, somewhat casually, am making huge claims. In order for them to be taken seriously justifications would of course be required for which I not only could, but would have to, appeal to works of other authors. But on this occasion I refrain from doing so. Rather, what alone is important for me here, and for the remainder of this essay, is to sketch hypothetically a broad contextual consideration for which I nurture only a heuristic hope. This is not a publication of results that are certain, but an attempt, a letter to friends, as it were, with a request for corroboration and correction.

2. *The Incommensurability of Three Relative Totalities: Nature, Sociality, and Self*

We began with the question: Through what causes is any human being (e.g., I myself), what he or she is? We have named three distinctive kinds or contexts of causes that may be brought forth as an answer to this question and have pointed out that each of these three causes has a tendency to become absolute, that is, to reduce all the others to itself and thereby to exclude the others. I have taken the liberty of doubting the claim of these three causal realms to be absolute.

But still one might say: Let us be both generous and just! Give to each its due! I am what I am through all three of these causes. There are three distinct causal factors that determine my reality. And then the question could arise: In what quantitative relationship do these three distinct factors stand to one another? Am I, as it were, determined one-third by nature, one-third by society, and one-third by myself? Or am I, as we might well be inclined to think in an atmosphere informed by the style of the natural and social sciences, determined to a small percent by myself but to a much larger percent by biological causes, with the remaining percentage determined by society? Or does another relationship obtain? Or is each individual human case different, the self-directed person determined primarily by him- or herself, another more gregarious, and a third chiefly a child of nature? The opinions on this matter, of course, vary considerably. The natural scientist would, indeed, highlight the biological factors and allow but a small consideration, if any, to self-determination. The ethician, on the other hand, would make extensive claims for self-determination, and the social scientist would claim similarly for society. The ethician will perhaps say that a human being who has become and is a 'merely natural being' like a ball caught in a game of catch played by his or her natural drives, bears the responsibility for this circumstance, and so on. The argument gets longer and more involved until one notes that this dialectic of views is wrong, that a quantitative argument about the three causalities is nonsensical. It is nonsensical because it is in principle undecidable in a rational way.

In order for this argument to be decidable, a common measure for the three kinds of causality must exist. Only in this way can they be weighed in relationship to one another, either with exact numbers or in a rough manner only. But this does not seem possible, because here it is a matter of three *distinct categories* of causality that are incommensurable with respect to one another.

The interests informing the prespectives that make available the natural, social, and egological causalities are completely different. The practical attitude placing natural causality at our disposal is completely different from the practical attitude through which access is gained to social causality and, again, completely different from that through which egological causality is available to us. What the three causal categories have in common is that they are theoretical objectifications of certain *techniques*. I mean by "technique" a certain capacity to do, a determinate power, a mastery of a determinate change, that is, of a becoming in a definite direction. Such a capacity or ready availability is originally acquired in experimentation and can be repeated in a consistent and stable way (method).

Natural causality is the guiding idea behind the principle of the domination of nature. Social causality is the guiding idea of such social techniques as pedagogy, politics, demagogy, and the like. And egological causality, the empowerment of the I, is a guiding idea of certain forms of experimentation, practice, and ability, as they are consistently pursued in ethical practice, ascetics, yoga, and so forth. One can, I presume, speak of natural, social, and egological causalities as particular contexts only when there is a technique at hand, an experientially learned and methodically repeatable control of certain changes. In each case one may consider the idea of causality itself as either empirical or as a heuristic maxim for the realm accessible to our experience. In a primitive, mythical culture where corresponding techniques are not cultivated in a differentiated manner, one does not find the ideas of natural, social, or egological causality as distinct contexts. Thus we may say that the natural practitioners, the social practitioners, and the ethicians, from the standpoints informed by their relative horizons of interest, are all correct when they seek to extend their base of power, the relevant causal context, as far as possible. The abilities corresponding to the three kinds of causality (i.e., the correlative techniques), seem to be completely distinct from one another, indeed independent of one another. A glance at the histories of cultures teaches the same thing. For example, in the culture of India the technique of self-causality, yoga, was developed to a high degree of efficiency. At the same time, however, less mental energy was invested in exploring the causal domination of nature or of society. The ideas of nature and society as practical causal systems were perhaps never explicitly projected. But in China, it seems interest in the domination of society prevailed. The standard-giving schools, those of the Confucianists and legalists, were concerned primarily with this, and no concentration of political power in human history endured so long as that found in China. It is not that there was no interest in the control of nature (as witnessed, for example, by Taoist alchemy, astrology, geomancy) or in self-control (as we can also find in Taoism, but more so in the Buddhism that came from India). Representatives of these interests, however, were mostly outsiders and were subordinated to the dominating interest of social control. And today we know that the great scientific-technical achievements of modern Western culture have in no way brought in their train equal successes in the areas of ethical self-control and social techniques such as education.

Perhaps, because of their incommensurability, we might say of the three technique-informed, empirical causal contexts—nature, society, and self—that they are in themselves closed contexts, self-contained systems. In this sense they are totalities. They are not absolute, however, but relative totalities. They are relative, namely, to particular goal-oriented points of view or attitudes; they are the global guiding ideas of particular practical interests. We shall soon have occasion to return to this feature of relativity.

3. The Immediate Correlation of Nature, Society, and Self as Three Dimensions Of Our Existence

In still another sense nature, society, and self are not absolute. They are not independent entities or substances. In this context I would like to recall the critique that Richard Avenarius' empirio-criticism, as well as ordinary language analysis and phenomenology, has directed against Cartesian dualism. In immediate everyday experience—which expresses itself in an unreflective way in ordinary language and which phenomenology wishes to describe reflectively and hermeneutics wants to interpret—nature and the I are not independent substances. Avenarius 'restores' the original unity of the 'natural conception of the world' in opposition to the dualist constructions of metaphysics. Also, Husserl's return to the life-world and life-world experience was motivated by an effort to rectify the metaphysical dualism of nature and spirit. Indeed, it seems to me that the entire phenomenology of Husserl can be understood as a reflective movement, going back to an experiencing in which nature, I myself, and the Other form a unity. In our concrete experience nature, self, and society form a unity of correlation. Sheer nature, sheer society, sheer self, as closed causal contexts, are only technical products of abstraction that grow out of practical interest-perspectives and that serve these interests. The sense of nature is nature experienced and dealt with by me in a social context; the Other in a concrete sense is only experienceable as the Other of my self within the context of nature, and so on.

In this unity of correlation, to which the self-contained, technique-informed causal systems are bent back as to their original concrete base, the distinctions of nature, society, and self are not dissolved. Here, however, they can no longer have the sense of self-contained, technique-informed causal systems.

I can find no better picture to express this than the following: Nature, society, and self are the three dimensions, the three coordinates, the three axes of the reality of our own life. They are not three distinct regions on a plane; each dimension is everywhere; each is in the whole and in each part. In this sense each dimension is total. In my concrete reality I am wholly and completely nature, wholly and completely body (*Leib*); but I myself am also wholly and completely an Other, a *socius* of my Others; In my concrete reality I am as much you or he as I am I. But I am also wholly and completely I, which may not be reduced to you or him. Each dimension is the whole, but not the whole in every respect (*totum sed non totaliter*).

There is no relation of causal or logical priority between any of these three dimensions. In a logical or causal sense no one of these can be derived either from another or from both of the others together. Furthermore, I do not see any possibility of deriving the three-dimensionality of nature, society, and self—that is, to be able to show on the basis of a principle that our own reality must manifest precisely these three dimensions and no others. Nature, society, and self are, as the fundamental dimensions of our existence, total (i.e., everywhere), and are not derivable from one another. They are not absolute, however, but are rather relative in the sense that they condition one another reciprocally. In my concrete existence I cannot be without nature; nature cannot be without me myself; I myself cannot be without sociality; sociality cannot be without nature, and vice-versa. Nature, society, and self—as distinct, technique-informed causal contexts— are therefore not only relative to particular practical points of view shaped by horizons of interest but are also, as the dimensions of our existence, relative to one another. In this sense also they are relative totalities.

The elucidation of the concrete context of experience, whether through the analysis of everyday language, through phenomenological reflection upon one's experience, or through the hermeneutics of the productions of the spirit, seems to be a kind of science completely different from the technique-informed causal sciences. These latter have a practical interest in the causal domination of certain changes. The former are, as has been said, useless; that is, they do not bring any power and in this sense are of no practical interest. Further, they are not under the sway of any of the guiding ideas behind the three empirical causalities, even though they can speak about them. Indeed, even history cannot be considered a causal science, for it is never in a position to say what really would have happened if this or that had not happened, or if something had happened that did not happen. Historical motivations are not necessarily to be understood through the causalities at one's disposal. Only when technique-informed sciences reconstruct cases in history to illustrate their own theoretical contexts do historical events enter into a relationship of technique-informed empirical causality.

Those sciences not characterized by technique-informed causal contexts, which attempt to shed light on the concrete reality of our life and thereby make visible the correlative unity of nature, society, and I, are not elevated above these three dimensions of our reality, but rather happen as expressions of this reality *in* these dimensions. These sciences are indeed not uniform. They do not make up a one-dimensional unity; rather, they arrange—and must arrange—themselves according to I, sociality, and nature.

Does not phenomenology in the Husserlian sense essentially thematize the point of view of the I? Is it not essentially egology? It shows, of course, the correlation of I, sociality, and nature, yet it does so from the point of view of the I. It shows how, in I-consciousness, nature and sociality 'present themselves', 'become evident'. Do not the hermeneutical sciences represent the point of view of the Others, of sociality, of the histories of culture that constitute the I as thinking and acting? There also exist attempts at a 'phenomenology of nature', of an 'ontology of intuited nature', that does not serve to dominate nature through a technique-informed causality but rather seeks to interpret the meaning of sensibly experienced nature as it appears within our life-context. We may here note in passing that our feeling and percipient bodiliness is an essential constitutive correlate of this sensibly experienced nature.

Thus we can say that the three dimensions of our life's concrete reality are the three possible viewpoints from which we can consider this reality and from which alone we can consider it. These viewpoints do not necessarily have to be interested in power and do not have to become locked up in interest-perspectives that construct technique-informed causal systems. Nevertheless, they are points of view, and the descriptions and theories based on them are always perspective-bound aspects, always relative expressions of our concrete reality.

It seems that no science exists that is sufficiently free of a particular point of view to be adequate in every respect to our concrete reality—an absolute description in which everything without remainder is included, and into which this reality in every respect would be taken up. There can be no simple theory elevated over the relativity of viewpoints; there is rather only the metatheoretical consciousness of the relativity of all our theories, that is the metatheoretical consciousness of the manifold of our knowledge—which manifold is conditioned by the plurality of different viewpoints.

Still, in different cultural traditions we find the idea or the ideal of the unity of truth or, as the case may be, the idea of an absolute knowledge that is one with this single truth. This idea points in a direction I would like to take in developing the following reflections.

4. The Question of the Metaphysical 'Cause' and the Three Basic Types of Metaphysics

In the course of human history there has been asked still another 'causal' question, completely different from the one that served as our point of departure. This question does not aim at technique-informed empirical causes in the sense proposed above. These previously considered causes of our mutable, originating, and passing reality are themselves originating and passing causal members of this reality. The other kind of 'cause', here in question, is supposed to be nontransitory and unconditioned, itself not a conditioned member of the world that has become and is becoming. In this sense it is a metaphysical cause. This metaphysical cause does not have, as the others do, the sense of a starting point enabling the attainment of definite changes (goals) in our transitory reality through practical mastery. Rather, this cause is supposed to be a ground, not accessible to us nor at our disposal, that gives our ephemeral reality its abiding meaning. It is not easy to say what occasions human beings to look for such a 'cause'. It is, I think, on the one hand the experience of the negative: of sorrow and evil; of the decline and death of all things born, of all nature; of injustice, or the powerlessness in society of the just; of one's own shortcomings and one's own failures. On the other hand there are the experiences of the sublime, the exalted: of the infinitely wonderful beauty of nature; of the unconditioned disarming goodness of one's fellow human beings; of one's unmerited ability and good fortune. Perhaps it is precisely this extreme two-sidedness of all the dimensions of our passing reality, the overwhelming sorrow and overwhelming bliss, that practically is not ours to ordain, that lets us inquire and hope beyond this reality to a perpetual ground in which we are liberated from the pain and dread of everything ephemeral and that makes definitive the bliss here hinted at and mirrored in a fleeting manner. Such a 'cause' is taught by the metaphysical religions and by religious metaphysics.

If this metaphysical cause is to be the nontransitory ground and meaning of our total three-dimensional reality in process, then one might assume that it is itself not to be sought in a single coordinate of this reality. It itself cannot be thought of as natural, social or egological. But when we consult the historical forms of metaphysics and the religious promise of salvation, we seem to bump into the old triad of nature, sociality, and self. It seems that we can arrange the traditional forms of metaphysics and religious promise of salvation into (1). the natural or cosmological form, (2). the normative-social form, and (3). the form of the spirit. Aristotle's metaphysics has, as is often said, a cosmological character. Its 'unmoved mover' is the ground of the natural order. The Stoic conception of God is also taken from nature: the world-reason, the vital principle of the cosmos, and so on. Likewise the *tao*, the principle of Chinese Taoism, is understood as the ground of nature. Other metaphysical philosophies and religions think of the eternal ground of things primarily as an extension of the social coordinate. Plato's idea of the good was perhaps formed originally as a principle of social order (*taxis*) or the origin of the social norm. That is certainly true in the case of the highest metaphysical principle of Neo-Confucianism, the *li*, which in terms of its content may be primarily interpreted to mean 'humanity', 'altruism' (*ren*). Finally Buddhism, especially in the forms it has undergone in China, is essentially a metaphysics of the spirit. The eternal is experienced in one's own 'interiority', in the spirit as the eternal ground of this interiority. And the same holds for the neoplatonic-Augustinian tradition of Europe, which extended beyond Eckhart and Cusa to Fichte. The absolute is sought in the 'ground of the soul', in the 'point of the soul', *abditum mentis*, in the spark of the soul (*scintilla animae*), in the transcendental I.

I do not wish to attempt the ridiculous here of putting all the metaphysical systems of history on parade. Rather, I only want to bring this consideration to your attention: Clearly the triad of nature, sociality, and self not only signifies the three dimensions of our passing reality—or, as the case may be, the three lines of empirical causality into which this reality can be analyzed—but also rubs off onto the metaphysical cause, which ought to be the eternal ground of all the dimensions of our ephemeral reality.

Bearing witness to this tendency to color the metaphysical cause, Chinese cultural history— which makes up a complete cosmos of possibilities of thinking— may serve as the finest and clearest voucher. From the latter part of the Tang dynasty (the beginning of the seventh century) until our century, the Chinese have regarded their tradition as determined through "The Three Doctrines," namely, Confucianism, Taoism, and Buddhism. But in its essentials this threefoldness, as we suggested above, exactly corresponds to sociality, nature, and self. Such arrangements are, of course, always *des terribles simplifications*. Nevertheless, they manifest basic tendencies.

5. *Unum Trinum*

The classification of metaphysical teachings that we have been discussing is still not the last word. In the intellectual tradition we also meet an attempt to bring this plurality of cosmological, social, and psychological metaphysics to a unity. This is clearly true of Chinese tradition since the time of the Tang dynasty, where we see the

'Unification of the Three Doctrines' presenting an increasingly vital intellectual tradition. This means that the eternal grounds of nature, sociality, and one's own spirit were thought of in terms of *one* ground.

Something corresponding to this is also found in European intellectual history. Spinoza's God has the attributes both of extension (nature) and of thought (self). Leibniz thinks of God as the ultimate ground of the harmony of corporeal and psychic events. Kant postulates God as the principle bringing the realm of nature to a unity with that of morality and freedom. Schelling conceives the identity-philosophy of the absolute as a unity of the philosophy of nature and of the (transcendental) I. Other examples of European thought might be added. I will refrain from pursuing the question why, in these European philosophemes, a duality appears instead of a triad; why the You is not recognized as an equiprimordial dimension of our actuality. For our present context it is more important that the eternal ground of our transitory reality not be thought of as a single dimension of this reality, but rather as the one ground of all the dimensions.

The single metaphysical ground of nature, sociality, and self can appear as a logical postulate, that is, as a mere thought, a mere idea; but this ground can also appear as reality. As an idea makes its appearance among the mere 'lovers of wisdom', the philosophers, when it is recognized that nature, sociality, and self are only relative, and when the requirement is put forth for a ground that surmounts all the dimensions of our transitoriness. This ground is experienced as an actual reality by the truly wise and by the saints, when the interests in the domination of nature, society, and the I are extinguished, and in this stillness, in this 'nothing' (emptiness: *sunyata, vanitas*), in which the transitory reality is submerged (i.e., becomes transparent as transitory), the nontransitory One shines. We have such testimonials from the wise of all metaphysical religions, even though this One is unanimously referred to by them as ineffable.

In these philosophical and relgious metaphysical traditions we also find the view that this One, as everlasting, is 'beyond' or 'above' the transitory; nevertheless, it is not outside of them, that is, not outside of nature, sociality, and self. This view was logically founded out of the consideration that, if such a being were outside, it would exist in opposition to the transitory; it would thereby draw limitation and relativity into its own being. The saints experienced the realization that the nontransitory does not exist apart from the destruction of the transitory but is rather only to be found in the middle of the transitory.

For example, Shakyamuni, after years in pursuit of a path of self-annihilation and *askesis* turned away from it and went 'the middle way'. The word of Jesus has been handed down: "The Kingdom of God is in your midst." Zen emphasizes that the beyond ('the other shore') is on this side, that transcendence is in immanence. In Taoism, according to the teaching of Chuang Tzu, the eternal Tao may be seen in the least and most ephemeral reality. It seems then that the eternal is really to be found only through the transitoriness of nature, of co-subjects, and of myself. Perhaps this is the realizable meaning in our human experience of the Christian doctrine of the trinity: The one God is "Almighty Father, creator of heaven and earth" (ground of nature), is Son, who is met in Jesus and in each fellow human being as the deepest ground ("what you have done unto the least of my brethren, that you have done unto me"), and is Holy Spirit, who dwells in my spirit as inmost ground. Of course, this by no means exhausts what has been thought about the trinity in the history of Christian theology. But the idea of the trinity has perhaps its closest, and as it were most elemental, experiential basis precisely in the fact that divinity can reveal itself to us only within the three dimensions of our transitory reality, so that these are to us, at the same time, the three 'persons' ('faces') of the One.

If this proposal were true, it would also have implications for religion. A religious attitude that seeks God only in the 'interior of the soul' would be just as one-sided as one that strives after God merely in society (in the neighbor) or merely in the cosmos (in the beauty of nature). Only a religion that discloses the everlasting in all three axes or dimensions of our ephemerality encompasses our entire concrete existence; only such a religion brings our existence in all of its dimensions into the saving perpetual ground and does not relinquish any aspects of our existence to the sorrow and anxiety of sheer ephemerality. Furthermore, only such an inclusive religion keeps the inner mysticism of the soul from sliding into an autistic quietism, the religious love of neighbor from sinking into mere social activism, the mysticism of nature from being aesthetic enthrallment by nature. Such an inclusive religion achieves this because it points in the direction of the One that is 'present' in all dimensions of our existence but that is not subsumed into any one of them. Although we can indeed become conscious of the transcendence of the everlasting in a single dimen-

sion of our transitory reality (the different one-sided religious traditions seem to make this clear), the divine transcendence is clearest as
the One of which we are aware within the three axes of our existence:
as trinity.

6. *Phenomenology and Theology*

I understand the term *phenomenology* to mean 'reflection on our
concrete experiential reality'. The theme of phenomenology is 'I,
nature, intersubjectivity', in their correlations. Although
phenomenology brings to light the correlative unity of these three
dimensions, it seems nevertheless in each case able to do this only
from the point of view of one dimension and therefore takes on the
forms of 'egology', 'hermeneutics of understanding', and 'ontology of
nature'. Phenomenology is a movement that counters the one-
sidedness and speciality of the practical, technique-informed, 'profes-
sional' interests that, because of their search for achievable results,
have fixed their vision only on a single dimension of the reality of our
life. In this respect they are abstract. As a reflection on the concretion
of our existence, phenomenology is a movement in opposition to the
abstract interests in power. It is thereby a critical corrective to the absolutizing of the causality of a single dimension of our transitory being, regardless of whether this absolutizing is naturalist, subjective-
idealist, or sociological. In this way phenomenology prepares for true
theology, because it sees through the false gods, through the absolutizing of relativities.

But phenomenology is not theology. It describes our transitory,
ever-becoming, ever-passing reality. Theology, or what I consider to
be the same, genuine metaphysics, has, as earlier suggested, two
forms: on the one hand the mere postulates of thought, and on the
other the actuality. Phenomenology as such describes; it does not
postulate. But on the basis of, and motivated by, its description,
metaphysical postulates can be raised, so that one may speak of a
phenomenologically motivated metaphysics. Thus for Husserl the
Kantian theory of postulates has a phenomenologically motivated
sense. As either phenomenology or as the hermeneutics of
metaphysical ideas, an attempt can be made to understand the meaning of these ideas from the concrete life-context within which they
emerge.

The metaphysics of actual realization occurs in the life-experience of the saints. According to their claims the saints experienced the revelation of the absolute as something beyond all possible description, indeed as the annihilation of all ideas and concepts. Their theology is ultimately one of negation and silence.

Phenomenology as hermeneutics can attempt to understand the lives and the testimony of the saints, but how is it to grasp within these phenomena the unsaid and ineffable, which are referred to as decisive? As 'phenomenology of mysticism' it can say something about the experiences of the saints; but it has much more to say about the transitory, physical, social, and psychological concommitant circumstances of the eternal than about the eternal itself.

Phenomenology cannot be indifferent or neutral toward theology. Just as it provides a critical corrective to the absolutizing of the relative dimensions of existence, so it also provides a corrective to a one-sided postulating, a pursuit of the eternal in but one of the axes of the reality of our life. To a mere mysticism of the depths of the soul, or to a mere metaphysics of love of neighbor or of ground of nature, it will call attention to the dimensions of our life that in each case are passed over and relinquished to the sorrow of sheer ephemerality. A phenomenologist can only hope for the salvation of our total reality from a religion of 'trinity'.

I would here like to thank James G. Hart (Indiana University), who translated this essay from the German, Guido Kueng (Freiburg, Switzerland), Eduard Marbach (Bern), and Robert Sokolowski (Catholic University of America). Through numerous comments and questions in regard to a first draft of this essay, they have aided me in preparing this present improved version.

J. N. FINDLAY

3. Some Thoughts Regarding The Holy Spirit

The aim of this paper is to deal with a type of theological object that is to be credited mainly with connective and mediatorial functions and that is only in an attenuated given hypostatic status: its role is to *relate* the central or apical hypostases (whichever analogy one may prefer) to one another, or to relate them and their zones to the remotest periphery of being. In the latter case, its role is to forge lines of transfiguration and living identification with this periphery. In Christianity this connective role is fulfilled by the Word, which is at once *with* God and yet also, by a logic peculiar to religion, is not different from Very God Himself; further, by the same logic, it is not different from a flesh-and-blood man who lived in Judaea two millennia ago and is further a light that lightens every man who comes into the world. But this connective role is even more eminently fulfilled by another hypostatic Persona known as the Holy Spirit, which not only spoke by the prophets, some of whom may not have belonged to the main fold of orthodox shepherds, but which was also, for one great theologian at least, not different from the reciprocal love that unites the supreme Paternal Hypostasis with His Word. None of these religious hypostases behave like ordinarily conceived things or persons, but it seems clear that the Word and the Spirit behave even less so than others: their whole being would seem to consist in connecting the Center of all being with its periphery, or in connecting one aspect of the absolute Center with another.

Wilhelm Wundt described the Holy Spirit as a *daimonenartiges Wesen*: it had the imperfect individuality attributed to daemons in antiquity. This Holy Spirit or Word—we need not for our narrow purposes discriminate between them—does not, however, restrict itself

39

to speaking by the prophets: it also illuminates and comforts less exalted individuals and becomes for each of them a fountain of water
welling forth unto everlasting life, or a flood of manna descending on
them in the wilderness, and so on. The Holy spirit becomes therefore,
especially for us modern men, the most central and sacred of religious
hypostases; not only does it not disdain a Virgin's womb but it does
not scorn even the most corrupt and disordered soul alive. It is, in fact,
the one wholly credible and indubitable member of the Divine Trinity.
Even if we doubt the existence of the sources from which it is alleged
to proceed, in a doubt which, in our twilight state, cannot but afflict us
at every moment of our life, we cannot yet doubt its living presence
within us, above all when we fall short of our higher aspirations, but
also when it confers upon us the guidance, strength, peace, and joy
that it at times does. It is, we may say, the divinity that shapes our
ends, rough-hew them as we will. This inner role of the Spirit is not
confined to Christianity. Buddhism also believes in a Body of Compas-
sion revealed in higher worlds, which mediates between the transcendent Body of the Law that is beyond all forms and the Body of Renunciation that the Enlightener wears in this world. In addition to its
Primal Buddha, who is the ultimate refuge of all beings, Buddhism also
posits a Buddha-eye or Buddha-nature latent in all of us, which if
raised to full enlightenment, can effect our salvation. The
Neoplatonists likewise have a hypostatic Soul that brings down, into
the zone of time and dispersion, the timelessness of Mind and its objects and of the Unity beyond Mind and its objects; it further nourishes
within itself all the little Logoi or genetic codes with which it programs
the forms of nature. The basic architecture of being is of necessity
ecumenical and has revealed itself to the Gentiles as much as to the
Christians.

I must, however, develop my own theology or Absolute-theory
more fully in order to give a better account of this connective,
dynamic aspect necessarily posited in Divinity. The approach to the
absolute object of religion that I shall attempt on this occasion will be
through Values. By Values I mean not merely the contingent goals pursued by contingent, finite persons, but higher-order goals that will
necessarily recommend themselves to every reflective person. They
spring from trends or features intrinsic to consciousness as such and to
its direction beyond itself, to objects that can also be objects to others
besides itself. Under Values I mean to include not merely the goals of
our interested or disinterested practice but also the goals pursued by

our cognition, the specification of the marks of a reality that can also be a possible and worthy object of rational acceptance. As regards Values in general, I hold that they can only be valid for anyone and everyone if they are Values of a higher order, which are indifferent to the particularity of contingent, personal interest, while being ready to organize and unify the latter. They must be goals that we can set up for ourselves and others, no matter what we may happen to desire personally or what others may happen to desire. They are goals that everyone can desire for everyone and can desire that everyone should desire for everyone, without affecting their contingent, personal desires, except to eliminate conflict among them. Under the conditions of such impartial universality, it is obvious that Satisfaction or Bliss is a goal that can validly, and without conflict, be pursued by everyone for everyone, without arbitrary partiality or the arbitrary imposition of one man's contingent, personal goals on another.

Bliss or Satisfaction or pure Pleasure is, however, only the lowest of the goals that everyone can, in freedom from his own particular, personal interests, desire for everyone and desire that everyone should desire for everyone. The quest for Bliss or Satisfaction leads on to the necessary quest for Power and Freedom for each and all, again with provisos against conflict, since without Power and Freedom, neither Bliss nor Satisfaction can be achieved nor enjoyed securely. But among such powers and freedoms there is none more important than the power to know and understand the world and the people who share it with us. In the condition of knowledge, the world no longer terrifies and oppresses us with unknown possibilities but is our own world, with the built-in limitation of variety and the subjection to rule that permits understanding and the realization of purpose.

I shall not here attempt to give a validation of the pursuit of Beauty, meaning thereby the Bliss in appearances that meets our cognitive, and particularly our perceptual, approaches halfway and does so with perspicuity and poignancy. Nor shall I seek to validate the various forms of interpersonal Love that, in their transcendence of the most obstinate of metaphysical barriers, enrich the finite, one-sided person with most remarkable extensions of Bliss, Power, and Understanding and can also, with suitable provisos, seek an extension from everyone to everyone. Nor shall I explore the validating conditions of a Justice that is little beyond the desire to rise beyond contingent personal desire and arbitrary preference, nor those of Virtue or Moral Value, which necessarily arise in the actions and intentions of those who pursue all or some of the Values I have enumerated and do so perhaps with great zeal and energy and perhaps in difficult circumstances.

For all the Values I have mentioned, something like a transcendental deduction is possible from the higher-order desire alone to pursue only those goals that can be pursued by everyone for everyone, and without inner conflict and without the arbitrary imposition of one man's goals on another. The sort of deduction I am sketching is much more fundamental than the deduction of imperatives and maxims of action attempted by Kant, although its method is similar. I have attempted to carry it out in my book *Values and Intentions*. In this connection, it is my belief that, while it is by no means difficult to map a system of truly nonarbitrary interpersonal Values, it is often overwhelmingly difficult to make use of such a map in practice; the Heads of Rational Value often come into conflict in their application and are, further, so disparate and incommensurable that there is no assured method of deciding which, in a case of conflict, should be made to yield to which. In such circumstances I should hold, with Hegel in the *Phenomenology*, that there is a Conscience that represents the deepest sincerity of a man's, or of a community's, moral personality and that simply cuts the Gordian knot of interpersonal conflict, such a cutting being interpersonally legitimate since it is the only way of reaching a decision at all. The decision is then recognized as valid *by* everyone, but yet only *for* the person in question. This is precisely how and why the conscientious decision is validated and respected.

My concern however, in this paper, is not with the problems of Value-theory but with the manner in which we should structure our objects of religious deference and devotion. For here I hold that reflection on our impersonal Values, and the integration of our aspirations towards them, necessarily leads to the constitution, for our thought and aspiration, of an object in which *all* suprapersonal Values will be present together, and in an absolutely transcendent, all-surpassing form. The aspiration towards such an object, and our unconditional deference to it, may be regarded as the defining mark of Worship or of religious deference. But the conditions of such a surpassing object are not such as can be fulfilled by any ordinary empirical object, in which no Value is maximal; most Values also involve realizational conflicts with other equally valid Values. The sort of synthesis required will be one of unlimited potency rather than of one-sided actualization: it will have to be something like, but only rather like, the way in which conflicting alternatives are surveyed by a single mind. We may further say of such a supreme synthesis that it will not be a *case* or an *instance* of such Values—not even a supreme case—but rather a unity of *those very Values themselves*, a unique, logical unity that not only places such a synthesis infinitely beyond any synthesis of instances but also opens its component excellences to infinite forms and degrees of participation. Such a conception, which transcends the distinction between subject and predicate or between existence and essence, certainly puts a strain on our understanding but is not one that can be avoided in the act of supreme deference to Values that we call Worship. The most glorious *instance* of Values is only one among others, and cannot be worshipped. Somehow, although we cannot understand how, such a non-instantial transcendence must be achieved.

The supreme religious object must, further, effect a synthesis of all the explanatory, cognitive Values as well as of all the other forms of rationally approved excellence. The object that embodies, and indeed *is*, all Values cannot itself exist in a dispensable, contingent manner: it must be such that it cannot validly be conceived away. It must cover all possibilities and forms of goodness and likewise, by negating them, all possibilities and forms of badness; hence it must exist certainly and necessarily. It could only *not* be if it represented an intrinsically incoherent plight of thought. This does not of course mean that *for us* the question of its coherence or incoherence might not be an open one, since we are here not dealing with the presence or absence of merely formal contradiction. For us, likewise, there are a great number of alternative notions as to what its basic nature might be, though it itself can permit of no alternatives or rivals alongside itself. It can, however, be permitted to permit of contingencies outside itself, provided that they in some fashion depend on some mode of free self-determination peculiar to itself. I shall not go further into these aspects of Absolute-theory nor consider the various postulates and theorems of such as Spinoza, Proclus, Hegel, Shankara, Aquinas, and Christian Wolff. It is only worth saying dogmatically that there can be no Absolute that is value-free and that refuses to embody the Anselmian notion of perfection. If this notion is incoherent, divinity is impossible and all religion idolatrous, except such as adores the impossible. I shall not explore this last alternative, which is undoubtedly a possibility *for us* and one that I once embraced. Nor shall I further attempt to justify Absolute-theory except on the pragmatic ground that everyone in fact falls back in thought on an irremovable Absolute of some sort, whether this be Matter or Spirit or Space-Time or Sense-data or Platonic *Eide* or Absolute Values or whatnot. Everyone thinks in terms of something or other that he *cannot* think away.

The perfect Being in Whom or in Which all values and possibilities nestle together cannot, however—on a respectable view embraced by such as Plotinus, Proclus, Angelus Silesius, Meister Eckhart, and Hegel—*be* at all, unless surrounded by an encompassing radiation of limited, dependent, contingent, mutually exclusive entities whose natures represent limited excerpts from its perfection, but which are also in some measure free to add to such excerpts perversions and distortions, such as cruelty, that are only present in the Supreme Perfection in the sense of being negated by it. (Much as the way in which certain abuses reveal their presence, in a well-ordered family, by *never* being permitted and *never* entertained, even in thought.) Towards such perversions and distortions the Perfection at the center of things must of necessity act correctively and redemptively, finding in such correction and redemption the supreme exercise of its perfecting powers. The mutual exclusion of contingent, finite entities (together with their interconnections in that they spring from a common source) will then necessarily demand the existence of an all-comprehending medium such as Space, which at once separates everything finite from everything else finite and at the same time connects them all with one another. Possibilities of deviation and correction likewise demand the existence of a comprehensive medium such as Time, which is at once supersessive and progressive: only in such a medium can there be a large lapse from perfection and an unending progress towards it. The unitary Perfection at the center of things must therefore in some manner imperfectly illustrate itself in imperfect beings variously stationed in something like Space and developing and changing in something like Time. And to the form of exclusion that we call Space must be added the further form of exclusion that may be called Spiritual Space, meaning thereby the mutual exclusion of minds and understandings, only which can, in an imperfect and imitative empathetic manner, have access to one another's experiences. We need not exclude unconscious things from the imperfect beings thus stationed in Space and Time, interacting with one another dynamically and also entering into an experimental dialogue with the conscious inhabitants, a dialogue in which, in reply to suitable test-questions, they are ready to declare their deeper natures. And we must extend the reach of Values to those unconscious things. Not only do they (as in the case of organisms) pursue definite goals but they are also, in the inorganic sphere, at least obedient to that limitation of variety, that repetition of pattern that, itself a Value, our understanding looks for in all objects of experienced and only looks for because it is itself a case of the selfsame limitation of variety.

It is here, we may say, that the aspect of Divinity that we may call the Holy Spirt, and also in some contexts the Word, enters the theological picture. For the Periphery of Being, with its necessary limitation, individuation, and mutual exclusiveness, as well as its mutability and manifold deviation from perfection, is at the opposite limit from the unity and simplicity of the Divine Center and requires what we may call a set of radial lifelines connecting it with the latter. Along these lifelines, the aspect of the Godhead that we may call the Holy Spirit (or in some contexts the Word) may be conceived as working, reaching *out* to the alienated peripheral instance and, in such reaching out, coalescing with whatever reaching *up* towards itself may be coming from the periphery. For a central Absolute cannot simply exclude its distanced periphery, which exclusion would mean giving the latter an absolute status alongside itself: it must endow the points on the periphery with all that they have of positive perfection and it must continuously sustain them in being, as Descartes argues in one of his proofs. If the Word itself is *with* God and also *is* God yet also *proceeds* from God and is related to God by reciprocated *Love*, so even the things on the periphery, with all their deviations, are also *with* God and even remotely *are* God, for there is nothing else at all for them to be. Pantheism, when it does not try to *compose* Divinity out of what streams from Divinity, is obviously an absolute aspect of truth. And it is along these radial lifelines linking the Divine Center with its periphery that God *qua* Holy spirit is ever active, steering peripheral beings towards those suprapersonal Values that, in their unity and totality and self-subsistence, simply *are* Divinity. Those radiating lifelines not only connect all peripheral being with the Center but at the same time connect them all with one another. Hence nowhere, not even on the periphery, are they ever wholly sundered: distance or irrelevance is only a limiting form of connection. Hence we cannot absolutely separate points or zones in Space and Time, but each is what it is by reason of its position in the great sum total, with all parts of which it is continuously linked. Hence, the occupants of Space and Time also have necessary patterns of covariance that link them with one another. Hence, some of the occupants of Space and Time are also sensitive to what lies around them and react to it in a fixed manner, which manifests both what they are and what the environing things are. Further, the higher exercises of cogitative experience do nothing but reflect this preestablished harmony, which is not to be regarded, in Humean fashion, as an inexplicable mystery but as the basic presupposition of all explanation.

I must, however, at this point reject as an exaggeration the idealistic dogma of universal internal relations, which requires a completely deterministic locking in of everything into its place in the whole. The absolute Center must plainly be credited with something like a freedom of decision, a power to take *one or another* of a number of paths in its expansion towards the periphery, and the items on the periphery can also be credited within limits with a similar freedom. Thus, while everything always makes some difference to everything, everything could within limits have been different in itself and could have made, also within limits, different differences to everything else. I shall not try to elucidate the distinctions of essence and accident predicated in the words "within certain limits," except to say that they represent necessities of thought and being, which have suffered at the hands of misplaced empiricistic criticism.

The lifelines leading from the periphery to the absolute Center are lines along which we, as well as the Holy Ghost, can travel, although in a reverse direction, and what we experience on that journey casts a dim analogical light on what must lie at or near the Center itself. We can, for example, freely imagine situations that bring out possibilities unrealized on the actual periphery, and we can grasp and savor, in an immediate, nutshell fashion, complex meanings and theorems that range over countless peripheral situations and that would perhaps, in cases such as that of the transfinite, not permit illustration for us at all. We are also able, even in our peripheral state, to perform the strange miracle of entering into other people's experiences; it seems plain that we are always in some measure performing this miracle, which is not based on any inference but rather serves as the permanent presupposition of the latter. In all such exercises we are traveling beyond the sheer periphery of being and along a lifeline to the center, along which, although in a reverse direction, the Holy Spirit may be thought to move. This means that, at the Center of being, there lies a state in which all lifelines converge and in which nothing can be remote from, or external to, anything else. It must also be a state in which, without blurring of content, there will be a total vanishing of the progressive, supersessive character of peripheral Time. Such supersession is in fact always overcome in some measure even at the periphery, as when we hold in mind the just past or vividly recall the remoter past, but at the Center progression and supersession must vanish completely, and any lapse of time, or the infinite lapse of all time, be grasped *uno obtutu*, in a single glance. As a shepherd can see the whole of his finite flock and know just how many they are, without counting them one after another, so at the Center, and for the vision there, all the finite cardinals will be seen as embodied in the transfinite sum total of all time and being. God, we may say, can give a fulfilled, intuitive sense to all these cardinals and to the distinct forms of transfinitude as well. At the Center the distinction of persons will likewise be no more than a nuance: everyone, we may say, will be everyone, although more centrally himself, much as God is everyone, although supremely Himself. And at the Center sensuous illustration and exemplification will languish and be replaced by pure cogitative gist, as it in fact always partially is, even in this peripheral life. One will grasp a whole system of interconnected truths in the utterly luminous, but also utterly wordless and imageless, manner in which, even in this life, one grasps such trivial truths as that someone is trying to deceive us or that a certain number is a product of two others. In the same way, at the Center, deliberation and planning will become merged in execution and satisfaction.

I shall not persist in these mystical excesses. Dante has done it much better when in the thirty-third Canto of his *Paradiso*, he describes the manner in which substances and accidents, and all their relations, are conflated together in the *semplice lume* of the Beatific Vision. Plotinus has also written unsurpassably on the same topic in his tractate on Intelligible Beauty. When one cannot hope to achieve anything as good, it will be well to remain silent, perhaps only uttering a *Veni Creator*. We may however believe, with an approach to rational certainty, in a whole spectrum of states between the sundered, sensuous, compulsive periphery, in which everything falls apart from everything else, and the absolute Center, in which all things come together in unity. And what is called disembodied life will be comprehended in that spectrum, although it should perhaps not be called 'disembodied' since, as in dreams and as in the myths of Plato, Dante, in the Apocalypse, and so on, many beautiful vestiges of the corporeal and the sensuous will survive. It will only be at the end of the journey that all things sundered and successive, bodily and sensuous, or personally dirempted will be wholly laid aside, and the connective functions of the Holy Ghost be reduced to pure Love.

Summary

I have great difficulty in summarizing papers I have written, so I apologize for any defects in this summary. The paper sketches the whole of my Neoplatonic-Hegelian theology: if you will read the Eighth Tractate of Plotinus's Sixth Ennead, Paragraph 18, you will have one of its sources, although it has other sources, eastern and western, ancient and modern, as well. I have also tried to work this theology out in my Gifford Lectures, *The Transcendence of the Cave*. The central point in my theology is logical and ontological: there are forms of being characterized by what Hegel calls *Ineinandersein*, or an *interpenetration* of aspects that are distinct and even opposed, and there are by contrast forms of being characterized by what he called *Aussersichsein*, or mutual externality. The contrast of these two modalities of being may best be illustrated by the contrast between a pregnant insight or resolve, in which an infinity of theoretical or practical reasoning or endeavor is present in a wholly clear but wholly concentrated 'nutshell', the sort of thought that Luther may have had when he pinned his theses on the cathedral door at Wittenberg, and the sort of experience that spells itself out in a series of states or objects separate in time or space, or is sensuously illustrated or imaged or filtered through the grossness of words. In this sort of experience there is no sense of a unifying conflation of all the separate givens; each stands isolated, *abgetrennt* from the others, although we are compelled to acknowledge a web of impalpable relation among them. There is, further, in human experience a whole spectrum of states, ranging from those of maximum concentration and interpenetration to those of maximum dispersion and diremption, and it is along this spectrum of states that our inner life regularly proceeds, the concentrated resolve or understanding being spelled out in observation or action, and the dispersed, fully spelled out version of experience being concentrated into interior interpenetration. In most of ordinary life we favor the exteriorizing dimension and think that we only achieve clearness and objectivity in following it: our language and logic likewise favor it. We want to isolate items everywhere and to say clear-cut things about them, Arguably, however, the interiorizing dimension is ultimately the more important: after hearing the symphony completed, it lives on, as Lotze said, for a little while at least as an abiding mood in the soul, and it is in such synthetic unity that symphonic enjoyment is consummated.

It is further arguable that the whole of our higher value-experience lies in the interiorizing dimension. When, for example, after long theoretical and experimental work we arrive at a synthesis that elucidates and unifies infinite detail, it is then that we have that experience of Insight or Knowing that is one of the highest of our values, precisely because it conflates and unifies, without the confusion of infinite detail. Another highest value is that of an aesthetic appreciation, which sees all the detail of some complex artwork or material object as contributing to a single harmonious integration. And another highest value is the love that binds all the scattered apprehensions of someone's varied acts and appearances, whether individually good or bad, into a single, total acceptance of everything; within the person in question, they are all entirely and intensely dear, simply because together they express the person in question. There is also a highest value in the achievement of a single, total reaction to the vast variety of needs, interests, and approaches of a whole group of persons, a reaction that seeks to do *justice* to them all and integrates its response to them in a single, unified piece of practice.

I shall not go on trying to deduce a complete cartography of the highest values. I have made such an endeavor in my book *Values and Intentions* and elsewhere. I believe that all the supreme values lie at the ends of lines, which break down peripheral outsideness and separateness and move towards a central unity in which all things come together, without thereby losing their distinctiveness. What is now important to stress is that all religious and mystical experience moves in this interiorizing, unitive direction, although much further and more pertinaciously than is done in our ordinary everydayness, and that there is a consummating point to the whole movement that may, if one likes, be given the quasi-personal name of God, although it may be thought of and pictured in widely differing ways, not all of which involve a loving personal relation. All comes together at the center of things, in goodness and harmony as well as in unity, since all evil and ugliness and unintelligibility lie along the exteriorizing path and consist in various forms of mutual incoherence, exclusiveness, indifference, hostility, and destructiveness. In my theology, however, the Divine Center depends on the outgoing creative movement, which permits the generation of mutual exclusion and evil, as much as on the ingoing movement, which overcomes them and redeems them. It is essentially bound up with redemptive, illuminating activity, and would, as Angelus Silesius says, give up the ghost in sheer need if it had nothing at all to redeem. There can be no beatific vision at the center if there is not also a periphery where incomprehension, disharmony, hostility, and other forms of evil are permittedly rampant, even though always counteracted and subordinated by the unity at the Center. The Word and the Holy Spirit seem alike to represent that theological aspect that not only, to quote Dante, binds all things by love into one volume at the Center but also represents the eternal radiation from the Center, which, in becoming dismembered on the periphery of being, gives to all things on the periphery the power to revert to their center and their source.

CHARLES COURTNEY

4. Henry Duméry's Phenomenology of Transcending

I. Philosophy as Critical Reflection

Among those inspired by phenomenology, Henry Duméry, Professor of Philosophy at the University of Paris (Nanterre), has come nearest to producing a systematic philosophy of religion. In the course of this essay on his account of transcending, I will present the main elements of his system and its method. But at the outset it is important to emphasize Duméry's conception of philosophy as a critical reflection on primary experience or action. Religious acts together with all other modes of human action—perceptual, imaginal, political, playful—are the subject matter for philosophical inquiry. Philosophy, according to Duméry, is a secondary enterprise which comes along after the fact, or the act, and attempts to discern an intelligible structure in the action. Duméry's position here echoes that of Husserl, who, in the final pages of the *Cartesian Meditations*, stressed that "phenomenological explication does nothing but *explicate the sense this world has for us all, prior to any philosophizing*, and obviously gets solely from our experience—*a sense which philosophy can uncover but never alter*, and which, because of an essential necessity, not because of our weakness, entails (in the case of any actual experience) horizons that need fundamental clarification" (1960:151, emphasis in the original). So, reflecting philosophically on loving your cat or your friend is not the same as, nor a substitute for, the act of loving your cat or your friend. And, though there may be such a thing as the intellectual love of God (Spinoza), intellectually loving God is different from the philosophical clarification of the nature of that act. Duméry's phenomenology of transcending is not itself a way of transcending. To clarify what Duméry's contribution to understanding transcending might be, let us say that he offers us a philosophical approach to approaches to transcendence; to cut it just a bit finer, since he reflects on human activity, we can say that he offers an approach to religious transcending.

II. The Principal Topics and Procedures of Duméry's Philosophy

Before we consider Duméry's account of religious transcending, we need to look at the three major topics of his philosophy and the three different procedures he follows for them. The reader will find complementary expositions of the main features of Duméry's philosophy in several chapters of two books by Professor Louis Dupré: *The Other Dimension* (1972) and *A Dubious Heritage* (1977).

The first topic is the category of the Absolute which he treats in *The Problem of God*, the first of his systematic works in the philosophy of religion. There, the author makes "an attempt at a critical dissolution" (1957b:1,4) of the idea of the Absolute. The issue is whether this idea can withstand rational efforts to render it superfluous or unintelligible. Duméry's procedure is to follow Husserl's reductive movement to the intending, constituting transcendental subject and then to prolong it with an additional reduction to a transcendent Absolute that is transordinal, beyond determination, and that he characterizes as pure unity or pure act (1957c,1964:Chap. II). Such an Absolute is, of course, beyond the grasp of the acting subject and the critical philosopher; nonetheless, Duméry concludes that it is rational to affirm a radically transcendent Absolute.

The second major topic, the acting human subject, is dealt with by another philosophical procedure, namely, a description of its unity and complexity. This is done in Part One of the *Philosophie de la Religion*. In this case a description is possible because the intentional, objectifying consciousness produces expressions that can be examined. Duméry's name for human consciousness is "act-law," by which he wants to indicate that the human subject is a free agent conditioned by its being incarnate, in community, and historical; that is, human consciousness is actual by reason of its taking form in situation. It is act-law, or one and multiple, in contrast to the Absolute, which is pure act or the One.

The third topic of Duméry's philosophy is that of human action in its different modes. A fully developed philosophy would study all the ways in which the act-law is expressed. One list of the principal kinds of action is this: mathematics, aesthetics, morals, religion (1957b:I,51). Duméry has, up to now, written only on religion. The procedure in this phase of philosophy is to describe and to order. A philosophy of religion would, for example, bring into view the religious object or objects, specify the particular intention of religion, show how the different levels of consciousness and powers of expression are employed in religious life, and trace the relations between religion and other forms of action.

This present study of religious transcending, while assuming that Duméry's philosophy of the Absolute is largely successful, will deal with the latter two topics of his philosophy, namely, philosophy of the subject and reflection on the religious category of faith.

III. Duméry's Philosophy of the Human Subject

The three principal influences on Duméry's thought are the French tradition of reflexive philosophy, phenomenology, and Plotinus. My exposition of his philosophy of the subject will be organized around the main contributions apparent from these influences. From reflexive philosophy, chiefly the work of Blondel, Duméry learned that consciousness is a constant presence to self. An immediate awareness of acting accompanies the act. In order to know *that* we are acting or *what* we are doing we do not need to step aside and gaze at ourselves as at an object. Nor are we simultaneously accomplishing two operations, both acting and knowing that we are acting. Acting, attending to, includes awareness. Thus Duméry speaks of consciousness of self rather than of knowledge of self. If we consciously tend toward an object, let us say of desire, we do not need, in addition, to tell ourselves that we desire the object. Desiring is a way of 'being conscious' (1957b:I,41). This omniconsciousness of self is what makes possible the reflexive recovery of self that is philosophy. That is, philosophical reflection does not start from scratch. We can say that it prolongs, while changing the direction of, immediate self-awareness.

From phenomenology Duméry learned that consciousness is intentional and constituting. He does not give an independent defense for the eidetic and transcendental-phenomenological reductions, nor does he work them out in detail. He adopts the main conclusions of the reductive movement. If consciousness is intentional, objects are not *in* consciousness, which fact would realize or substantialize consciousness. Nor are objects opposed to the subject such that their being-in-relation is suppressed, that is, unthought, paradoxical, or problematic. If consciousness is constituting, then the subject is a giver of meaning and value. Consciousness is objectifying; through consciousness, meanings and values come to be. Duméry puts the two theses together when he says that "the only objects are *intentional* objects because the only consciousness is *objectifying* consciousness" (1957b:I,41). Naturalism is the great enemy of true spiritualism, and Duméry credits phenomenology's suspension of the natural attitude with providing the most effective philosophical antidote.

From Plotinus Duméry took his emphasis on the subject as act and the differentiation of the several levels of consciousness. The latter he specifies as intelligible, rational, and sensible. Every concrete act involves all of these, but reflective analysis can distinguish them. The intelligible (or spiritual) level is that of the act-law, the unseen ground of all expression, immediately present to the Absolute. The sensible plane arises from the relation of subjectivity to the external world. This relation, mediated by the body, is the locus of sensation. The rational plane interacts with both of the others to create the many varieties of expression. The rational and the intelligible together produce categories of expression. The rational and the intelligible together produce categories, concepts, so-called pure ideas. These two, together with the sensible plane, produce natural language and symbols, and schemes. Duméry's philosophy is ordered according to pairs of categories and schemes. Thus we have the category of the Absolute and the scheme of transcendence, the category of the subject and the schemes of the soul, the category of grace and the schemes of the supernatural. Just as we never see the seeing eye, we never experience the creative act at the intelligible level. Nonetheless, the expressions show its effects and we, banking on the prereflexive presence to self, have reason to affirm the free agency of the subject. The subject *is* bound to express itself, but it is not bound to any certain expressions. Thus, we see the subject continually challenging and changing the given forms.

This complex unity, the structure of the subject, never, of course, appears as such. What has been presented so far is a philosophical product, the result of a reflection that has sought, in Husserl's words, to exhibit horizons of experience, aspects that natural experiencing will never attend to but that, if the philosophical work has been done well, are ingredient to every experience whatsoever. Now it is time to study in more detail one of the kinds of human activity.

IV. The Religious Act

The philosopher who begins the work of critical reflection without prejudice would do well to accept initially the conventional mapping of the kinds of human action. Though many would want to revise Duméry's list of mathematics, asthetics, morals, and religion, I submit that nearly all lists would include religion. Religious acts, then, are appropriate objects of philosophical inquiry. In his book on method, *Critique et religion*, Duméry says that it is not philosophy's place to make judgments concerning reality or value. Philosophy can, however, specify the conditions according to which a religion or a religious act is not unreasonable. He elaborates the point in *Philosophie de la religion* by saying that the philosopher of religion is concerned only with problems of meaning and modality. No judgments are made as to religious truth or falsity; such judgments are religious or theological. Neither does the philosopher seek to dissolve a doctrine such as the Incarnation into a philosophical equivalent; that would be to put philosophy into competition with religion. The philosopher has a threefold task with reference to religious phenomena: (1) to give a rational statement of the meaning, (2) to show how it is constituted, and (3) to state under what conditions it can become a norm for the thought and practice of a religious person (1957b:I,103,n.3).

The religious act is specified by the intention and by the object intended. Duméry says that the singular mark of religion is that it has to do with the relation of the soul (or person) to God (1957a:141n). Now if the transcendental subject as act is immediately present to the Absolute, it would *seem* that the religious relation is the simplest of all, so simple that the qualifications of intention and object do not even apply. In fact, the religious relation is the most complex of all. The reason is that the human subject, though an agent and free, is actual only by being expressed across the planes of consciousness and toward objects. But the Absolute is not an object. It is that by which there are objects and cannot, therefore, be directly intended as an object. It must be reached, if it is reached, indirectly. Already-constituted objects must be taken as indices of the Absolute; thus, the Absolute is named the Lord, the Almighty, the Eternal, and so on. The religious actor seeks to focus the whole person—body, mind, and soul—on God, and thus the entire range of expressive capacities come into play. And, since the Absolute is the ground of all that is, every object can in principle become a springboard for the religious intention. Such objects are called sacred. The immediate focus of religious transcending is on sacred things, on those objects that are revelatory of God.

Duméry defines revelation as "God present to the spirit-which-speaks-this-presence" (1957a:144). Since all expressive speech is on 'this side' of both the Absolute and the act of speaking, the entirety of revelatory expression will come from man and will have mundane content. This may appear to destroy utterly the transcendent aspect of religion. To the contrary, Duméry contends that this account of the matter is the one that best makes sense of the worldliness of religious language and preserves the radical transcendence of the divine.

Let us now look at some examples of the sacralizing of objects and of religious expression.

V. Sacralizing and the Projective Mentality

Sacralization is the objectivation of an inner disposition. It is projecting onto a thing the intention of, or aspiration for, the Absolute. The intention is primary; without it there would be nothing sacred. Sacredness is not a natural quality of certain things, for (1) any object can receive it, (2) not all objects of a certain kind are sacred, and (3) objects may lose their sacredness and also regain it. We have sacred objects only when we have subjects aspiring to the transcendent.

Still, it is no surprise, Duméry notes, that the sacralizing projection often attaches to the extraordinary, the weird, the powerful. Whatever breaks the regular flow of phenomena suggests another realm, which it is impossible to control. And that is a characteristic of the genuinely transcendent. But the religious person can mistakenly conclude that there is a supernatural realm, structured like nature, but more powerful. This doubling may happen, but it need not; if the intentionality is sufficiently strong and clear, it will not.

Since the human subject becomes actual only as it is corporeal, social, temporal, and so on, Dumèry says that human consciousness is projective. What are the features of this projective mentality in the religious act? The religious agent is one who does not need to know *that* the consciousness has a projective structure but who knows *how* to use it to intend the divine. The religious person is constituted in the function of, and starting from, a situation. All the levels of consciousness—bodily, rational, and intelligible—are employed to intend transcendence via various constituted objectivities. The religious person seeks light, pure light, but can get at the light only by means of objects from which light can be reflected.

Dumèry distinguishes four levels or planes of religious expression and illustrates them with reference to the Christian category of redemption. First, there is the psychological plane. The religious consciousness operating on this plane senses guilt over its breaking of the relation between the soul and God. The contraries are not moral (vice-virtue) but religious (sin-love). Redemption, at this level, will be brought about when an innocent one takes the guilt, the sin, upon himself. Thus, Jesus' passion—which is experienced, Dumèry says, as a violent and salutary sentimental shock. The freeing act of the redeemer gives the guilty one a chance to turn inward and to discover the divine presence.

On the mythological plane the problem of guilt is objectified temporally in terms of an origin and an eschaton. The operative pair of figures here is Adam-Christ, the one the source of death and the entry of sin into the world, the other the source of life and the principle of resurrection in the future.

Third is the institutional plane, where the emphasis is on the significance of redemption for relations among persons. The key Christian expression in this context is the Eucharist. Persons are enabled to establish community and thereby to actualize themselves more fully, by participating in the symbolic act of the Eucharist. Since the rite brings into play body (through kneeling and eating and drinking), emotion, imagination, mind, and spirit, it is the richest mode of expression. Dumèry even says that religion is primarily cultural and that the least mass is worth all the councils (1957b:II,219). Since the purpose of all religious expression is to achieve interiority, adherence to the Absolute, it is pertinent in this connection to note Dumèry's observation that the faithful community in the various events of Holy Week can, in attitude, follow Christ.

The historical plane, for Duméry the most important, gives a factual point of attachment for the religious consciousness. He acknowledges that our historical knowledge of Jesus of Nazareth is scanty, but that what we do know is enough to suggest (to Duméry) that Jesus was totally faithful and that his religion was as nearly interior as possible.

A fifth plane is mentioned, but not discussed extensively. It is called the conceptual plane, and apparently in it the doctrinal element of religion is worked out. In it, also, the religious person with a rational bent works out a major part of his or her salvation.

Note that on each plane there is a movement that we can call interiorization. The circumstances of history, the legacy of tradition, and the capacities of the subject are gathered in a spiritual act that refers all to the transcendent. And the movement is not necessarily bound to the theme of redemption. The different planes of expression could be illustrated by other Christian themes. Or, by a religion for which redemption is not central—Islam, for example.

It may be helpful to supplement the preceding 'epistemological' exposition concerning redemption with a more 'existential' account. In *La foi n'est pas un cri (Faith is not a Cry)*, a less technical book, Duméry touches on many of these same points while seeking to comprehend "the first Christian experience" (1959:17). Christianity is situated historically. Jesus is a real person who manifested God, "whose life, death, and religious attitude express the presence of God preeminently, personally, and immediately" (1959:72). This religious reality, or fact, was discerned by the disciples, and with that we have the irreducible historical dimension of Christian faith. To *historical* faith is added *cultural* faith, when the reality of Jesus is linked with the deepest religious meanings of the Jewish tradition (Christ, Messiah, Suffering Servant, Son of God, etc.) and receives catechetical and liturgical form. A third, and decisive, dimension of faith is the *theophanic*. By this Duméry means that those who see Jesus as the Revealer discern not only the Anointed of the Lord, but in doing so they see God. God is present to them (1959:72). Just as Jesus is revealer as an actual human being, so faith, for the disciples and all who come after, is a living intentionality of the God of love and should produce acts of love.

These parallel summary presentations of projective religious mentality have perhaps left the impression that Duméry has a subjectivist view of religion. If so, the impression should be corrected. Religious projections are grounded in the acts of subjects, but the acts are objectifying. The religious person does not objectify his or her psychological states; the religious intention is actualized and manifested through the constitution of religious objects. The objects as bearers of essence and signification are resistant to subjective manipulation, while being subject to a spiritual intention.

This emphasis on the primacy of the intentional act does not imply, however, that all persons are the makers of their religious objects, that they are or must be spiritual geniuses. They are born into and confront already-constituted religious forms and institutions. They are not forced to start from scratch. Persons are, however, called to make the available religious expressions the instruments of their religious intention. The religious facts that are already there will remain just that, facts, if they are not incorporated into an actual religious intention, if they are not resacralized. As facts or as deposits of the past, religious things lack religious reality; association with the intention of a living person makes them actual. We can find an analogy in the difference between the textbook geometric proof and the proof worked out and thought through, or in that between the musical score and the music played.

VI. Superstition: A Test Case for a Philosophy of Religion

Now that our exposition is complete, let us turn briefly to a critical question. Can Duméry's account of religion handle instances of superstition and perversion? It should be able to, if it is an adequate account of the nature of religion. Lived religion, of course, has its own perception of and response to superstition. What does rational criticism have to say about it? I think Duméry would say that when the expressive planes are mixed, nonesense will result. For example, mixing the historical and mythological planes is a mistake, as is trying to force the forms of cult into those of doctrine. I think Duméry holds that each of the planes of expression, left to itself, is able to carry religious intention to term. But things miscarry when the planes are mixed. The perversions of idolatry and superstition emerge when the religious intention is fixed on an object rather than on using the object as a springboard for attaining the Absolute. Just as any object can be sacralized, any sacred object can become an idol. Examples are Scripture, doctrine, institution, rite, Redeemer—the list could continue indefinitely.

VII. Concluding Comments and Questions

It is one of the paradoxes of the religious life, says Duméry, that human beings, in order to convert toward transcendence, must move among objects and thus appear to move away from the goal. The paradox is lessened somewhat, it seems to me, if we regard the already-constituted forms of expression as potential instruments to serve the religious intention. Thus, certain political expressions such as Kingdom and Lord could be used for a religious purpose. This way of appropriating available forms could be called the way of invocation. But what about those acts that are not specifically directed toward the divine? Do they have no religious significance? Does the religious attitude have no bearing on them? I am asking a question about the religious vocation of worldly acts. Duméry might answer in the following way: If the religious attitude is sufficiently integrated into a person's life, then all that he or she does will be done with the awareness of the transcendent dimension. This will prevent the absolutization of any worldly power or form and will make it possible to refer all ways of acting to the transcendent. Whereas the way of invocation will seek to draw one into the presence of the transcendent through worldly forms, the way of vocation will place one *in* the world *before* the transcendent.

Finally, I want to ask about the range of application of Duméry's philosophy of religion. He claims that it is universally applicable and that he has worked it out with reference to Christianity only because that is the religion he knows best. Debate on this issue could well focus on the primacy Duméry gives to the historical plane of expression. If he claims that the life of Jesus of Nazareth is a historical fact and that the Vedas, the life of Gautama Buddha and the Qur'an, are not, then there is a problem. But if he claims that there must be a set of empirical conditions for every act of sacralization and allows that the range of possible valid conditions is indefinite, then there would seem to be no problem. He would simply be reasserting something about what is involved when a worldling makes a religious discernment. Then the question would be whether it is appropriate to say that the historical plane is the most important of all. My own preliminary efforts to extend Dumėry's approach to other religions indicate that it has promise, especially insofar as the emphasis on intention and projection gives us ways of getting behind the surface of symbolizations to see how religion functions in the lives of persons.

References

Dumėry, Henry

1957a   *Critique et religion: problèmes de méthode en philosophie de la religion.* Paris: Société d'Édition d'Enseignement Supérieur.

1957b   *Philosophie de la religion: essaie sur la signification du Christianisme,* Tomes I-II. Paris: Presses Universitaires de France.

1957c   *Le problèm de dieu en philosophie de la religion: examen*
1964   *critique de la catégorie d'Absolu et du schème de transcendance.* Paris: Desclée de Brouwer. English translation by Charles Courtney, *The Problem of God.* Evanston: Northwestern University Press.

1959   *La foi n'est pas un cri* suivi de *Foi et institution.* Paris: Éditions de Seuil.

Husserl, Edmund

1960   *Cartesian Meditations: An Introduction to Phenomenology,* trans. Dorion Cairns. The Hague: Martinus Nijhoff.

5. Creation, Solitude, and Publicity

Naturam expellas furca, tamen usque recurret.

God alone, not choosing the possible alternative, being alone, without looking to any other as model, using no material, and not enriched either by achieving the result or by the result achieved, causes others to be.

The one who is best creates, but creating is not what is best—because the one who creates would be just as good if he did not create. Creativity and generosity are not necessarily, although they are in fact, one with the necessary one who is best.

Nature, in the secondary sense, is creatures created by God, but nature in the primary sense is God—whether he choose to create or not to create, and therefore whether or not there be creatures at all, whether or not there be nature, in the secondary sense.

If God were to choose the condition that-creatures-not-be (that-creatures-not-be is possible because that-creatures-are is chosen as an alternative and for no other reason than the choosing itself: the plenitude of goodness would not be diminished, nor would goodness be impugned for lack of generosity, if creatures were not), then all that 'being' would mean would be God alone: the extreme of solitude.

The fact (that-creatures-are) to which the conditional (if . . ., then . . .) is contrary is the extreme of publicity: for creatures to be is for them to be both chosen by and manifest to another, the creator. Thus everything creaturely is gratuitiously, and nothing creaturely is secretly.

If the creator chooses to manifest himself to creatures, especially if he chooses to manifest himself both as the one by whom creatures are gratuitiously chosen to be and as the one to whom they are exhaustively manifest, then some creatures—all being called to imitate the creator—answer by choosing to manifest themselves both to the creator and to each other both as both chosen and choosing and as both manifest and manifesting.

Publicity, both choosing to manifest and manifesting choice, becomes in the extreme both the gratuitous establishment of the plurality of being and the gratuitous revelation of the gratuitousness of this establishment—a gratuitousness that could have remained secret, the revelation of it being gratuitous—and, in turn, imitation both of this establishment and this revelation.

Hiddenness is thus manifested as the unchosen alternative to that chosen manifestation that does away with hiddenness. In overcoming hiddenness, manifestation brings to light the hiddenness which would have prevailed had it not been overcome.

The created thinking of the possibility that-creatures-not-be must include itself in this possibility and thus think itself both as being gratuitously willed by another and as being exhaustively thought by another.

The extremes of solitude and publicity first become meaningful in a theological context. When this context is weakened or ignored or attacked but the extremes which it made meaningful by conjoining them in the teaching of creation are retained, then there is modernity.

The rejection, in turn, of modernity takes two forms: either the return of the extremes to their theological context or the recovery of senses of solitude and publicity which have not been pushed to the extremes, extremes conjoined in the teaching that God alone, not choosing the alternative and using no material, causes others to be: that God is all that 'being' means is meaningful—although false—and that all that is which is not God is only because it is both gratuitously chosen by and exhaustively manifest to God.

But we can use the words 'chosen by God' and 'manifest to God' while cancelling, for what 'God' means, the connotations alternative being left out and overcoming being hidden? Lack? Triumph? Good poor and victorious *ex parte connotati?*[1]

The Trinity is giving and receiving of plenitude, plenitude to which no being created could be adequate, giving and receiving 'without connotation' of anything created, generosity and gratitude which are meaningful 'without connotation' of a possible but unchosen alternative, the alternative of not-giving-and-receiving.

And so the contingency said of the created, human nature of Christ is not said of the uncreated divine nature, although that contingency is truly said of one who is one of the Trinity, one in undivided necessary uncreated divine nature.[2]

Notes

1. ". . . actus purus cum connotatione ad aliqua volita, aut sine illa; et ex parte hujus connotati recipit contingentiam, non ex parte intrinsicae entitatis et perfectionis. . . ." John of St. Thomas, Commentary on Aquinas, *Summa theologiae* I, 19: *Cursus theologicus* XXIV, 2 (Solesmes edition, III, 76b).

2. See Thomas Prufer, "Notes for a Reading of Augustine, *Confessions,* Book X," *Interpretaton: A Journal of Political Philosophy,* Volume X, Number 1 (January 1982), 197–200. (In footnote 5 *Ordinato* should read *Ordinatio.*)

ROBERT R. WILLIAMS

6. *Phenomenology* And *Theology: Hegel's Alternative to Dogmatism and Idealism*

Paul Ricoeur's conversion from Husserlian phenomenology to hermeneutics has produced a negative assessment of Husserl's transcendental phenomenology. In his earlier work as translator of and commentator on Husserl, Ricoeur characterized Husserl's thought as a methodological rather than an ontological idealism. The problem of the ultimate philosophical interpretation of Husserlian phenomenology, the turn from phenomenology to ontology, was bracketed. Hence phenomenology appeared as a method that was pre-ontological, or metaphysically neutral, even if Husserl himself had certain metaphysical ambitions and tendencies towards idealism. Ricoeur also noted tensions and ambiguities in Husserl's thought that render simple classification difficult if not impossible. There is a fundamental tension between the so-called transcendental idealism of the *Ideas* and *Cartesian Meditations* and the so-called existentialism and historicity of the *Crisis*. In the former literature it seems clear that the foundational stratum of Husserl's thought is trancendental consciousness; in the latter literature a similar case can be made for the *Lebenswelt* and/or for history. The problem of the foundation stratum becomes acute when Husserl's thought is queried in respect to the problem of God. Nowhere does the meaning of Husserl's operative concept of constitution appear murkier than in this case, as Ricoeur has noted:

> In what sense at and what level of . . . phenomenology is subjectivity still a plurality of consciousnesses, an intersubjectivity? Is the most radical subject God? Or does the question of the "origin" scientifically elaborated by transcendental phenomenology, dissipate that natural man and problems of religion as if they were myths?[1]

Ricoeur has apparently made up his mind, for he now claims that Husserl's phenomenological idealism leads to the atheistic interpretation of religion and theology: "the transcendental idealism of Husserl contains implicitly the same atheistic consequences as does the idealism . . . of Feuerbach. If consciousness posits itself, it must be the 'subject' and the divine must be the 'predicate', and it can only be through an alienation subsequent to this power of (human) self-production that God is projected as the 'subject' for whom the human being becomes 'predicate'."[2] Such an interpretation of transcendental idealism is both clear and controversial: once transcendental subjectivity is identified with human subjectivity, human subjectivity seems to be rendered absolute, for nothing can be prior to transcendental subjectivity. Thus God is reduced to the status of a constituted object or projection. To introduce a transcendental method into theology is like inviting an atheistic Trojan horse.

Ricoeur has raised anew an old, perhaps perennial, question. His negative assessment of transcendental idealism is reminiscent of the notorious *Atheismusstreit* provoked by Fichte nearly two centuries ago. For such a question was directed at Fichte when he sought to give systematic expression to Kant's transcentental philosophy, and thereby raised the question of the status of the transcendental subject.[3] The question concerning the identity of the transcendental subject is also thematized in a recent study of Hegel. Professor Merold Westphal interprets Hegel's *Phenomenology* through Husserlian concepts—notably those of the life-world and the critique of natural science. Westphal's reading of Hegel confirms that the transcendental subject is human society.[4] This conclusion is virtually indistinguishable from Feuerbach's. Moreover, another study, that of Professor Howard Burkle, levels the charge of atheism at the whole phenomenological tradition, from Hegel through Henry Duméry.[5] The transcendental turn, and accompanying derivation of objectivity from subjectivity, deprive God of any existence apart from transcendental consciousness. Thus transcendental method implies the nonexistence of God.

To be sure, on the other side of this debate stand Schleiermacher, Schelling, and Hegel. In this view transcendental philosophy spells the demise of precritical metaphysics and theology, but not of ontology and not of theology as such. Hence there is a third alternative to classical theism on the one hand and critical finitism on the other, an alternative that acknowledges and goes beyond transcendental philosophy. This third alternative can be broadly characterized as phenomenological theology, a view that interprets God as positively related to, even given in, religious experience and that grounds transcendental method in this larger, concretely historical view of experience. What follows is a brief historical and philosophical review of the encounter of German Idealism, represented principally by Hegel, with critical finitism. The focus will be on two questions: (1) What is the ontological interpretation of transcendental method? and (2) Is there a forced choice between phenomenology and theology? Hegel's concrete theism provides an answer to the first and a rejection of the second question. However, the problem is to determine the sense of Hegel's alternative, that is, whether there is a difference between Hegel and Feuerbach.

I. The Phenomenological Moment in German Idealism

Both Hegel and Husserl agree that Kant's transcendental inquiry into the conditions of possible experience includes a phenomenology of experience.[6] Yet Kant's account of experience is truncated because it seeks transcendental justification only for theoretical knowledge (there is no transcendental deduction of other types of experience); hence Kant's transcendental subject is essentially mundane in character.[7] Moreover, Kant's transcendental subject is highly abstract in that it is neither historical nor conscious. When Fichte sought to reformulate Kant's critical philosophy as a system, he saw the need for, and introduced more clearly than Kant, a phenomenological moment into transcendental philosophical method. This step implies that the very meaning of the word *transcendental* and that access to the transcendental region have become problematic. The phenomenological moment, therefore, is necessary for at least two reasons: (1) to overcome the abstract, ahistorical character of Kant's transcendental subject by situating it in a history, and (2) to clarify and provide a relative justification for the *choice* of transcendental idealism in opposition to dogmatic realism.

In his introduction to the *Wissenschaftslehre*, Fichte indicates that the task of philosophy is to explain experience, that is, to account for those connections of subject with object that are experienced as necessary, as not originating from the empirical self.[8] Philosophy, therefore, is a search for the grounds, the conditions, that make experience possible. There are two possible grounds for explaining experience. The first seeks to maintain the realism of the immediate or natural consciousness. It abstracts from the subject-pole of experience and explains experience by reference to a transcendent object. This is dogmatic realism. The second possibility abstracts from the object-pole of experience and explains experience by reference to a transcendental subject; it is transcendental-critical idealism. Between such radically divergent explanations there is nothing in common; hence neither can refute the other. Further, refutation is impossible because first principles can neither be defined nor explained.[9] To define or explain a first principle is to make the tacit assumption that there is something prior to the 'first' principle—a self-contradiction. Hence, the import of Fichte's portrayal of the antitheses idealism and dogmatic realism is that there is no absolutely self-evident first principle. Philosophy does not begin with an absolute principle or with absolute truth; philosophy rather finds itself in the midst of a conflict between two principles, each mutually exclusive and each presuming to be absolute. The initial conflict of principles cannot be resolved by argument (for argument always proceeds in terms of and on the presupposition of a first principle), but only by appeal to interests, namely, to the sort of man one is or would like to be. Theoretical knowledge, including the choice of a philosophical system, is thus at least in part dependent on pretheoretical interests and concerns.[10]

The importance of pretheoretical consciousness is underscored by Fichte's characterization of the *Wissenschaftslehre* not as absolute knowledge but rather as a pragmatic history of human consciousness.[11] This step presupposes a distinction between the pretheoretical, or natural, consciousness (cf. Husserl's *natuerliche Einstellung*) and the theoretical consciousness. According to Fichte, the pragmatic history will consist in the transcendental philosopher's describing the development and transition of pretheoretical consciousness according to the theoretical and transcendental standpoint. The pragmatic history of consciousness therefore thematizes the problem of the attainment and taking up of the transcendental standpoint. Hence, Fichte both continues and deepens Kant's critical thrust, rendering metaphysics problematic.

To be sure, as a transcendental philosopher Fichte already knows in advance that the goal of the development of pretheoretical consciousness, the *telos* of the pragmatic history, is transcendental idealism. But transcendental idealism is merely a hypothesis to be tested in the phenomenology of the history of consciousness. The transcendental idealist must not dogmatically impose his explanation of experience upon ordinary consciousness. The description of ordinary, or pretheoretical, consciousness is phenomenological in the sense that "philosophical reflection . . . can only follow it [namely, pretheoretical consciousness] but can give it no law."[12] The pragmatic history of consciousness is supposed to show that ordinary consciousness itself interprets its realistic conviction (that there are objects and a world out there transcendent to consciousness) in an idealistic fashion. Hence, unlike dogmatic realism, transcendental idealism does not remain a mere hypothesis—it is pragmatically, if not absolutely, justified by ordinary consciousness itself.

However, although Fichte calls for a phenomenological description of ordinary consciousness, he does not really provide such in the *Wissenschaftslehre*.[13] His attention is concentrated more on philosophically interpreted experience than on pretheoretical experience. Consequently it is difficult to avoid the impression that Fichte's concern to ground theoretical knowledge and his choice of transcendental idealism as the solution to this problem predetermine his description of ordinary consciousness. Instead of an independent phenomenological-existential exhibition and confirmation of the hypothesis of transcendental idealism, pretheoretical consciousness plays no actual role. Fichte's discussion tends to be abstract and circular:

> This fact, that the finite spirit must necessarily posit something absolute outside itself (a thing in itself) and yet must recognize from the other side that the latter exists only for it (as a necessary noumenon) is that circle which it is able to extend to infinity but can never escape.[14]

Although Fichte may have remained in the circle of transcendental or subjective idealism, he nevertheless opened up a new domain of philosophical inquiry, which Hegel and others were to exploit.

Hegel took up the idea of a phenomenological description of ordinary, pretheoretical consciousness in his *Phaenomenologie des Geistes* and extended it far beyond anything envisioned by Fichte. Hegel actually provided descriptions of ordinary consciousness, of which sense-certainty and Master-Slave are brilliant examples. Hegel saw that Fichte's idea of a pragmatic history of the human consciousness required an expansion of philosophical concern beyond the problem of grounding theoretical knowledge. After all, experience is something more than a means of verifying scientific hypotheses.[15] Kant's efforts to provide transcendental grounding for science must be set within a larger historical context. Hence, Fichte's pragmatic history must be opened up to all forms of experience—aesthetic, social, religious. And this expansion of experience will require, in turn, an expansion of the transcendental region beyond the Kantian transcendental ego.

Not only does Hegel take up the idea of a phenomenological description of ordinary consciousness but he also intends that such descriptions be genuine, not determined in advance. Fichte had said that philosophy should not impose criteria or laws upon natural consciousness, although he may have done just that. However, not only does Hegel insist upon this point of phenomenological neutrality but he further claims that for just this reason no external philosophical criteria are needed. Ordinary consciousness itself provides its own criteria of truth and objectivity—and then discovers the inadequacy of its original criteria. Hence, ordinary consciousness is self-transcending, and this is all that is needed to start it on the voyage of philosophical discovery. The philosopher need but observe and explicate the dialectical process of experience:

> The essential point to keep in mind throughout the whole inquiry is that these two elements—concept and object, being-for-another and being-in-itself—both fall within the knowledge that we are here undertaking. Consequently it is not necessary for us to bring a criterion with us or to apply our own ideas and opinions to the investigation. On the contrary, precisely because we lay these aside, we are able to consider the matter as it is in and for itself.[16]

In the *Phenomenology* Hegel accords a certain methodological priority to the phenomenological moment of description of ordinary consciousness. [17] Such priority implies that there is no self-evident starting point for philosophical reflection, whether it be an absolute object, or substance (Spinoza), or an absolute subject (Descartes, Kant, Fichte). Hegel's turn toward experience is a turn away from Cartesianism and the priority of the epistemological standpoint. That is a dead end, a vain effort to know before one knows. Equally it must be said that Hegel's phenomenological method involves a break with Schelling's version of absolute identity. Even though Hegel himself holds a version of the identity principle, the *Phenomenology* attests to the fact that philosophy cannot simply begin with absolute identity, shot, as it were, from a pistol. For that appears to be a relapse into dogmatism. Even though it may call itself idealism, it is no different in principle from what Spinoza says. Absolute identity, therefore, requires an existential introduction in order to distinguish it from dogmatism.[18] Hence, the methodological priority of phenomenology signals that philosophical reflection begins, not with absolute certitude or with apodictic self-evidence, but with a given, namely, with the inadequate, often-conflicting, preontological comprehension of Being belonging to ordinary consciousness. It is precisely the inadequacy of pretheoretical consciousness, the discrepancy between concept and object and between the consciousness of being and the self-consciousness of such, that constitutes the dialectical movement and development that Hegel terms experience (*Erfahrung*).[19]

However, despite such genuine differences from Fichte, Hegel's *Phenomenology* is no less shot through with a metaphysical thesis and with precomprehension. For although it is true that pretheoretical consciousness must be described without the imposition of external philosophical criteria—especially not the criteria that express the primacy of epistemology—it is no less true that for Hegel experience is speculatively precomprehended as the internal division of the *Begriff*.[20] Hence negation and self-transcendence are not absolute but develop towards a final goal in which the self-surpassing of knowledge will no longer be necessary, in which there will be a full correspondence of concept with object and of object with concept.[21] Hence, the absolute standpoint, to which the *Phenomenology* is supposed to lead us, is at the same time presupposed by the *Phenomenology*. Yet such a presupposition is not something absolutely known in advance, that is, it is not really a presupposition in the naive, uncritical sense, because it receives its critical justification only through the actual unfolding of the argument of the *Phenomenology* as a whole. That is why a traversal of all the forms of consciousness is necessary. The 'presupposition' of absolute identity is attained and justified only as a result. Hegel himself characterizes the structure of the argument of the *Phenomenology* as a "circle turning back upon itself, which presupposes its beginning and yet attains its beginning only at the end."[22] Philosophy can be actual only as a system, a system of experience in which nothing is known that is not already present in experience.[23]

Here is a tremendous, if problematic and elusive, expansion of the concepts of experience and philosophy. What makes such an expansion both possible and necessary is the initial detour away from transcendental subjectivity and epistemology as foundations. The *Phenomenology* instead grounds transcendental subjectivity in social experience and history. Consequently there occurs a displacement of the Cartesian problem of getting from consciousness to being. For consciousness is already, if naively, on the ontological level. It is not yet a self-consciousness. The *Geist* of the *Phenomenology* attains self-consciousness only in and through a consciousness of the other.

II. The Ontological Turn of Transcendental Philosophy

Beyond a Philosophy of Finitude

Hegel was well acquainted with the claim that transcendental philosophy makes possible only an ontology of finitude. His second published essay, *Glauben und Wissen*, is an exposition and critique of this thesis as presented in the philosophies of Kant, Fichte, and Jacobi.[24] Hegel interprets these thinkers as expressing the fundamental attitude of Enlightenment culture, whose central theme is anthropocentrism, or the absolutization of human finitude. Hegel writes:

> The fixed standpoint which the all-powerful culture of our time has established for philosophy is that of a Reason affected by sensibility. In this situation philosophy cannot aim at the cognition of God, but only at what is called the cognition of man. This so-called man and his humanity, conceived as a rigidly insuperably finite sort of Reason, form philosophy's absolute standpoint.[25]

What has elevated anthropologism to the absolute standpoint is the critical philosophy, or the transcendental turn to the subject:

> The one self-certifying certainty . . . is that there exists a thinking subject, a Reason affected with finitude: and the whole of philosophy consists in determining the universe with respect to this finite reason. Kant's so-called critique of the cognitive faculties, Fichte's [doctrine that] consciousness cannot be transcended or become transcendent . . . all amount to nothing but an absolute restriction of Reason to the form of finitude, [an injunction] never to forget the absoluteness of the subject in every rational cognition.[26]

The result of the attempt to determine the bounds of knowledge is the absolutizing of human subjectivity, such that consciousness itself is grasped as an obstacle to knowledge. Hence consciousness is shut up, solipsistic, and incapable of transcending its self-imposed limits. Thought is restricted to finitude and attains its concreteness in actual knowledge only within the bounds of finitude. From such a perspective God, or infinite Being, appears as a wholly abstract, transcendent Beyond, a 'bad infinite' that stands in opposition and contrast to the finite self-certifying subject and its experience. In the case of Kant, infinite being cannot be known, for it is wholly transcendent to experience. To be sure, the concept of God can be thought, and it is a subjective necessity of thought to think of the infinite as existing. But this thought is merely abstract; the concept of existence adds nothing to the original concept and is certainly not an intuition of the object. Hence, the existence of God is at most a postulate of moral faith.

Hegel comments critically on Kant's postulates. The content of the theological postulate is the identity principle of thought and being, which is the same as the ontological proof.[27] The question is, whether this *content* can possibly be something merely subjective, something that exists only in thought as a mere postulate:

> According to Kant himself the postulates and the faith that goes with them are subjective; the only question is how to take this "subjective". Is it the identity of infinite thought and being, of Reason and its reality, that is subjective? Or is it only the postulating and the believing of them? Is it the content or the form of the postulates that is subjective? It cannot be the content that is subjective, for the negative content of the postulates immediately suspends everything subjective. Hence it is the form, or in other words, it is something subjective and contingent that the Idea is only a subjective thing.[28]

If God, or absolute identity, has merely a postulated existence, then it has no existence beyond or independent of the postulating consciousness. The existence of God would thus be subjective, merely possible. However, the form of the postulate (as relative to the finite subject), contradicts the content of the postulate. Hegel thus advances a modal version of the ontological proof for God against Kant: the idea of God excludes the status of merely possible existence, or of merely subjective existence.

Hegel thus sees some version of the ontological argument as constituting the decisive ontological development of transcendental philosophy. However, although Hegel defends the ontological proof repeatedly against Kant's attack, he concedes that the traditional form of the proof is defective. Moreover, Hegel never completes his discussion of the theological proofs in general, nor of the ontological proof in particular. Although he sides with the theological tradition against Kant and his followers, it is equally clear that the tradition must be conceptually revised. What the revised and reconstructed version of the ontological proof would look like remains conjectural, for Hegel never positively reformulated the proof per se. Yet the entire Hegelian system rests upon and is an exhibition of the ontological argument interpreted as absolute identity. Hence, while it is correct to characterize Hegel as seeking to combine a version of the ontological proof with transcendental philosophy, this formulation is not Hegel's own but is an external one drawn from terms current in the history of philosophy. Some glimpse of how these apparently disparate elements are integrated within the Hegelian system is provided by Hegel's discussion of three attitudes of thought towards objectivity.

Three Attitudes of Thought Towards Objectivity

In the *Encyclopedia* Hegel introduces his ontological logic through a synoptic review of the history of philosophy.[29] The latter is portrayed as constituted by three successive phases, three distinct attitudes of thought towards objectivity. The different concepts of objectivity embody different conceptions of Being and thus constitute a phenomenological history of Being. The first concept of objectivity is realistic. It interprets the object as a thing in the external world. To be an object is to have external existence transcendent to and independent of subjectivity. The second concept of objectivity is idealistic. To be an object is to exist for and to be constituted by a subject. However, the transcentental turn of idealism reverses the meanings of the terms *subjective* and *objective*. For only what is constituted by transcendental subjectivity is universal and necessary, and so objective. The third concept of objectivity is roughly the view of identity theory; it corrects the one-sided abstractions of the other two by grasping their implicit presupposition and bringing it to expression.

The background of Hegel's classification—at least for the first two attitudes of thought—lies in Fichte's contrast of dogmatism and idealism.[30] The former view abstracts from the subject-pole of experience and explains experience by reference to an absolute object. To be is to be a thing. This view is the dogmatic expression of naive realism. It passes over or explains away freedom and subjectivity. In contrast, idealism abstracts from the object-pole of experience and explains experience by reference to the transcendental subject, or pure act. To be is to be an object for this transcendental subject. As pure act, the transcendental subject is the condition of possible objects. This view expresses the absolute claims of freedom and autonomy, but at the expense of a separation between the transcendental subject and nature.

Hegel applies Fichte's antithesis of dogmatism to idealism to the history of philosophy and theology. Dogmatism and idealism become at once types of thought as well as successive periods of thought. Hence Hegel charges pre-Kantian metaphysics with dogmatism. Its principle is abstract identity, and it thinks of everything as the same, that is, it thinks of everything as a thing, or external object.[31] Hence everything in the universe, as well as the universe as a whole, is regarded as a ready-made object. The human mind is conceived as a thing, and God is conceived as an absolutely existing object, or *ens realissimum*. Such an absolute object has an abstract existence; it is relegated to a beyond. From there it predetermines everything here below. Such a view fails to acknowledge freedom and the constituting role played by subjectivity. To be sure, freedom is not entirely absent, but it is dominated by the ready-made objective universe. Such a view is not as bloodless and neutral as it might seem:

> As Fichte in modern times has especially and with justice insisted, the theory which regards the Absolute or God as the object and stops there, expresses the point of view taken by superstition and slavish fear.[32]

When faith understands itself and its object naively in terms of substance-metaphysics and its categories, the corresponding image of God is one of absolute, inscrutable master, and the correlative image of man is one of slave. Such a situation is characterized by heteronomy and false consciousness. Abstract eternity is in part the objectifying correlate of false consciousness.

The second attitude of thought towards objectivity, that of idealism, is a critical negation of the first. Instead of conceiving Being as thing, idealism conceives Being as subject and contrasts subjectivity with the world of objects. Transcendental subjectivity is not a mundane object; it is not an object at all, but rather an act. The principle of idealism is not identity but opposition; in Kant and Fichte "non-identity is raised to an absolute principle."[33] In such philosophies, consciousness discovers itself, becomes aware of its own nothingness, and elevates this nothingness into a system.[34] Thus subjectivity is negative, critical. Sharply separated from the world, subjectivity has no content, and the world is denied intrinsic meaning and reduced to a mere object of utility. When this critical subjectivity is turned to religion, the sacred Beyond is brought down to earth. The *ens realissimum*, or absolute object of dogmatic faith, becomes a mere object, a block of wood or stone. Thus the sacred grove is reduced to mere timber.[35] "And if the Ideals cannot be reduced to the block and stones of a wholly explicable reality, they are made into fictions."[36] Thus the Enlightenment culminates in a naturalism that makes theology a projection, a play without substance.

F.H. Jacobi interpreted the opposition between critical and precritical thought in the following way: "*Either* God exists and exists outside of me, a living being subsisting apart; *or else* I am God. There is no third way."[37] Jacobi's either/or again raises the initial problem posed by this paper. Apparently Jacobi, Burkle, and Ricoeur see things the same way: transcendental philosophy either makes God dependent on transcendental subjectivity or simply identifies God with such. Hence it is atheistic. Presumably theism is committed to the alternative staked out by Jacobi, namely, that God exists as an object outside of and transcendent to consciousness. However, this appears to be simply a return to precritical thinking in which God is absolute object. If Jacobi's either/or is final, then the alternatives appear to be either to return to precritical thinking, the abstract identity in which all cows are black, or to acknowledge that Feuerbach is right.

However, Hegel contends that these alternatives are not exhaustive but that there is an alternative:

> Philosophy says there is a third way . . . For philosophy predicates of God not only being but also thought, that is, ego, and recognizes him as the absolute identity of being and thought.[38]

Hegel's alternative of identity returns to and appropriates the central insight of the ontological argument, namely, that genuine Being exists not merely in a subjective, but also in an objective, mode.[39] *The ontological proof constitutes the third post-Enlightenment attitude of thought towards objectivity.* It dispels the illusion of subjective-psychological immanence, to which transcendental philosophy is prone, and resurrects objectivity, as the self-objectivating concreteness of thought itself. In such a concrete identity "the claims of separation must be admitted just as much as those of identity."[40] Hence the object of consciousness must be really transcendent and independent. It cannot be reducible to consciousness nor have merely subjective being. However, this is not to speak of an absolute object in the precritical sense, for this necessity of self-transcendence is a necessity of thought itself. Hence it is also a fully mediated self-transcendence; in other words, in the ontological proof thought attains concreteness and thus becomes its own other: "The Idea is the eternal vision of itself in the other."[41]

Hegel's concrete identity involves a concrete rationalism, a comprehensive system of thought and experience. The concrete identity that admits the claims of separation makes possible, and requires, the radical openness of thought to experience manifest in the *Phenomenology*. Hence, the concrete identity is the ultimate condition of possible experience. But here the transcendental is not opposed to history and experience. It leads to history, for experience is the concretion of the identity itself. However, the infinite idea is not concretized all at once, nor is its concreteness ready-made. History is necessary in order for *Geist* to become what it already is. This means that the concrete identity is experienced naively before it is apprehended in thought:

> It does no good to treat with condescension either the so-called ontological proof or Anselm's concept of the perfect as necessarily existent. For the argument itself is latent in every unsophisticated consciousness, and it recurs in every philosophy even against its wish and knowledge—as may be seen in the principle of immediate knowledge.[42]

Hence, the concrete identity is not the invention of philosophy; there is an existential precomprehension of it in religious consciousness.[43] Phenomenological theology is the explication of this pretheoretical apprehension of Being:

> Consciousness . . . does not start from its inner life, abstract thought, and connect existence with the abstract concept of God merely in thought; on the contrary, it starts from an existence that is immediately present and *recognizes* God therein.[44]

Phenomenological theology is the explication of a *social ontology*.

III. The Problem of Divine Transcendence

The ontological turn of identity theory is supposed to be a third alternative to the abstract theism of the tradition, and the equally one-sided anthropocentrism of the Enlightenment. Hegel seeks to penetrate beneath such one-sided, reductive abstractions to a more fundamental stratum. The *Phenomenology* has neither the abstract God nor abstract man, but rather *Geist* as its central concept. For Hegel, *Geist* is an intersubjective-social reality, an I that is also a We, and a We that is also an I.[45] *Geist* resists reduction to the alternatives of either a first-person account of consciousness or a third-person account. Likewise, the alternatives of abstract theism and absolute finitism are equally *aufgehoben* and translated into the language of *Geist*, that is, social-intersubjective relations. Hence according to Hegel, "The absolute Being of faith is essentially not the abstract being, the Beyond of believing consciousness; rather it is the *Geist* of the community, the unity of abstract being and self-consciousness."[46] *Geist* is supposed to suspend all rigid antitheses in a social whole that is reciprocally mediated. However, the question arises whether *Geist* is a human-anthropological reality or whether it is a theological concept. The former view leads towards Feuerbach, and the latter view leads towards abstract metaphysical theology.

In his recent book, *History and Truth in Hegel's Phenomenology*, Professor Westphal has tried to interpret Hegel in the direction of Feuerbach-Durkheim. Thus when Hegel says that the object of faith is not the abstract Beyond but rather the *Geist* of the community, he may be understood to mean that the highest contrast within the concept of *Geist* is the contrast between the human individual and the human species. The *Geist* of the community has no being transcendent to, or independent of, the human community. Consequently it is merely an aspect of the human community and/or species. Conversely, to interpret the object of faith as an eternal, abstract Transcendent, as the theological tradition does, is merely to engage in projection and to suffer the pain of alienation. This traditional view is therefore essentially accompanied by the unhappy consciousness. Westphal defends his interpretation of Hegel by appealing to the (apparent) Hegelian interpretation of the orthodox doctrine of the Incarnation: "For Hegel . . the divine nature is the same as the human, and it is this oneness which is intuited in the incarnation."[47] Moreover, such an interpretation of Hegel is required, according to Westphal, in order to solve some puzzles surrounding the transition from Chapter Six (Spirit) to Chapter Seven (Religion) in the *Phenomenology*. This problematic transition is not to be understood as a transition from a phenomenology of human consciousness to a purely speculative noumenology. The so-called 'transition' from Chapter Six to Seven is not a transition from ordinary human consciousness to a superhuman reality transcendent to the world. Rather, the transition from Spirit to Religion is to be understood immanently as a natural transition, which deepens, but does not transcend, human consciousness.[48]

Professor Westphal is correct in sensing Hegel's departure from classical theism. However, the question is whether this departure is a 'deconstruction' of theology as such or only a critique of one form of theology, namely, classical theology, with its dogmatically asserted, abstract eternity and transcendence. As Westphal rightly says, the text must be the final arbiter; however, there are few texts as elusive and difficult as the *Phenomenology of Spirit*. I do not believe that the text Westphal appeals to for his Feuerbach-Durkheim interpretation supports such an interpretation. Westphal's reading can be maintained only by suppressing the crucial conclusion of the text. The full passage runs thus:

> But the absolute being of faith is essentially not the abstract being, the Beyond of believing consciousness. Rather it is the *Geist* of the community, the unity of the abstract being and of self-consciousness. That this *Geist* is the *Geist* of the community depends essentially on the doing of the community. For this *Geist* exists only through the productive action of consciousness—or rather it does not exist without having been brought forth by consciousness. For although such doing is essential, nevertheless it is not the sole essential ground of that being, but merely one moment. The being (*das Wesen*) exists at the same time in and for itself.[49]

The first part of the above quotation points in the direction of Feuerbach, as Westphal suggests. But this tendency is then so substantially qualified and modified that the Feuerbach reading appears to be a mere caricature of Hegel's actual position. Rather than a one-sided assertion of the primacy of the human consciousness which produces the object of faith, the above passage signifies a combination of the transcendental-productive activity of consciousness with the ontological proof or principle. What is 'produced' by consciousness is not dependent on consciousness, but rather exists "in and for itself."

The object of faith is not produced by consciousness; rather consciousness and its object here are equiprimordial.

We have previously argued that the proper execution of the ontological turn in transcendental philosophy requires the overcoming of the one-sided abstractions of an absolute object and an absolute finite subject. Such views are one-sided in that each posits only one side of the divine-human relationship as real and explains the other away. For example, classical theism is dominated by the category of substance and so tends to posit God as absolute object, that is, as real, outside of all relation. The relation of God to world is merely ideal. On the other hand, critical philosophy makes substance a category of thought and so inverts the divine-human relationship as traditionally conceived. Human subjectivity is the absolute self-certifying reality, and God is merely ideal, a fiction or projection.

However, Hegel sees in the ontological proof, properly interpreted, a way around the above impasse. His interpretation of the ontological proof is not that of the classical theological tradition, which confuses the being established by the proof with abstract transcendence. Hegel contends that the ontological proof establishes a reciprocal relationship of the divine and the human, a divine-human community:

> In such a relation at least this much is implied, namely that not only do we stand in a relation to God, but also that God stands in a relation to us. In an excess of zeal for religion our relation to God is emphasized to the virtual exclusion of the other side, such that we grasp only our relation to God, and Know nothing of God himself. However, a one-sided relationship is no relation at all. If in fact religion is supposed to be understood only as a relation from us to God, this appears to deny that God has an independent being of his own. God would then exist only in religion as something posited and produced by us.[50]

Since the ontological proof is understood in terms of identity, it is necessary to consider it from both sides or in both aspects. Viewed from the standpoint of consciousness, the ontological proof signifies that consciousness transcends itself towards an independent other. So interpreted, the ontological proof becomes virtually synonymous with the basic axiom of Husserlian intentionality, namely, that consciousness is consciousness–of. As Sartre realized, this means that intentional consciousness is already on the ontological level. Deny that consciousness transcends itself towards an independent, transcendent other, and you deny the ontological proof.

Further, the fact that intentional consciousness is already on the ontological level and is equiprimordial with its object has important implications for the object. The relation is not simply a connection of consciousness to its object, but also a connection of the object to consciousness. Hence the transcendent object is not a mere object, but a self-relating other, which is able to (1) relate itself and manifest itself to others, and (2) maintain itself in this relationship. In Hegel's reformulation, the ontological proof grounds not an abstract ontology of substance, but a concrete social ontology in which the paradigm case of sociality is the social, self-relating absolute. Hegel moves beyond the ruins of the perceptual model of being (Being as mundane object) and the ruins of the reflective model of being (Being as self-negating subject) to a social model of being. The ontological proof establishes that consciousness transcends itself towards an independent other and that the absolute qua other is capable of entering into relation and capable of maintaining itself in relation. Hence the absolute is not simply substance, or simply subject, but both: "In my view . . . everything turns on grasping and expressing the True not only as Substance, but equally as Subject."[51]

Hegel's social ontology is a third alternative to classical theism and to Feuerbach. Hegel does not, like Feuerbach, simply collapse the divine into the human. The absolute is not contradicted by relation, but maintains itself in relation. Hegel's treatment of the Incarnation as the identity of the divine and the human must be interpreted more circumspectly than Feuerbach and Westphal have done. However, the Feuerbach reading of Hegel focuses attention on a difficult interpretive issue, namely, the sense in which Hegel's social theism retains a plausible sense of divine transcendence. This issue comes to the fore in Hegel's formulation of the death of God as a theological issue. In the death of the incarnate God, what dies is the abstraction of the divine Being, insofar as it is not subjectivity.[52] Hegel writes:

> This is the painful feeling of the unhappy consciousness that God himself has perished. This hard saying is the expression of the innermost self-knowledge, the return of consciousness into the depths of the night of the abstract I = I, a subjectivity which distinguishes and knows nothing besides itself. This feeling is therefore in fact the loss of the divine substance and its standing over and against con-

sciousness. But at the same time it is the pure subjectivity of substance, or the pure certainty of itself which it lacked as absolute object or pure being. This knowledge of the death of God is the inspiration (*Begeistung*) through which substance becomes subject, through which substance loses its abstraction and becomes actual, simple, becomes the universal self-consciousness.[53]

The death of God signifies that God as absolute object is *aufgehoben*, that through such annihilation abstract transcendence is also *aufgehoben*. However, this is not an absolute negation, as Feuerbach seems to think, but only a determinate negation: absolute substance becomes subject. But what subject? Does this mean that henceforth the absolute exists only as the spirit of the community? Such an interpretation would lean in Feuerbach's direction.

But perhaps not. A passage from the *Lectures on the Philosophy of Religion* may clarify matters somewhat:

> God has died, God is dead: this is the most frightful of all thoughts, that everything eternal and true does not exist, that negation itself is to be found in God . . . However, the process does not come to a halt at this place . . . God . . . maintains himself in this process, and the latter is only the death of death.[54]

The death of God is a critique and negation of *one type of theism*, abstract dogmatic theism, but not of theism per se. The death of God is not simply a migration of the absolute object into finite subjectivity. The death of God means that negation or subjectivity itself is in God. Because God is social, God is God's own other. Since God is God's own other, God can maintain himself in the process of self-othering self-negation. In short, the death of God does not necessrily violate Hegel's social absolute; rather, it illustrates the latter. Stated otherwise, Hegel's social absolute involves a trinitarian conception of social process, for only a trinitarian absolute can preserve and unite the opposites of substance and subject.

Although Hegel identifies God with the Spirit of the Christian community, this does not imply a reduction of theology to anthropology. For God maintains himself in relation. Obviously this does not entirely clarify the sense of the divine transcendence. But it at least clarifies the central thrust of Hegel's thought. Moreover, it is clear that for Hegel the *Phenomenology of Spirit* does not culminate in noumenology or in dogmatic metaphysics and that what supports the transition from the chapter on Spirit to the chapter on Religion is the ontological proof interpreted as a social ontology. Hegel's description of the church as a community based on love and forgiveness of sins is an intriguing, if elusive, phenomenological theology:

> The "yes" of reconciliation, in which the two egos renounce their opposition, is the existence of an ego expanded into duality, while nevertheless remaining identical with itself. Yet in its complete externalization in and through its counterpart it has the certainty of itself. This is the appearing God manifest in the midst of those who know themselves even as they are known.[55]

Whatever the ultimate import of this passage, it is clear that the theological notion of forgiveness of sins is for Hegel the clue to the phenomenological genesis or 'appearance' of absolute spirit.

Notes

1. Paul Ricoeur, *Husserl: An Analysis of His Phenomenology*, trans. E.G. Ballard and L.E. Embree (Northwestern University Press, 1967), 28.

2. Paul Ricoeur, "Toward a Hermeneutic of the Idea of Revelation," *Essays on Biblical Interpretation* (Fortress Press, 1978), 109.

3. J. G. Fichte *Grundlage der gesamten Wissenschaftslehre*, in Fichtes Werke, hrsg. I.H. Fichte, Band I: *Zur theoretischen Philosophie* (Berlin: Walter de Gruyter & Co., 1971). English translation: Fichte, *Science of Knowledge*, with the First and Second Introductions, ed. and trans. Peter Heath and John Lachs (Appleton-Century-Crofts, 1970).

4. Merold Westphal, *History and Truth in Hegel's Phenomenology*, (Humanities Press, 1980).

5. Howard Burkle, *The Non-Existence of God: Anti-Theism from Hegel to Duméry* (Herder, 1970).

6. Hegel, *The Logic of Hegel*, trans. from the *Encyclopedia of the Philosophical Sciences* by W. Wallace (Oxford University Press, 1959), 370. This reference occurs in Jean Hyppolite, *Genesis and Structure of Hegel's Phenomenology of Spirit*, trans. Cherniak and Heckman (Northwestern University Press, 1974), 9. I am unable to confirm the reference. For Husserl, cf. *The Crisis of European Sciences and Transcendental Phenomenology*, trans. David Carr (Northwestern University Press, 1970), sections 25–33.

7. Husserl, *Crisis, Ibid. See also*: Eugen Fink, "The Phenomenological Philosophy of Edmund Husserl and Contemporary criticism," in *The Phenomenology of Husserl*, ed. and trans. R.O. Elveton (Quadrangle, 1970), 100.

8. Fichte, *First Introduction to the Science of Knowledge.*

9. Fichte, *Grundlage der gesamten Wissenschaftslehre*, section 1; English translation, 93.

10. Fichte, *First Introduction*, section 5; English translation, 12–16.

11. Fichte, *Wissenschaftslehre, Werke* I, 222; English translation, 198.

12. *Ibid.*, 223; English translation, 199.

13. Jean Hyppolite, *Genesis and Structure*, 9.

14. Fichte, *Wissenschaftslehre, Werke* I, 281; English translation, 247.

15. The problem is comparable to Husserl's argument in the *Crisis*, which traces the objectively true world of science back to the foundational but subject-relative life-world. Once this step is taken, philosophy is confronted with the enigma of objectivity and truth: "The idea of a true world in any sense, and within it our own being, becomes an enigma in respect to the sense of this being. In our attempts to attain clarity we shall suddenly become aware, in the face of emerging paradoxes, that all of our philosophizing up to now has been without a ground." *Crisis*, 131–132. Hence philosophy is thrust back upon human interests, thereby becoming *Weltanschauungphilosophie*. Hegel and Husserl are both after something more than this, a concrete rationalism.

16. Hegel, *Phenomenologie des Geistes*, hrsg. Hoffmeister (Hamburg: Meiner Verlag, 1952), English translation *Phenomenology of Spirit*, trans. A.V. Miller (New York: Oxford University Press, 1979). The German original will hence forth be abbreviated as PhG, the English translation as PhS. All translations are my own, although I have made use of the English translation, PhG, 71; PhS, 53.

17. This methodological priority is due to the fact "that in point of time the mind makes general images of objects, long before it makes notions of them, and that it is only through these mental images and by recourse to them that the thinking mind rises to know and comprehend thinkingly." Hegel, *Enzyklopaedie der philosophischen Wissenschaften*, hrsg. Nicolin and Poeggler (Hamburg; Meiner Verlag, 1969), English translation *Encyclopedia* (hereafter the German original will be abbreviated as *Enz* and the translation by *Enc.* section 1.

18. This is a point that Hegel never abandoned, even though the place of the *Phenomenology* as an introduction is a matter of dispute. In his *Encyclopedia* the Phenomenology is given a subordinate place within the system, while the task of introducing the system is carried out by a meditation on the history of philosophy organized around the three attitudes of thought to objectivity. This situation is comparable therefore to Husserl's various attempts to introduce his phenomenology through the Cartesian way of the *Ideas*, the critique of psychology, and the critique of the sciences (*Crisis*). Hegel's *Phenomenology*, and through the history of philosophy in his *Encyclopedia*.

19. PhG, 73; PhS, 55.

20. Hyppolite, *Genesis and Structure*, 576.

21. PhG, 69; PhS, 51.

22. PhG, 559; PhS, 488.

23. PhG, 558; PhS, 487.

24. Hegel, *Faith and Knowledge*: An English Translation of Hegel's *Glauben und Wissen*, ed. and trans. W. Cerf and H.S. Harris (Albany: State University of New York Press, 1977) (hereafter, *Faith*).

25. Hegel, *Faith*, 65.

26. *Ibid.*, 64.

27. *Ibid.*, 94.

28. *Ibid.*, 95 cf. p. 68: "This absolute identity is not a universal subjective postulate never to be realized. It is the only authentic reality."

29. Hegel, *Encyclopedia*, sections 26–83.

30. Although Hegel does not mention Fichte in the three attitudes of thought to objectivity section of the *Encyclopedia*, he does refer to Fichte in his later discussion of Objectivity sections 193–4. It is difficult to overestimate the importance of Fichte for Hegel, despite Hegel's critical disagreement with Fichte.

31. Hegel, *Encyclopedia*, sections 34–36.

32. *Ibid.*, section 194.

33. Hegel, *The Difference Between Fichte's and Schelling's System of Philosophy* (An English Translation of Hegel's *Differenz des Fichteschen und Schellingschen Systems der Philosophie*) trans. W. Cerf and H.S. Harris (Albany: State University of New York Press, 1977), 81.

34. Hegel, *Faith*, 56.

35. *Ibid.*, 58.

36. *Ibid.*

37. *Ibid.*, 169.

38. *Ibid.*

39. Hegel, *Encyclopedia*, section 193.

40. Hegel, *Difference*, 156.

41. Hegel, *Encyclopedia*, section 214.

42. *Ibid.*, section 193.

43. *Ibid.*, section 1; religion and philosophy have the same content. Moreover, the religious consciousness as pretheoretical is prior to and independent of philosophical reflection: "Religion can exist without philosophy, but philosophy cannot exist without religion, for it includes religion in itself" (*Enz.*, Vorrede zur zweiten Ausgabe, 12).

44. PhG, 527; PhS, 458.

45. PhG, 140; PhS, 110.

46. PhG, 391; PhS, 335.

47. Westphal, *History and Truth*, 192.

48. HT, 199; cf. Hyppolite, *Genesis and Structure*, 541ff.

49. PhG, 391; PhS, 335.

50. Hegel, *Vorlesungen ueber die Beweise von Dasein Gottes*, hrsg. G. Lasson (Hamburg: Meiner Verlag, 1973), 46.

51. PhG, 19; PhS, 10.

52. PhG, 546; PhS, 476.

53. *Ibid.*

54. Hegel, *Vorlesungen ueber die Philosophie der Religion* Zweiter Band, Hrsg. G. Lasson (Hamburg: Meiner Verlag, 1966), Zweiter Halbband, 167, English translation *The Christian Religion*, ed. and trans. Peter C. Hodgson (AAR Texts and Translations No. 2) (Scholars Press, 1979), 212.

55. PhG, 472; PhS, 409.

JAMES G. HART

7. *A Précis of an Husserlian Philosophical Theology*

Contents

Introduction

This essay is, in part, a condensation and occasionally doctrinal presentation of a larger project showing the religious and theological dimensions of transcendental phenomenology. Here the focus is on what motivates Husserl to introduce a divine principle at the foundation of the world's appearing and on how experience discloses an intrinsic 'piety'. Transcendental phenomenology culminates in an analysis of the 'living present' (*lebendige Gegenwart*) or primal presencing (*Urgegenwaertigung*). This is the concrete whole for all transcendental phenomenological considerations and can therefore be called, in a sense proper to this mode of reflection, the absolute substance because it needs nothing else in order to be. Transcendental phenomenological reflection and reconstructive speculations (see below) on this ultimate theme enable Husserl's thought to gain the lineaments of a comprehensive philosophy. Whereas the scaffold for this philosophy is taken from Leibniz's monadology, several fundamental motifs are Aristotelian: The universe of monads is most elementally a *byle* whose sense is to be understood in a phenomenological analysis of the difference between wakefulness and its privation; the universe of waking monads is pervaded by a teleology over which a divine entelechy holds sway.[1]

According to Husserl, we cannot be misled by any conceivable theory if we hold fast to the principle of all principles: that every originary intuition (*originaer gebende Anschauung*) is a legitimate source of knowledge (*Ideas* I, section 24). The originary intuition is a beginning of all beginnings *quoad nos phaenomenologicos*; but in what sense is it the beginning of all beginnings? Is the primal presencing that is at the heart of all originary intuitions and that is called 'absolute substance' the principle of all principles, even of the divine? In *Ideas* (sections 51 and 58) we have another sense of principle to which we are necessarily led, about which we are *compelled* to inquire ("*fuehrt notwendig zur Frage nach dem Grund. . . . Das Faktum als Quelle . . . zwingt die Frage nach dem 'Grund'*"). Whether and how this principle or ground is subordinated to the originary intuition will occupy us in later sections of this essay. Our first task is to see in what sense the originating primal presencing, which founds 'inner time-consciousness', is a principle.

1. Primal Presencing as Principle: A Surmounting of Opposites

The originary intuitions of the natural attitude are principles for knowledge within this realm of naïveté, but they are already-begun beginnings whose sources are brought to light through reflection. The apperceiving, constituting, meaning-giving acts that inform the materials of perception have become part of a spontaneous, associational, dispositional system; that is, the beginnings of originary intuitions are founded in already-begun beginnings or already-originated principles. The stuff or materials of perception themselves are, as identities in manifolds (of colors, bodies, movements, shapes, sounds, etc.), begun beginnings. And the dispositional schematic principles that, as acts (*Auffassungen*), come into play in the informing of the materials are able to be principles relevant to an actual present because of an ongoing prior beginning that incessantly relates pasts to presents, potentialities (habitualities) to actualities. And the coming into play and playing out of the particular apperceivings, in conjunction with past achievements, is a concentration from out of the unified web of achievements, which is the apperception of 'world'. 'World' is not merely the frame and motivational principle for the particular meaning-acts, but as *noema* of noemata, as base/horizon of the mind's intentions, it is itself incessantly in a process of revision, confirmation, incremental growth, and decline as a result of these achievements, which are rooted in the primal presencing.

The living present is, for properly transcendental phenomenological reflection, the principle of all principles, in the sense of being the source of all the moments of constitution that lead to the originary intuitions of the natural attitude. As such, the description of its basic features combines qualities that are distinct and exclusive in the principles of which it is the source. Just as philosophers have envisaged genera as the sources and higher unifications of distinct and exclusive species, which are their instantiation, so Husserl analogously places features together in the primal presencing that are exclusive and separate in the constituted-constituting realm. Let us attend in a doctrinal fashion to some of these surmountings of opposites into a higher, constituting unity, keeping in mind, however, that Husserl's procedure is not deliberately that of a dialectic of concepts.

(1). A Surmounting of Phenomenon and Noumenon, of Dative and Genitive of Manifestation

The primal presencing is the *living* present, that is, it is named 'vital' because, although it is a *nunc stans*, an abiding present, it is self-renewing and *fluens*. As (to use Thomas Prufer's apt expression) the ultimate "dative of manifestation," that to which everything appears, the *mihi* to which everything that can be presenced is brought to presence, it is the absolute phenomenon. As such it is not an appearing of what appears; that is, there is no genitive of manifestation (no appearing 'of'), no apperception of something that appears through appearings. Therefore it is 'noumenal', and transcendental phenomenology is, as Iso Kern has suggested, a noumenology. But only in this ultimate reflection does this coincidence obtain; only here is there a sense of the 'in itself' that admits of no naiveté of no further constitutional theme. Only here is there a coincidence of the in-itself and the for-itself.[2] There is relative naïveté in the reflection on acts and *sensa* because these, in contrast to transcendent spatial-temporal bodies, may be taken as beings-in-themselves, indifferent to and independent of the mind aware of them; they may be taken as having their essential determination in themselves, whether or not the mind is presencing them, and thereby they may be taken as the foundation for a rigorous phenomenological philosophy. But acts and *sensa* are functional simplifications of the living present's retentional and protentional motivational web and thus find their sense in a wider sense-structure, which is the ongoing apperception of 'world'. Furthermore, the view of them as in-themselves, apart from the functioning constituting mind, is naive with respect to their temporal, durational identity rooted in the conscious *punctum saliens* of the living present. This consideration is the fundamental justification for transcendental phenomenological *idealism*. If immanent being as a temporal unity could exist without the correlation of an experiencing, then transcendental idealism is refuted; immanent being would simply be there as a result of an unconscious process. But the immanent temporal unities have their *esse* in their *percipi*. Without the *percipi* of prereflective awareness, immanent temporal unities are inconceivable. Every experience is conscious, and the prereflective awareness of experience is conscious and is constitutive of the temporal unities.[3]

(2). A Coincidence of Act and Sensum, Auffassung and Hyle

The reduction to the primal presencing may be envisaged as a dismantling of every form of apperception back to the originating pulsing 'intentionality' wherein originates the emergence of the distinction between *Hyle* and *Auffassung, sensum* and apperception. Even though no 'datum' is animated, this absolute flow of consciousness is characterized by a proto-intentionality, a protorationality, suggestive of the (constituted) phenomenon of *instinct*. Here the primer, the ABC's, the grammar of essences, that is, the most basic ingredients of the structure of the world, are uncovered. This entelechial feature of the primal presencing, as we shall see, is of fundamental importance for theological reflections.

(3). A Coincidence of the Egological and the Nonegological

Whereas there is a coincidence of for-itself and in-itself, noumenon and phenomenon, act and *hyle* in the prior unifying dimension of the primal presencing, something approaching a dualism rather than a prior, not-yet-differentiated unity characterizes the egological and non- or preegological dimensions of the living present. Yet this living primal presencing is a whole comprising these two parts; they are therefore to be envisaged as abstract moments in themselves. The ultimate dative of appearing, although never a mere phenomenon for reflection, still enjoys a mode of objectivity (an identity in a manifold) inasmuch as reflection on a sensing or an act (e.g., an act of reflection) discloses a sameness between the 'I'-poles (or datives of manifestation, including the preindexical 'living-pole') of the present reflecting-on and the prior reflected-on sensing or acts. Its sameness is thereby seen to be a result of an always-possible egological act (of reflection) as well as of an ongoing, anonymous, temporalizing, 'streaming' living-pole, the sameness of which is independent of any egological act. Reflection is possible because of this anonymous dative of manifestation (living-pole), which itself enjoys a self-displacing, prereflective (improperly named) 'reflection' of retained and protended, anonymous living presents in the 'present' living present. The prereflective awareness of the life of the mind, which is the sourcing of the temporal duration of the mind in any of its waking attitudes and acts or sleeping attitudes, is always a readiness for reflection, because the prior retained and the not-yet-present living presents are profiled ('reflected') in the ongoing, anonymous streaming. Although this relentless hyletic stream goes on its own, apart from any participation of the I, it prereflectively affects the living I-pole (dative of appearing), thereby realizing a feeble, self-displacing, or ongoing, passive 'reflection' of former and protended profiles. Thereby is the mind alive to itself and capable of explicit self-displacing reflection and thematization. The living primal presencing is at once the source of the passive 'reflections' of the stream of retentions and protentions and of the properly named egological acts that build on and presuppose this prior passivity. Even though the 'living I-pole' of the present act of reflection is necessarily anonymous, owing its identity to the streaming, passive synthesizing and not to any act of the I, it always involves a preflective 'reflecting' to that which is itself always capable of becoming the source, and even the oblique referent, of an egological act. Therefore, the primal presencing is never simply and absolutely nonegological.[4]

(4). The Source of 'I' and 'The Others'

A most important aspiration of the ultimate transcendental reduction is to establish how 'I', as the self-referring or reflecting I and 'the Others' (other I's) are borne by, and constituted in, the primal originary presencing, an 'I' only in a misleading sense; it is therefore most commonly named the *Ur-ich*. 'I', as an occasional (or indexical) expression tied to self-referential acts (all acts as *Stellungnahmen* are self-referential) that obliquely relate to Others ('I' refers implicitly to 'you', 'they', 'we', etc., as 'here' implicitly refers to 'there' and 'now' to 'then'), exists necessarily in relation to Others. Not only is 'the Other' the first 'I' in the order of *personal* constitution, but the actualization of the capacity of indexical achievements is dependent on the initiating, gracious presence of others.[5] Nevertheless, this constituting presence of Others is itself constituted, not by an already-constituted, personal, self-referring I, but by the empathic functioning of the primal presencing of the (improperly named) 'primal I'. This latter, anonymous and silent, is not an occasional expression, not bound to the circumstance of speaking, not at a time or in a place. Nor does this primal I have Others to whom it signals. Rather, it is unique.

This is not the uniqueness of 'someone', because no one can lay claim to possessing this uniqueness as a personal identity or achievement.[6] Just as the first-person expression 'I' is the more fundamental implied reference of all occasional expressions whatsoever (i.e., 'here', 'there', 'then', 'now', 'you', 'we', etc.), so the ultimate dative of manifestation, the primal presencing, is the source of all occasional expressions of the first person.[7] While in this 'standpoint' of the reduction, we are prevented from saying that 'in each case' of the transcendental I there is uniqueness. With *everything* reduced to an appearance of what appears, everything is reduced to an occasional-indexical 'expression' that refers to the non-occasional primal I as that to which everything appears. The following may serve as a formulation of the aspired to, but not achieved, resolution of Husserl's meditations: The primal presencing is a transcendental, intersubjective 'instinct' wherein the primally present modifies itself by bearing the 'past' primal presencings in itself, and this 'process' is coincident with the primal I's bearing in itself the plurality of I's as modifications of itself. Through the originating self-othering of the primal presencing's retention, the primal I becomes for-itself through its self-modification; this implicit community of the primal I with itself is the foundation for the explicit possession of 'myself' in memory and reflection. This implicit community founds the basis for the analogous empathy or analogous sympathetic appresentation of the remembering act, whereby the remembered I is experienced to be the same as the remembering I. In the proper acts of empathy or sympathetic appresentation, Husserl's view tends toward (postulating? uncovering?) a prior instinctual communalization, so that when empathy occurs, the intersubjective community is already 'there', and empathy is merely an explication of this communalization as memory is an explication of the passive self-communalization of retentions, and expectation is the explication of the passive self-communalization of protentions.[8]

(5). The Coincidence of the Temporal and the Transtemporal

As there is a problematic dualism of egological and nonegological moments, so there is a difficult dualism of the transtemporal and the temporal within primal presencing. A first difficulty is that there is an important sense in which this 'flux' is not temporal: the 'ongoing' primal presencing of the present is not present, the retaining of the past is not past, and the protending of the future is not future. We neglect this important problem in favor of another one: it would be inappropriate to hold that the perception of succession or change requires *simpliciter* an unchanging, subsistent mind, transcendent to the flux, simultaneously relating and enjoying objects that exist only in succession. On the contrary, Husserl holds that the awareness of change presupposes a succession of consciousness, or more precisely, the perception of change, succession, and so forth presupposes the succession of perceptions.[9] But the succession of perceptions is not a flux of discrete, unsynthesized impressions. The flux of 'differents' is a unifying and differentiating achievement. But if this achievement is ascribed to a timeless mind subsisting transcendently to the succession of perceptions, the perception of change would seem to be a magical affair.

The ultimate, irreducible egological moment, as the living-pole or *Ur-stand* affected by the hyletic flux, is not eternal mind subsistently transcendent to the flux. But neither is it best envisaged as a substanceless 'sequence of minds' or 'society of occasions' which are incessantly being born and, as owners of an inheritance, are bequeathing this inherited inheritance in turn to their offspring upon their expiring. The egological moment is always there (*dabei, mihi*), and in being affected by the flux, it is a self-displacing that surmounts the flux.

Husserl's view would seem to be that we have in the primal presencing as a *punctum saliens* the coincidence of a *punctum stans* (egological movement) and *punctum fluens* (hyletic moment). We have flux at the heart of mind, that is, at the primal presencing; but the flux has the ideal form of the standing-streaming. Although it is true that the all-temporality or transtemporality of ideality or of ideal objects is a mode of temporality and in this sense constituted, it would seem that the all-temporality of the form of the primal presencing, that is, the standing-streaming, is constitutive and uniquely transtemporal. Further, the being of the self-displacing egological moment, or the living-pole, is transtemporal in a nonconstituted way that perhaps only theological speculation can make clear.[10]

(6). The Principle of the Unified Medium of Consciousness

The final, and perhaps most important, consideration (because it is presupposed by all the preceding issues) is how the primal presencing may be said to be the principle of consciousness, that is, of *Bewusst-sein* or Being's diaphanousness. We are not only aware of what appears; the (achieving) appearing of what appears is also a matter of awareness. Husserl founds the traditional theory of prereflexive 'inner perception' (improperly so called) of our act-life in the elemental primal presencing, which constitutes this act-life as a temporal identity. The ongoing, streaming primal presencing is the immanent awareness of the stream of consciousness. But in what sense does this primal streaming serve as a principle of consciousness? If the profilings of the retained and the protended presents are an othering and an identifying of the same, it is because they are already conscious, present to themselves as the same, and this self-same presence is coincident with, and not a result of, the retentional-protentational othering (profiling) and identifying (profiling) as the same. To explain being-consciousness by the self-relating, self-profiling identifications of the primal presencing presupposes either that the primal presencing/self-relating (profiling) is already conscious of itself (and therefore we have no explanation) or that the primal presencing is not aware of itself, "in which case it cannot be understood how it could ever come to be in a position to . . . recognize anything it encountered as itself."[11] A consideration such as this might have led Husserl to maintain, in the spirit of Fichte (and of Dieter Henrich), that consciousness is prior to all production and that the unity of consciousness is the medium in which the I lives, and is, prior to all I-relating.[12] However, even though each pulse of experience is conscious, the unity of consciousness (which is a unity of the intentional streams) is a constituted unity, and this is the medium in which the I lives and that it always presupposes. The primal presencing of the living present is never not a profiling of retentions and protentions. And, therefore, as we can never speak of the experience of a first or last experience, so we can never speak of a primal presencing initiating a relation to a retention as if it were not already a retention and protention. In this respect the living present, or primal presencing, is not a principle by which consciousness is constituted. And yet it is this unbegun and unending stream of presencings that produces the unity of consciousness, which is the relatively diaphanous medium of acts of the I. The medium is unevenly delineated, and is therefore only relatively diaphanous, because the horizon of retentions and protentions pulls toward oblivion or obscurity. Depending upon whether one is talking about the center by itself or in relation to the periphery of this medium the two contradictory views hold: 'Either you are conscious or you are not'; 'Consciousness admits of degrees'. Like its diaphanous character, the absoluteness of the medium (i.e., that it admits of no prior constituting elements, no inside or outside, transcendence or immanence) may be highlighted when one focuses on the unity of the moments of the life of the mind as a finished accomplishment. As Augustine put it, in any knowledge, either of itself or of something else, the whole of the mind knows; and in any knowledge about itself, the whole mind knows that the mind as a whole knows itself as a whole ("tota se scit" or "totam se scit" in *De Trinitate* X,6 [iv]). But this absolute, diaphanous medium is an ongoing achievement with lights and shadows, delineations and obscurities; it can appear as a comprehensive, homogeneous atmosphere only when one abstracts from its essential contours of temporality and contrast. The medium is diaphanous only in the sense that its unity and continuity of continua are already achieved; but the contingency and facticity of this achievement insert at the heart of this luminosity something like blind spots and cracks that, however, *de facto* are incessantly healed. We may now turn to the way in which Husserl integrates such considerations within transcendental phenomenology.

2. Metaphysics and Phenomenological Theology

The metaphysical, reconstructive, and ultimate features of philosophy are the concerns of most immediate interest to phenomenological theology. If we attempt to unify Husserl's varied and recurrent descriptions of this metaphysical turn of transcendental phenomenology, we may single out three aspects: (1). the *application* of the principles of transcendental, eidetic phenomenology to the empirical, transcendent world; (2). the *reconstruction* of the transcendent world in terms of transcendental, phenomenological, essential structures; and (3). the *speculation* on the conditions for reason as it is manifest in the originating primal presencing as well as in the originated and explicit achievements and structures of the scientific, moral, and political community.[13]

1. Very early we find the distinction between *first philosophy* and second philosophy, which is also called *metaphysics*, and last/ultimate (*letzte*) philosophy. First philosophy is what philosophy must first of all be: a disclosure of the a priori structures of the basic regions of 'world' (e.g., physical thingliness, animality, spirit, objective spirit or culture, etc.) upon which all of the positive and natural

sciences build. Further, it uncovers the constituting, correlative realm of these basic regions in terms of the essential modes of intentionality. Finally, it works out the a priori structures of transcendental subjectivity in its most elemental founding dimension. In short, first philosophy is the eidetic of transcendental subjectivity, its intentional life, and its worldly constituted correlate. Included in this eidetic is an essence analysis of perfect being as the ideal of transcendental subjectivity. This is a study of 'God' as the idea of perfection and as the *telos* of human life in terms of its essential features—and not in terms of its actuality or existence.[14] The only trace of a theological 'ontological proof' is in the question whether the realizability of the ideal of life is necessary for a present meaningful life, and whether only an actual 'God' can secure the conditions for this meaningfulness. This is a rich issue in Husserlian theology, which we here simply pass by. The proper ontological proof is that of the primal I whose nonexistence is inconceivable; but this we also merely mention.

Metaphysics as second or last philosophy is the interpretation of the positive sciences, of factual reality in the light of first philosophy's normative essential features. This is also called an application of the eidetic-ideal disclosures of transcendental reflection to the empirical, factual being known in the natural attitude and through the positive sciences. Thus metaphysics is not only regional ontology (as normative, conceptual horizon-analysis) but also eidetics in the realm of constitution of such phenomena as religion, language, nature, soul, art, law, mathematics, and so on.

Such an approach introduces strict, normative considerations into areas usually thought to be immune to such claims.[15] Of immediate interest to this work is the way in which Husserl envisaged the phenomenology of religion. As it has been typically executed (e.g., in Eliade and Van der Leeuw), Husserl would perhaps note a kind of naïveté, although doubtless the enormous learning and richness of insights would be credited. The regions disclosed by disciplines such as anthropology, the history of religions, folklore, and so forth, as a rule, occlude the fundamental concepts that guide their disclosure. The basic concepts of nature, life, spirit, humanity, community, language, culture, and so forth tend to be used in a nonthematic and uncritical way. Doubtless the recent sensitivity to precisely this point, as occasioned by the writings of Heidegger, Kuhn, Hanson, *et alii*, has increased sophistication in the approach to religious studies. But for Husserl, the new contextualism is incomplete until it becomes more radically aware of its nature. This awareness gives birth to the transcendental context, which is unlike the perspectives that it articulates and is normative with respect to these contexts.

In a letter to Dilthey, we have perhaps Husserl's most elaborate discussion of the 'eidetic ontology' of religion.[16] On the one hand we have a principle of openness, but on the other, one of norms that might seem to lend themselves easily to the appearance of being imperious. The first holds that every experience has its own describable features, and that every experience of evidence has its own legitimacy and must be analyzed on that basis.[17] The second holds that we can measure the 'facts' of historical religions against both the 'ideals' emergent in religious experience and the experience in the context of religion. Husserl illustrates this latter through his favorite example of the transcendent spatial-temporal thing as the foundation of a study of nature. On the one hand, the natural sciences do not examine 'nature' as the sameness of spatial-temporal thingliness, which is manifest across an infinity of profiles (i.e., they are oblivious to this foundation because of the veil of ideas, *Ideenkleid*, of post-Galilean methodology). On the other hand, this sense of nature is the basis upon which all the modern natural-scientific determinations build. When we come to the physicality of physics, then, we must acknowledge the *idea* 'corporeal thing', which serves as the comprehensive ideal context for endless 'relativities', that is instances, exemplifications, variations, modifications, and specifications: solids, liquids, gases, particles, subparticles, waves, planets, fields, and so forth. Operative throughout the variety of these relativities, with all the laws peculiar to them, are the ideal laws governing the *eidos* of 'corporeal thing'. All objective validity in the a posteriori realm, that is, laws, regularities, presumptive features, and so on, has its principles founded in the a priori regional realm, which defines the field of phenomena. In more contemporary parlance, we might say that the paradigmatic frame of research founds the progress and the coherent debate within a field. Yet for Husserl, as we have earlier noted, transcendental reflection enables one to talk about paradigm shifts or revolutions; thereby does the true ultimacy of regional ontological principles become disclosed.[18]

Husserl finds an analogous situation in the realm of religion. Here ideas of 'divinity', 'heaven', 'nature', 'humanity', 'transcendence', and so on are functioning. Furthermore, in each historical religion there is operative a system of motivation, association, legitimation, and so forth that characterizes in a typical way the life of the individual in this society. The comparative study of religions brings together religions a, b, c, . . . with respect fo a feature, X. Whereas such a study typically assumes the obviousness of that feature, the eidetic study would pursue precisely what the idea is that bears the comparison. It might be that there is no such idea, that the religious beliefs or practices are incommensurate or heterogeneous. Such radical contextualist claims are not an easy matter for a transcendental foundationalism such as Husserl's. Religions in their variegatedness provide typical considerations that comprise the essential noematic context and intentional 'life-style' for the particular religions. If we loosely use 'the truth' for the ideal of each relevant religious content as well as for the mode of intentional 'life-style' we can say that every historical religion necessarily has its share of 'the truth', but always only to a relative degree. However, it is doubtless the case for Husserl that there are hierarchies of religion, in terms of their approximation to the eidetic ideals, that are emergent in experience as such. We see, then, that the task of phenomenological theory of religions is to investigate intentionality as well as the piety that is intrinsic to intentionality and to which the religion-constituting consciousness gives expression. Or, to use Dilthey's term, the phenomenology of religions must investigate "the inner life" with its various forms. Husserl hailed Rudolf Otto's *Das Heilige* as 'original' in the sense that it goes to the noematic and noetic material of historical religious experience. But Otto's work is preparatory for a genuine philosophical theory of religious consciousness, and Husserl hints that it has not reached the genuine origin (*Ursprung*), or essential necessities, of religious consciousness.[19]

Thus Husserl, in accord with Dilthey, recommends the study of the 'inner life' through a reflective appreciation that involves, on the one hand, an empathic study of the historical religious material by means of the appropriate historical, linguistic, or other available tools; on the other hand, it also involves a critique of this inner life and its motivations, in terms of ideals emergent in the concrete phenomena. The religious consciousness—our own or that of another, which we are reflectively appreciating—is the concrete, intuitive phenomenon out of which we generate the ideal-eidetic unities with their essential distinguishing features. The legislating spaces of the purely ideal (e.g., cult versus magic, prayer versus extortion, etc.) become evident through free, imaginative variation. Having achieved this, the historical factual instances serve as exemplifications. But doubtless the imaginative variation is aided by the extraordinary differentness provided by the historical material. The particulars can then be appreciated critically, in terms of their approximation to the ideals.

What prevents Husserl's procedure from becoming either naive or imperialistic in a cultural-religious sense is his concern with strict eidetic necessity and transcendental constitution. The comparative-phenomenological study of religions poses the difficult foundational task of disclosing the generic ideas that permit comparison. As modern contextualists are quick to point out, this is by no means an evident possibility. Where the comparative phenomenologist is ready to claim a collection of 'universals' with instantiations in regard to femininity and masculinity, heaven and earth, angels and demons, the holy and weird, and so forth, the contextualist is inclined to name this collection an arbitrary uniting of heterogeneous differents. And it is clear that if these are empirical universals, that is, generalities and conventional necessities that have come to be and hold for an historical people, it might well be the case that in numerous instances there are incommensurables. Yet the transcendental-phenomenological thesis is that there are foundational considerations, which have a strict eidetic necessity, that unite all human experiences. Although the work in a philosophical phenomenology of religion is just beginning, we find attempts at eidetic constitutional necessities in the analysis of being-in-the-world and in the discussions of dread, nausea, eeriness, limit situations, and so on. Further, there are well-begun efforts toward a theory of constitution of the symbolic consciousness through an 'archaeology' and 'teleology' of the imagination. Perhaps Husserl's distinctive contribution will turn out to be his analysis of bodiliness and the correlate *noema* of the heavenly and earthly, the remote and near, the up and down, and so on and his disclosure of the piety intrinsic to experiencing (see sections 8 and 10 below).

The proper distinctive theme of religion, the divine, is not to be reached through providing the noematic regional ontology that founds the empirical universals of religions. The divine as the 'source', the 'best', the 'highest', and so forth is referred to in the myriad meanings of the history of religions. But, Husserl insists, it is only through reflection on transcendental constitution that the proper ideal sense of this referent is disclosed. This means that, in the matter of religion, the third sense of 'metaphysics', as the speculative reflection on the conditions of reason, is the foundation for the (first) sense of metaphysics, as the application of the principles of transcendental eidetic phenomenology to the transcendent world of experience. Thus, it must ultimately be said that "only when the nature of transcendental consciousness is understood, can the transcendence of God be understood. Thus all religion has been naive . . . but in the phenomenological attitude, the naive theses of religion receive not only intelligibility but also a certain validity."[20] This rather imperious sounding claim, on the one hand, does not imply that transcendental phenomenology has nothing to learn about religion, any more than that the transcendental attitude can dispense with the natural attitude; on the other hand, the claims of 'positive' or revealed religion are subordinated to the transcendental attitude, and this, in turn gives rise to a rational theology, a *Logos* theology, which has kinship with many forms of Western mystical and Eastern religions. In this respect the transcendental phenomenology of religion itself becomes a 'type' of religiosity for the discipline known as the comparative phenomenology of religions. In the course of this work we will return to some topics of interest to the phenomenology of religion. The 'type' of religious thought 'represented' by Husserl will become clearer as our discussion unfolds. An abiding question that Husserl would have to ask these typologists is whether the transcendental phenomenological attitude merits a special case, or whether the Rhineland mystics, Vedanta philosophy, some Buddhist discussions, and so on, have indeed surmounted the natural attitude? But for now our purpose has merely been to use the regional ontology of religion to illustrate what Husserl means by 'metaphysics' as the application of eidetic ontology to the 'positive sciences'.

2. Perhaps because of the pull toward the question of the source of all constitution, metaphysics as the application of the results of eidetic analysis, received little attention from Husserl. In later writings, however, when aspects of Leibniz's monadology served as a skeleton for his efforts to flesh out transcendental phenomenology as a complete philosophy, the theme of the application of the results of transcendental reflection reappeared. Whereas second philosophy, or metaphysics, envisages regional horizons and the eidetics of intentional life as the implicit legislating spaces for the accounts of the regions of the world of the natural attitude, as well as for the various attitudes, acts, and so on that comprise the life of the natural attitude, in later writings we find a sense of metaphysics as an analogous extension of the a priori features of transcendental subjectivity (thus the frequent use of the term *Ich-All*) to realms *that are not accessible to*

phenomenological reflection. Here, too, there is an attentiveness to the claims of humanity in the natural attitude and a desire to have transcendental reflection serve as a guide to these interpretations of the world. Similarly, transcendental phenomenology points out that these interpretations of the world, because they are characterized by naïveté, inadequacy, presumption, and corrigibility, are not in a position to provide ultimate categories for their own enterprise. Yet this later reconstructive metaphysics is not an essence-analysis of the implicit legislating logical-formal spaces within which the determinations of the scientific and everyday claims of the natural attitude unfold. Rather, here the fundamental egological categories, or metaphors, are 'reconstructively' applied. Reconstruction is required because transcendental reflection cannot, as such, speak about the coming-to-be of reason; as such it is not in a position to account for the mind in states of dormancy, infancy, prehumanity, subhumanity, and distorting pathology. A task of reconstruction of great importance for philosophical theology is that of the primal presencing before individual persons and collective humanity appear on the scene. A similar task is the reconstruction of this presencing in the face of the intersubjective phenomenon of death. The death and birth of the primal presencing in the sense of its absolute cessation and beginning are inconceivable for phenomenological reflection: to presence its beginning, to presence its experienced beginning, it would have to take advantage of a prior, now-retained experience; to presence an experience of its end, it would have to presence a filling of the protention of what is after its end and thereby not be at its end.[21] What the beginninglessness and immortality of the primal presencing mean for example, in the face of the finiteness of the personal I, the species-unity of persons, the ecological fragility of the human species, the generic unity of human beings with animals, the phenomena of generations and inheritance, the teleological directedness of the historical-natural web that binds the human community, and so on—these are all tasks for reconstruction, and Leibniz's monadology provides the scaffold.[22]

The efforts of process philosophers to apply a theory of experience to subhuman entities have their parallels in Husserl's work. Perhaps the topic of reconstruction is a way to help decide the controversy over whether Whitehead's speculative philosophy is precritical, that is, whether he takes his categories in a naive way from sources that are mediated by more fundamental considerations of a transcendental order. In Whitehead one finds a running critique of a critical philosophy "for which a genuine philosophy of nature is impossible." According to such a critical point of view, we cannot expect any final metaphysical truths by scanning the order of nature. Nature, for this view, is a mere 'derivative appearance' of the transcendental mind's constituting agency.[23] And yet Whitehead's own position is far from being a naive appropriation of the deliverances of the natural sciences, followed by theorizing about them. Rather, there is a critical-transcendental motif functioning in his quest for an appropriate way to frame the experiences of everyday common sense as well as those of the natural sciences. The creation of such a frame, a scheme, which, so to speak, anticipates all charges of naïveté or category mistakes, "is the major effort of speculative reason." The speculative goal is to reach a scheme of interpretation that is sufficiently universal to comprehend everything and sufficiently concrete to be evident in and illustrative of the minutest items of experience and research.[24] The articulation of this scheme in terms of human experience as the prime analogate plus the 'subjectivist principle', "that the whole universe consists of elements disclosed in the analysis of the experience of subjects," would seem to suggest a greater affinity to transcendental thought than Whitehead was usually wont to acknowledge.[25]

Although Husserl would have to acknowledge that Whitehead's 'reconstructive metaphysics' was an achievement and his own but an aspiration, and that Whitehead reconstructed in rich detail whereas he scarcely got beyond the proposal, we can nevertheless surmise that he would have some basic reservations. The first would be general, concerning the analogical, reconstructive nature of process philosophy. One is never quite clear what the primary analogate is, that is, whether we have, for example, a biology of the mind or a psychology of organisms. Such interpenetration of concerns creates, indeed, rich metaphors, and it is appropriate for a philosophy in which the continuum of structures is a theme; but one may, nevertheless, wonder whether the price is a fusion of philosophy with poetry, with empirical universals, and with world-view advocacy. Without the founding of first philosophy's eidetics, there can be for Husserl, no genuine analogical reconstruction. And a philosophy of nature that is not such a construction is either naive or dogmatic. As a matter of fact, however, there are some fascinating coincidences between Husserl's sparse sketches and Whitehead's massive canvas. Of course in terms of the details, such as the particulars of the phenomenology of time-consciousness, there would be much to discuss. On another occasion we will turn to a consideration of the way in which Whitehead's principles might illuminate transcendental phenomenology. Let us here turn to the third sense of metaphysics to be found in Husserl.

3. The most proper theological task of metaphysics, as second or ultimate philosophy, emerges from the consideration of the contingency of the constituted world and the contingency of the constituting mind. Here, as Iso Kern has noted, the focal point is not the application, or even the reconstruction, of the eidetically necessary (rational) structures of transcendental reflection in relation to the experienced world's rationality, but is the very condition of rationality itself.[26] What is at issue is generated from the wonder that there is a cosmos rather than a chaos, in light of the contingency that permeates the region of worldly bodies. I can perform a phenomenological experiment that undoes the integrity and regularity of this transcndent world; strictly speaking it need not be a cosmos. Furthermore, it is rational in such a way as to permit a relative, if precarious, satisfaction and fulfillment of the desires of the heart and mind. Indeed, in light of the abyss of meaning that separates the transcendent from the immanent realm,[27] it is a *Wunder* that this correspondence exists and brings about a relative fulfillment of the most intimate desires of the heart. But this fulfillment is a relative and precarious one, and it is not death alone that is our ever insurmountable, fateful horizon. We live in the midst and horizon of a *universum* of irrationalities and fatal events[28] and are consequently entitled to speak equally of the surprise of goodness (fulfillment) and of evil (disappointment). Not only is the world's rationality thus an occasion for wonder but there is also the marvellous, if tenuous, harmony between our hearts and minds on the one hand and the world's responsiveness to our hearts and minds on the other. Furthermore, not only need the world not be a cosmos, not only does such correspondence need not exist, but the realm of spirit is also laced with contingency and facticity. This is not merely to say that, without the regularity and predictability of the constituted styles of the world's forms and events, my human personality would disintegrate because its identity and solidity are tied to positions taken with respect to the identity and solidity of a particular world (consider a world wherein the bodily, apperceptive base of the Others incessantly dissolved); rather (and more fundamentally, because the world's rationality is less fundamental, i.e., it is con-

stituted), there is a contingency at the heart of the flow of primal presencings.[29] That this contingency is at the core or essence of the mind is made clear by the consideration that the stream of primal presencings enjoys a kind of ghostly protorationality when we experimentally dissolve the body-based apperceptions that constitute the world. In spite of this total destruction of transcendent identities in manifolds, there is still the primal presencing's constituting of immanent identities, samenesses across manifolds, the thingliness or bodliness of which we, in our experimental madness, may immediately negate. The elemental, instinctual streaming, a kind of 'being-driven', continues 'irrationally' in spite of the dissolution of the world's rationality.[30] This establishing of identities in manifolds is irrepressible, and there is an ineradicable 'condemnation' to meaning and rationality: "In the total intentionality there prevails a 'causality': Transcendental subjectivity is not free in its possibility of constitution of being or nonbeing; it must constitute being" (KIII1 VIII, 4). the primal presencing, whose beginning and end are not conceivable, must constitute being; yet this 'must' is a fact, a contingency, the elucidation of which leads to a divine principle.

We have here at least two considerations: (1) the world's integrity dissolves; we reach a limit-situation wherein there is nothing in which we can trust—and nevertheless there is the irrepressible primal streaming, always on the verge of constituting being, that is, an ideal sameness; and (2) we ask, "What good is it if, through all the worldly-natural anomalies and even throughout the collapse of the practical, human milieu, the world preserves an identity that rests on a style (*Stilform*) in which the natural laws can passively be fulfilled?"[31] That is, granted this 'condemnation to meaning', this 'irrational rationality', what is there to be said about it in light of the thought-experiment (or nuclear holocaust) that undermines this irrepressible being-formation?

Before we turn to Husserl's motivations for the divine principle, a consideration relative to (perceptions of) German idealism will help to delineate his position. With Iso Kern we may note the consequences of collapsing the distinctions between the essential-necessary realm of transcendental reflection (first philosophy); the factual, contingent realm to which application of the essential-necessary is made (second philosophy); and the reflective 'speculation' on the contingency within and the founding rationality (ultimate philosophy). If transcendental reflection does not have occasion to heed these distinctions, it may well be tempted by an idealist-monist position in which reason or consciousness is thought of as metaphysically absolute or total. Everything would thereby become determined by reason and out of reason, and there would be nothing in the formation of reason that would not be caused by it. Reason would be the sufficient reason for all its formations. Accordingly, there would be no need for a second philosophy to deal with transcendent and empirical being. Reason would be absolutely intelligible, and there would be nothing 'accidental' affecting its functioning or essence. And because everything would have to be understood out of reason, it would be necessary; that is, the real would be the rational.[32]

In unpublished *Nachlass* manuscripts as well as in the published lectures on the history of philosophy [*Erste Philosophie* I (1923–24)], Husserl interpreted certain Neo-Kantian and unspecified post-Kantian idealist philosophers as espousing the view outlined above. He termed it a "metaphysics of reconciliation" and a "reconstructing metaphysics." It was a harmonization of the dogmatically accepted truths of the positive sciences with the theological requirement that the content and regularity of all factual being, as well as the meaning and validity of all rational norms, must find their teleological foundations in the creative divine spirit. A unity was thereby sought, between the divine being and the being of finite essences, between reason and the will of God, and between reason and the will of human beings. The transcendental procedural question was, How are we to arrange the world, presented as it is by the natural sciences, so that we can understand it in a teleological way and can pursue our moral lives? The answer is that pure consciousness posits itself, as well as a world, in a necessary dialectical process. The ideal ethical demand or moral imperative requires the appearing of a rational world in consciousness—and out of this, everything is deduced. It is essential to this view that thought is in no way contingent, but necessary. Similarly, science is not merely a matter of fact; rather, it is necessary that science be. Knowledge is envisaged as absolute and involves necessary thought, which adequately accounts for whatever being there is. Nature thereby becomes the necessary correlate of the necessity of thought. Philosophy thus rethinks what an absolute mind is creatively thinking.[33]

For Husserl, such metaphysics does not do justice to the facticity of the flow of the world nor to the facticity of the flow of consciousness. The rationality of each is genuine but not necessary. From very early on in Husserl's philosophical-theological meditations, the rationality of consciousness is portrayed as laced with contingency and facticity and is never, in this sense, transparent to itself. Husserl's view is idealist in the sense that no consideration surmounts the dative of appearing (cf. our subsequent discussions); but a monist-rationalist view can hardly be laid at his door. Reason struggles and, in this sense, is ever in the presence of its other (see the discussion in section 9).

Furthermore, should we be tempted to appropriate Kern's more fundamental critique of Husserl's 'intellectualism' (in his excellent *Idee und Methode der Philosophie*) and grant that the streaming primal presencing that founds consciousness (but, cf. our earlier caution, in sections 1.6 and 1.3 above) is more properly called *sensibility* rather than the protorational 'passive synthesis' (because, argues Kern, quite in harmony with numerous discussions of Husserl, the proper sense of identity synthesis involves distinct acts with respect to the same object, as in remembering the geese as the same perceived yesterday), we have an even more radical statement of the miracle of reason: The rational act-life is discontinuous and essentially distinguished from the realm of prerational sensibility, which, in its turn, establishes consciousness as the ongoing, nonobjective, temporal unity of the self with itself and the world. Sensibility thereby provides the potential materials (*sensa*, kinestheses, associations, etc.) for the act-life. Here reason's foundations are wondrously produced by preestablished achievements, which are both harmonious and discontinuous with it.

A second, very brief reference to German idealism will further help to delineate Husserl's position. We have just seen, in Husserl's version of the reconciliating metaphysics of German idealism, an implicit critique of the method of postulation. Yet, as we know from his letter to Cassirer, he called it perhaps the greatest of all Kantian discoveries (see Kern, *Husserl und Kant*, 302). Manifestly, then, there is a proper sphere and occasion for its employment. We shall discuss this matter on another occasion. (See also Kern's and Williams'; essays in this volume.)

3. Primal Presencing as Principle: Neither Sheer Intellectual Form nor Nothing

Husserl's theological position may be initially indicated by stating that it is an alternative to the views criticized and proposed by Hans Wagner and J.-P. Sartre. In Wagner's view, Husserl reduces all theory to pretheory because he locates the ultimate explanatory principle in prepredicative experience, that is, in the contingent, passive, synthetic primal presencing. If this primal streaming is the genuine origin, the ultimate philosophical *principle*, we cannot distinguish the principle from that of which it is a principle. The primal, pretheoretical evidence might well be a necessary condition for the evidence of the principle that accounts for the world, but it cannot be the sufficient condition or the ultimate explanatory dimension, that is, a metaphysical principle.[34]

For Sartre, Husserl places at the heart of consciousness an ego, which creates an impossible opacity in what is spontaneous, transparent, and luminous. At the heart of consciousness, maintains Sartre, and ultimately constitutive of any sense of 'I', is the impersonal, spontaneous primal presencing, which determines its own existence at each instant. This is a *creatio ex nihilo*, with respect to which *we* are in no way responsible nor are we agents.[35]

Thus Wagner determines transcendental subjectivity as an ontological principle (albeit one that is relatively absolute) and assigns to it thereby the status of *subjectum veritatis*, a being whose essence is to ex-sist, to transcend itself intentionally, and to be mentally united with the world. This is a status that subjectivity in no way constitutes but that is the suffcient condition of subjectivity's power to constitute and to know what it constitutes as not merely constituted. Sartre, on the other hand, fends off any such principles behind or within consciousness as opacity-creating gratuities. At the center of consciousness is only the pure spontaneity of the primal presencing, whose originatings are 'from nothing'. This 'nothing' from which consciousness originates is the absolute source, in the sense that there is no mode of reflection or assumable standpoint that would enable us to assign a prior generating principle. The origin of primal presencing is total darkness, just as the source of all reflection is total anonymity. For Wagner, we are the way we are because of an ontological, constituting, formal principle that prevails over our total being; yet this principle is disclosed not through the investigation of origins, *Ursprungsforschung* (i.e., going back to the sources of the noeses and constituted layers), but by a noematic analysis: Because we, on occasion (e.g., in instances of transcendental reflection), know through our acts what is in-itself and indifferent to these constituting acts, we must be a being that ex-sists in intentional union with Being. In effect, constitutional analyses have no philosophical significance. For Sartre, the absolute spontaneity and nonobjectifiability of the sourcing primal presencing make such a consideration impossible. The dative of manifestation cannot be regarded as one would the unfolding of a regional ontology, as though characterizable by its a priori, legislating space, in manner resembling the way it frames the world. There is *nothing* that can serve as a prescriptive, essential horizon for primal presencing.

But, Husserl insists, we still grasp the primal presencing obliquely (see, e.g., *Ideen* II, section 23) and thereby do not do violence to the radical nonobjectifiability of the primal presencing. As long as I am directed to any object, even the I as the source of a remembered act, the 'I', as that to which appears that to which I am directed, is not an object. In this sense, the dative of manifestation (as that to which appears whatever appears, as the 'to me' and the improperly named 'I', out of which all self-referential senses of 'I' emerge) is nonobjectifiable. And in this respect Husserl agrees with Sartre (and Natorp). But it is still something about which we can talk and think. Husserl grants that the experiencing I, as nominative of reflection and dative of manifestation, the I that thinks and the 'to me' to which objects appear, is not an object in the act of reflecting and manifesting; as primordially constituting, it is not constituted. But I can determine it as primordially constituting and as nonconstituted; I can in this sense know it, have it as an object of thought. We must avoid the temptation to treat the experiencing agent's nonobjectifiability or the dative of manifestation's irreducible subjectivity as unknowable and as prior, or this side of *all* thoughts and articulations, that is, as 'nothing'. The determination of "this side of thoughts and determinations while thinking and determining" is an important essential thought about, and determination of, subjectivity. Having said this however, we must be aware of and beware of simplifications. When we regard the 'I' of self-reference and the anonymous dative of manifestation as sources of constituted being, we cannot thereby relent to the disposition to find their determination within the meaning-spaces of constituted being.

Husserl's view is aligned with Wagner's insofar as the (noematic) validity of the knowledge of transcendent being, in correlation with the life of the mind, occasions a wonderment in need of an explanation. Whereas the explanation can never be one that is indifferent to constitution-analysis, it is still not to be found simply in the ultimate 'principle' of constitution, the primal presencing, even though this fulfills all the requirements of the principle of all principles; that is, it is the absolute phenomenon and is thereby noumenal. The reason is that this noumenon is soaked with facticity and contingency. In effect, Husserl implicitly sees the option of Sartre, that at the origin of the mind's presencing—a world with science, logic, art, values, imperatives—we have sheer facticity. But he is not motivated to speak of the nothingness out of which the primal facticity arises; nor does he give up the search for origins, the constitutional analysis, and resort to pointing to an essence that accounts for the mind's transcendence but that has the consequence of nullifying the significance of constitutional analyses. Rather, faithful to the principle of all principles of originary intuitive evidence as well as to his predilection for the investigation of the origins of constitution, Husserl proposes an analysis of the originary and developed functionings of the mind in terms of this very facticity, and in terms of the development out of this facticity. When we do this we are necessarily led, compelled, to ask about the ground of this functioning, foremost about how the primal presencing is indeed the source (see *Ideas*, section 58).

4. *The Mode of Demonstration of the Divine Principle*

We said that, according to Husserl, we cannot be misled by any conceivable theory, if we hold fast to the principle of all principles: that every originary intuition (*originaer gebende Anschauung*) is a legitimate source of knowledge (*Ideas* I, section 24). The originary intuitions of the natural attitude are principles for knowledge within this realm of naïveté, but they are already-begun beginnings whose sources are brought to light through reflection. The apperceiving, constituting, meaning-giving acts that inform the materials of perception have become part of a spontaneous, associational, dispositional system; that is, the beginnings of originary intuitions are founded in already-begun beginnings or already-originated principles. And the coming into play and playing out of the particular apperceivings, in conjunction with past achievements is a concentration from out of the unified web of achievements that is the apperception of 'world'. World is not merely the frame and motivational principle for the particular meaning-acts, but it itself, as *noema* of noemata, as base/horizon of the mind's intentions, is incessantly in a process or revision, confirmation, incremental growth, and decline as a result of these achievements. Acts are, in spite of their eidetic typicality and particular temporal identity, functional achievements by way of a concentration or simplification of the massive apperception that, although hidden to reflection on the individual acts, provides the meaning-giving underground and background of the particular acts. Husserl is not far removed from Heidegger, in the view that transcendence, that is, being-in-the-*world*, founds the intentional act-life.[36] But the particular act/apperception, as well as the massive synthetic apperception ('world'), like (and in a functional relation with) the materials of perception, are already-begun beginnings rooted in the primal presencing, the living present, which is the ultimate discovery of the transcendental reduction. For properly transcendental, phenomenological reflection, the primal presencing is the principle of all principles, in the sense of being the source of all moments of constitution, which lead to the originary intuitions of the natural attitude.

The originary intuition of the primal presencing is the beginning of all principles *quoad nos phaenomenologicos.* But even if we take the primal presencing as unbegun and are able to claim for it the self-luminosity of a primal evidence, it is not the beginning of all beginings; it is not the source of the wondrous fact of rationality that is at the heart of all originary intuitions; it is not the source of the protorationality of the 'living present', or primal presencing. In *Ideas* I (sections 51 and 58) we learn of another sense of the principle to which we are *necessarily led*, about which we are *compelled* to inquire ("fuehrt notwendig zur Frage nach dem Grund . . . Das Faktum als Quelle . . . zwingt die Frage nach dem 'Grund' "). (Whether and how this principle or ground is subordinated to the originary intuition of primal presencing will occupy us in section 7 below.)

According to these texts, what compels the search for a divine principle is the "element of fact in the given order of the course of consciousness, in its differentiations into individuals and the teleology immanent in them."[37] What is forceful for theological topics in transcendental reflection upon the life of the mind is the factual connectedness of the flow of experience that establishes kinds of specific, splendidly regulated organizations by which, as intentional correlates, there is constituted for intuitive experience a morphologically ordered world, which lends itself to scientific classifications and descriptions. Thus what *founds* the theological speculation for transcendental phenomenology is primal presencing's facticity—not facticity or contingency in general, as in Aquinas's *tertia via*, for example, but the primal presencing's facticity as source (*Faktum als Quelle*) of the possible and real values that may be envisaged as extending indefinitely and mounting ever higher. Primal presencing occasions theological themes because it is, although as sheer contingency, the source of a constituted world, which

> so far as its material basis is concerned, permits at once of being determined in the theoretical thought of the mathematically grounded natural sciences as the "appearance" of a *physical nature* that conforms to exact natural laws. And since *the rationality* which the facticity realizes is not in any sense such as the essence demands, there lies concealed in all this a wonderful *teleology*.

In this text (from *Ideas* I, section 58), the context requires that we be astonished at a twofold rationality-in-facticity: that of the flow of the constituting consciousness *and* that of the constituted flow of appearings of a world of transcendent, spatial, temporal objects. The text continues:

> Further, the systematic study of all teleologies which are to be found in the empirical world itself, e.g., the factual evolution of the series of organisms up to man, and within the evolution of humanity, the growth of culture with its treasures of the spirit and so forth, is not exhausted by the explanations of all such creations by the natural sciences out of the given factual environment and in conformity with natural laws. On the contrary, the transition to pure consciousness through the method of transcendental reduction leads necessarily to the question concerning the ground of what now presents itself as the intuitable facticity of the corresponding constituting consciousness. It is not facticity in general, but facticity as the source of possible and real values extending indefinitely, which compels us to ask after the "ground"—which, of course, has not then the meaning of substantive cause.

An early (1908–09) text centers *metaphysics* on this issue. In a vein similar to that in *Ideas*, sections 51 and 58, Husserl observes that nature becomes constituted through rational motivations that belong to the essence of consciousness. On the one hand, these norms have their ideal meaning and validity. Yet it is not necessary that consciousness be rational; its essential and necessary rationality cannot be demonstrated. Of course, that it is subordinate to norms is evident from the essence of acts. Given such and such an act, like memory, judgment, picturing, and so forth, there are such and such features, which instance norms. But that consciousness *must* constitute a rational order so that there ensues a nature, a culture, an evolution of culture—that is not ultimately necessary at all. If we uncovered sources that could account for the contingent rationality of the primal streaming, then we would have a kind of *demonstration of the existence of God.*[38]

In the light of Husserl's principle of all principles, this demonstration would be a *monstrans*; that is, it would be original, intuitive evidence. Insofar as it involved a reference to what was absent, it would be a *speculation*; but the speculation would be neither the result of a conclusion from premises nor a postulation of what was not presently evident. The *speculans* would be a mirroring of the transcendent in the immanent. In the earlier version of *Ideas*, section 58, Husserl wrote that the transcendence of God comes mediately (*mittelbar*) to light (*Erkenntnis*).[39] Thus the *demonstratio* would be a showing of the *divinity as such* in what appears. It would not merely be one way of taking what appears; rather, it would be an essential feature of the dative of appearing, in such a way that it could not be taken otherwise, except by reference to this divine principle. (For 'divinity as such', see section 8 below.) But where do we look? Where is this *monstrans*? The answer, of course, has repeatedly been indicated in the course of this essay. But let us here review what perhaps are Husserl's least tentative statements on this matter, from his "Texts on Axiology and Ethics" (1909–23, FI 24 of the *Nachlass*). The context is asking, "What, then, is God, the theological principle?", a principle that is to account for the *Faktum* of the theoretical rationality of the world in its being-in-itself (from the viewpoint of the natural attitude) and is to account for its ethical-practical rationality, thereby providing a field for our endeavors in which we may realize ever-increasing value and fulfillment. But what does "account for" mean here? If we say that God creates the world just as an artist creates a work, we could say that the reason for the creation is tied to the artist's motive. Something within a person is related to an object of which the person is aware. But, Husserl observes, this parallel is not useful for understanding the *Faktum* of the rationality of the world. In this context he does not elaborate on this uselessness. Of course, we might add, there are the obvious difficulties of the inaccessibility of the divine mind, of comparing the factual rationality to a work; and we can ask with what and how is the world made? is it always being made? Are the materials made? How can the transcendental I be made?

From another context (KIII 1), we know that Husserl regards as unsatisfactory such attempts as Aristotle's (and more immediately, those of Brentano), which appeal to a mundane teleology in order to derive a divine mind, while at the same time remaining totally oblivious of an account of the world that takes its bearings from the immanent teleology of subjectivity. Such Aristotelian accounts only make sense insofar as they reconstructively proceed from the human personality and its typical deeds. Further, God is thereby accounted for in human terms, whereas the actual task is to account for subjectivity as originating in God. Thus, transcendental phenomenology enables the appreciation of the divine as the source and beginning of humanity rather than as a metaphorical version of humanity. This divine *Ausweis* is not from the constituted cosmos, but from that cosmos-constituting principle, transcendental subjectivity. Furthermore, if we grant that in some sense the world is a product, a result, of a constituting *poesis*, this sense must be determined by the fundamental distinctions (of both the natural and transcendental attitudes) between knowing, doing/acting, and making. The sense in which constitution is making must account for the fundamental fact that we act and make on the basis of the conviction that it is only through our actions and our making that the thing, event, state of affairs, and the like will be realized in the future. But inquiry rests on our conviction that although knowledge is, indeed, a result of our agency, that which we know or want to know is not a mere result of our agency. On the other hand, the sense in which constitution is a 'knowing' must account for the fact that the *noema* is always an achievement, the nature of which cannot be determined by the nascent, naive realism of the natural attitude. In short, in the face of the wondrous fact of the world's rationality, the appeal to a divine artisan to account for this fact not only overlooks the constituting role of intersubjectivity by sliding into the natural attitude, but it also tends to blur the most difficult distinctions between knowing, making, doing, and constituting.

What, then, is the appropriate reflection? Husserl's response is:

> Here the answer can only be given by immersing ourselves in the *Faktum* and in the essence of the irrational and rational ingredients found there. The I cannot be made nor can the life of the I. The I can only be in that it develops itself, in that it becomes through an uninterrupted motivation and thereby it develops itself to freedom. And then, in full consciousness, it takes a stand and is thereby motivated by awakened reason (FI 24, 40b–41a).

The procedure is an immersion (*Vertiefung*) in the gossamer of the primal presencing, in terms of its rational and irrational ingredients. The primal presencings in their problematic synthesis of uniqueness and community (of 'I' and the 'others') are "the primal waters of creation," the unbegun materials of the world. In this light we can say that a good part of Husserl's later discussions of passive synthesis and the constitution of internal time-consciousness are indeed theological texts "showing from below how God creates the world in a perpetual creating (*im ewigen Schaffen*)."[40] Or, perhaps more precisely, as Cairns has recorded it, showing from below "how God created that absolute world of transcendental intersubjectivity and continues to create it, even as the transcendental intersubjectivity creates its world."[41] Thus there is no one text that is a demonstration for God's existence; rather, the massive effort to wrestle with the protorationality of the primal presencing is a theological effort. That is, it is a manifesting of the functioning of the divine principle within the facticity of reason in the primal presencing.

Here is the text that best summarizes the results of this massive *demonstratio* "from below":

Each of our hyletic data is already a "developmental product" and therefore it has a hidden intentionality which refers back to a synthesis. Everything refers back to a *prote hyle* which is a completely undifferentiated material (*Stoff*) and to primal-constitutive processes with intentional motivations which belong therein. But all development is permeated by guiding "ideas." The ultimate guiding idea is that of the total development. That would be the system of ideas of the formal "Mathesis" in the widest sense (encompassing the axiological and practical sphere); this would be the system of principles and the ideal unity of all formations.

The development is not to be seen as a beginning and terminating process, as a tiny tale; rather there is continuously a primal *hyle* there and it adheres in all developed *hyle*; and, therefore, conscious I-ness transforms itself continuously into dying, i.e., everything is deposited into a form of passivity (loss of memory, etc.). The central issue is this: When inquiring about the ground of a development, the only reasonable manner of questioning is found in describing the development at its deepest level and in describing its guiding ideal-goal. God is the entelechy and outside of him there is "nothing"; he is the all-forming. And the irrational material (*Stoff*) is not something made but precisely that: stuff. And the world has its being from out of God and is otherwise "nothing." and God is only as the guiding and besouling principle of perfection, etc.[42]

5. *The Evidence for the Divine Entelechy*

This very important text opens up numerous themes, which will busy us in the following pages. Here we will operate with, but not explore, the concept of the divine entelechy: God as the guiding and besouling principle of perfection. In this section we wish to make as clear as possible what it is that motivates Husserl to claim that one is necessarily led to a divine principle from the primal presencing's facticity as source. In the above-cited text the primal presencing is referred to as having two moments: the *proto hyle*, as completely undifferentiated material, and the guiding ideas, which are expressed in the motivational, constitutive processes. Qua phenomenologists, we do not apprehend the primal *hyle* as completely undifferentiated material. We have mentioned the difficulties of this position in connection with the doctrine of the beginninglessness and endlessness of the primal presencing. In spite of the difficulties we saw that, with respect to the primal presencing's approaching zero-degree discrimination, the 'life' of the primal presencing (which is improperly named 'the I') does not come to be. In the nonwaking circumstance, we approach the absence of differentiation and discrimination and approximate the sheer 'continuity' of indiscernibly different presencings. Here the issue of a divine principle does *not* arise, because we do not yet have the *Wunder* of rationality, wherein one identifiable phase can be distinguished from the next and whereby an emptily intended, not-actual phase can be intended as capable of actuality. In the state of zero-degree discrimination, there is no *eros* toward the filling of empty intentions, nor is there development as the filling of these intentions and the awakening of new ones. The monad excised from the world is curiously sufficient to itself and not in need of the gracious divine guidance. With its birth, or contact with the world's appearances, it gains the capacity to distinguish one moment from the next; thereby primal presencing becomes present to itself or conscious, insofar as being present to oneself is enjoying otherness as such or difference with respect to the same. That is, if we think of zero-degree discrimination as total loss of consciousness (because discrimination as the enjoying of sameness in difference is dissolved into a confusion of the differents), then the capacity to appreciate sameness and difference is at least a necessary, if not sufficient, condition for consciousness. But as soon as the monad is awake, we find degrees of discrimination. The mind cannot help being 'mindful', cannot help attending or 'minding', in the minimal sense of the ongoing filling of the protended, the retaining of the filled protended, and the protending of the filling-retaining. Thus, Husserl says, the mind cannot help constituting being, and as an awake mind, it is "irrationally driven" to do so and cannot constitute nonbeing.[43]

By way of elucidating how we *must*, as waking minds, achieve identity syntheses or sameness across differences (which is the sense of 'being' in these texts of Husserl), we can turn to an argument by Franz Brentano. Brentano shows that because we cannot help but envisage (Husserl: *constitute*) the world and its entities as having temporal identity (duration), we must rule out any doctrine of 'pure chance' and hold to a theory of 'universal causation' (Husserl: *proto*rationality). Brentano begins with the consideration that there is an equivalence between 'something is' and 'something is present' (in contrast to the attitude of the reduction: not as present *to me*, but 'now'). What is, is simultaneous with everything else that is; the temporal differences are, of course, that some are ending while others are beginning, some are closer to their beginnings while others are closer to their ends, some have longer durations than others, and so on. Things have different durations. Whatever we are dealing with, even something described as having 'unchanging continuity', it is undergoing continuous temporal change; otherwise, we could not speak of what is present as having a longer or shorter duration, nor of this phase of the duration as being before that, and so forth. Of course, when we say that what is present has duration as a continuous temporal change, we need not mean that the connection, or continuity, necessarily extends in both directions at once. For example, what is present may have just begun or just ended. (Here it is clear that we are dealing with what for Husserl is a constituted realm, and not the primal streaming.)

> Yet that which is present cannot lack both directions simultaneously; one connection or the other must be preserved. In other words, it is impossible for something to begin and end abruptly within the same moment, but what begins abruptly now may end abruptly at a later moment, and likewise, it is possible for what ends abruptly now to have begun abruptly at an earlier moment.[44]

Between the beginning and the end we always find an intervening duration, regardless of how small we may envisage it.

Now, argues Brentano, if we could envisage pure chance as a

possibility, we could entertain something like a white dot's coming by chance into being, and further, we might assume its passing out of existence to be absolutely incidental (i.e., 'by pure chance'); thus it could pass out of existence at any arbitrarily designated moment.

> But this is the precise opposite of what we established earlier for each thing existing, without exception; namely that it must remain free from abrupt change for some time, be it ever so short, for one moment of abrupt change cannot directly follow another. They must be separated by a period during which no change occurs, and this can be subdivided *ad infinitum*![45]

This argues Husserl's point well, that the waking mind necessarily constitutes being and that it is not free to introduce chaos—even though it might well be confronted with events that undermine this inveterate drive to establish a cosmos. In order for something to pass 'capriciously' out of existence, it must first be; that is, it must appear as the same throughout different phases. It cannot become and be extinguished in the same 'moment', but only in different ones. This holds for the mind's own life as well; the identity of an act's constituting phases are not amenable to absolute caprice or chance.

But granted that when the mind constitutes anything, there are laws and necessities, and granted that the mind inveterately churns out temporal identity syntheses or beings with duration, nevertheless, the sameness that is constitutive of duration is evident only in the achieved sameness of the waking mind's achieving. This achieving builds on the hyletic streaming, which founds the being of the world. This founding is necessary in odd ways, which we must now touch on.

The founding is necessary because duration must be; that is, the sameness must endure across the span of temporal differents, and the beginning and ending of the streaming are inconceivable. Yet this is odd, because the sameness is evident only in the flux of phases as temporal individuatings of the wakeful mind's self-displacing, re-presenting, surmounting of the flux. In the absence of the self-displacing achieving (act) or of the achieved (white dot), the differentiation ceases. The necessity of the hyletic streaming is only evident in the wakeful achieving of the I.

Furthermore, the flux is contingent in an odd sense. Although it is necessary that *something* be—silence, 'nothing' in some form or other, nothing expected or recognizable—it is not necessary that some*thing* be, that is, something of the same 'nature' as the achieving being or as the achieved being. The 'phases' of immanent awareness must 'be'; they are the necessary base. But, there need not be that of which they are presently the 'phases', that of which we are presently aware: things, sensa, acts, and so forth. And when these are not, then this wakefulness, or immanent self-presence of intentional life as a discriminating awareness, is dissolved. If this dissolution does not directly result in unconsciousness proper, it provides at least the limbo created by a sensory deprivation chamber.

This discussion points to a final sense of the odd necessity of the hyletic streaming to be prior, founding, and presumed apart from waking mind. The cessation, or beginning, of the production of presencings is inconceivable, and yet each primal presencing is a fact. The beginning and cessation of anything is thinkable only in the process of the primal presencing, but it is not thinkable as the beginning and ending of the process of the primal presencing. Yet the process involves novelty. Although the cessation of the experience of what is now is inconceivable, each now is the filling of a protended not-yet now, which is contingent in that it is not necessitated by what preceded it. Although these novel pulsations are the founding presuppositions for all constituted worldly necessities, they are *Fakta*, contingents, whose cessation or beginning, nevertheless, is inconceivable because all cessation or beginning is thinkable only within, and presupposing the process of, the primal presencing (see *Analysen zur passiven Synthesis*, 377ff). Thus the beginninglessness and continuation are necessary; but this is always a necessity of novelty and fact. Consequently, the form of the primal presencing necessarily involves contingency. (In the C-manuscripts, Husserl also names this form the form of the standing-streaming.)

It is not necessary either that the *waking* mind involve necessities or that it constitute necessities. Although it is necessary that the terminating phase of a passive experiencing, an act of the mind, or a white dot be preceded by beginning/middle phases and that it cannot be simultaneous with these phases, it is still not necessary that these phases continue as differents of the same experience, act, or white dot. That the self-displacing *be* (perdure) is a *Faktum*, which enables that the passive or active taking of the differents be the same and that the same (white dot) *is* (e.g., abides as the same). All are contingents; none have a sufficient reason in the hyletic streaming for their being.

Here again, we may note a fundamental difficulty in describing the necessity or contingency of the primal presencing, inasmuch as it is the source of all senses of necessity and contingency and may not, therefore, be understood in terms of the necessity and contingency of constituted realms (see *Husserliana* XV, 385–386, 668–669).

If by necessity we mean what we cannot change, then the primal presencing's drive to constitute being, that is, its ongoing, self-displacing, re-presenting, establishing of sameness across differents, upon the base of the irrepressible, passive synthesizing of the hyletic flux, is necessary. But if by necessity we mean what cannot not be, then the constituting and constituted being are not necessary, because there is no intrinsic reason in the primal presencing, as hyletic streaming, why the being, the constituting or constituted sameness across the differents, must be. Of course, we cannot genuinely imagine or conceive another state of affairs, and even our maddest life or most chaotic world is parasitic on rudimentary identity syntheses. And in this sense as we can say with Brentano), the very chance of its being otherwise is inconceivable. Nevertheless, ultimately the factual flow of contingent, novel pulsations establishes the necessary hyletic duration as the base of the factual achievement of the being, that is, of the sameness across the differents of the achieving mind and of its worldly achievements.

Yet the self-displacing achieving and the achievement do not have a foundation in themselves. First of all, and most obviously, the achieving mind cannot account for the continued duration and regularity of the realm of relative being or that of the worldly noemata. This is no small consideration, but it is not the major interest of transcendental constitutional theory. Rather, what is of utmost importance is that the being of reason, as the self-displacing that establishes being or sameness across differents, can neither be accounted for by the necessary hyletic base, with its factual phases, nor can it (assuming that it is 'there' and is an egological achieving self-displacing) account for itself and its own achieving.

As to the former point: Until the egological principle is 'there' (*dabei*), there is no surmounting of the flux of the pre-being of the continuum of indiscernible differents. Not yet awakened is the capacity for being (cf. the Aristotelian *intellectus agens*), as the transcending of the differents, which lets them be—*as* differents of the same. Of course, Husserl's view is that the ultimate reduction leads to transcendental subjectivity, or 'I', as a coincidence of egological and hyletic moments. That is, we never have the hyletic streaming apart from what it affects, the egological moment (see, e.g., the text in section 7 below). Furthermore, we have clear indications that Husserl renounced the temptation to envisage primal presencing as more fundamentally hyletic and derivatively egological (see, e.g., C 17 IV, in Held, *Lebendige Gegenwart*, 97ff.). Yet, our systematic interpretation attempts to integrate the doctrine that transcendental subjectivity is 'in some sense' perpetual and necessary. One sense is the nonthinkability of its beginning or ending. This cannot mean that it is always wakeful, always 'dabei'. We must acknowledge the "pull towards death," or the emergent oblivion of retentional consciousness. (See *Husserliana* X, 365). Further, we must deal with the deprivations of the possibility of the standpoint of phenomenological reflection; that is, we must treat (reconstruct) the cases, in the Other and in oneself, in which wakeful consciousness appears to be absent, as in sickness, sleep, and death. If Husserl's doctrine is not merely that an individual experiencing of experiencing's beginning and ending is inconceivable, but that the being of a transcendental monad is without beginning or ending, then we have reason ultimately to conceive transcendental subjectivity as necessary *prote hyle*, as hyletic "streaming" of indiscernible differents, deprived of its wakeful egological principle (cf. section 6 below.)

Clearly this sense of ultimacy and necessity has aspects that do not derive from phenomenological reflection in a proper sense, even though they are motivated by transcendental phenomenology's aspiration to be metaphysics. The more proper reflection on the contingency of the primal presencing requires, of course, the wakeful egological principle of the dative of appearing. For this reflection the transcendental "I" is necessary vis-à-vis the world and its ingredients, in the sense evident within the transcendental reduction: Whereas everything in the world, and the world itself as a cosmos, can be thought out of existence, the transcendental I, understood as dative of manifestation and not yet a token-reflexive, cannot be mentally eliminated. It is always silently, anonymously 'there' (*dabei*).[46] Our present discussion assumes this mental noneliminability of the dative of manifestation as a necessity and focuses on the feature of contingency, which is constitutive of this dative as primal presencing, with its egological and hyletic moments. The theological dimension surfaces when one is moved to consider that the properly egological achieving builds on, and is constituted by, a transcendent domination (*Walten*) of the hyletic streaming, which domination is constitutive of egological being and wakefulness. The act of self-displacing in retentions and protentions, apperceptions and perceptions, associations and anticipations, and so forth, by which being is established, is something that 'I' both do and yet presuppose as involving something for which I am not responsible but which I count on. Thus, for example, both the achieving of (nonthematized) acts, through which we inform the present by drawing on relevant pasts through appropriate associations, and the thematized being of the acts, as temporal identity syntheses, build upon the ongoing hyletic streaming that 'I' do not achieve. The being of the wakeful experiencing, the achieving (e.g., acts) and my achievements (e.g., white dots) presuppose the facticity of the hyletic flux as functioning on their behalf, but for which they in no way account. The life of the I is, in this sense, a trusting in its own being (therefore it is a 'self-trust') but also a trusting in a functioning that 'holds sway' and enables it to be and to achieve; but 'I' cannot account for this holding sway (see section 10 below). We here come upon what Husserl calls the 'wonder' of reason.

6. *The Wonder of Rationality*

Our interpretation has attempted to conceive the divine 'holding sway' (*Walten*) in relation to Husserl's claims that, in some sense, transcendental subjectivity is necessarily perpetual. This is transcendental subjectivity as the factual hyletic streaming, a *prote hyle* that is a moment along with the dative of appearing ('I') in transcendental reflection. We have urged that the contingency be understood not with respect to the ongoingness or perpetuity of the stream of presencings, but with respect to the rationality and teleology that pervades this stream of presencings. Husserl clearly locates the cause of the *Wunder* in the rationality and the teleology, the forms of necessity, causality, probability, reliability, lawfulness, and so on, which ride on the facticity of the primal streaming. Presumably, the primal streaming does not have this rationality and this teleology in its excision from the world, nor when it has arrived at zero-degree discrimination. But the nature of an excised monad (i.e., not yet, or no longer, part of the world, dead, comatose, etc.) is a fundamental speculative problem for transcendental phenomenological reconstruction. Our interpretation urges that the (monadological) *prote hyle* is a principle that is coefficient with the divine; it is not created. But its distinguishing mark seems to be a creative (hyletic) flux; does not this flow always involve discrimination? As to be expected, for Husserl there are distinctions in forms of dullness and absence of consciousness. A basic issue is the following: If we are to argue for the perpetuity of the primal presencing on the basis of the non-conceivability of its beginning or ending, must we not assume a perpetual flux? And if the flow is necessarily characterized by a pro-torationality established by the divine *Walten*, is not the *prote hyle* itself then a product of the divine? And if it is not to be so characterized, how do we characterize it? On another occasion we hope to do more justice to the issues. What Husserl clearly wants to say is that wakeful primal presencing, regardless of how close it is to zero-degree discrimination, is still a self-unifying and self-differentiating streaming. As wakeful primal streaming it is still a 'flow', and this flowing is necessary both in the Brentanoian sense of non-chance and in the sense that its cessation or beginning is inconceivable. But this necessity of the flow is still a flow of nonnecessarily connected 'phases' or *Fakta*, and in and of themselves they do not account for their connectedness. The *prote hyle* abstracted from the divine *Walten* would seem to have as well the contingency of the elemental 'flux': the hyletic phases or *Fakta* simply happen, and there is no 'reason' that accounts for them. This contingency is that of the novelty and creativity of the eternal hyletic principle, which is the eternal correlate of divinity and whose perpetual sourcing is formally able to be considered apart from divinity. But the evidence for the divine in primal presencing rests on seeing the 'pulsating synthesizing', wherein each phase contingently follows upon the other; *furthermore*, this factual linkage of phases manifests rational 'style' and results in a manifold of structures, which together make up what we call rationality, culture, and progress. In other words, the evidence for the 'divine entelechy' is concentrated in the fundamental rhythm of empty intention/filled intention—wider empty intention/wider filled intention, always synthesizing, always pushing toward *excelsior*. That this rhythm obtains, however, is not necessary; it is neither automatic nor without occasional cruel setbacks. Still it has this typicality. That it is there at all, that it can claim achievements, and that it promises much more is astonishing, in the sense that (a) a good is at work that is not only in our behalf, but constitutes us as rational, and (b) this good precariously, delicately, rides on or is effected through a contingency that cannot guarantee the achievement of this goodness. It is important to remember that what is in need of a principle is not the coming-to-be of

the primal presencing. For Husserl, in this context, its beginninglessness is taken as established. Rather, what is in need of a principle is the
ongoing functioning rationality and teleology, which permeate the
primal streaming in its contingency. The Husserlian version of the
question, Why is there something rather than nothing? is not a
reference to *creatio ex nihilo*, not to the 'existential' (*actus essendi*)
fact that there is a mind presencing, but to the rational-teleological
way in which the primal presencing occurs.[47]

Experience is the pursuit of the world's promise of ever richer
meaning and is based on our capacity to connect the achieved meanings and to enable the former ones to function relevantly in the present. The fundamental feature of primal presencing (i.e., that it
establishes sameness through differences) must therefore be
understood such that the idea of the same is capable of infinite in-
crease. 'Experience', *Erfahrung*, and *Erleben* all have etymologies that
suggest journeying through unknown territory, facing the perils of all
differents, no sameness, or the deadly lull of all sameness and
no difference; there is a suggestion both of the danger of undoing the
sameness by difference and of the darkness of the absorption of the
differents and novelty by sameness. Every achievement of meaning is a triumph in the *ad-ventura* of experience, because it avoids the
twofold peril. The heroic adventures not only take place in the eerie,
upsetting unknown, for which we have no handy categories or
frames, but they also entail remaining attentive, wakeful, and
discriminating.

We achieve meaning when the cosmos is established, that is,
when sequences of events (*post hoc*) can be related in terms of patterns, styles, and familiar and necessary features of larger contexts
(*propter hoc*). Yet the miracle (*Wunder*) of primal presencing's rationality is that the *propter hoc* pervading the established cosmos is
rooted in the factual *post hoc*. At bottom, instead of the familiarity of
the rationally constituted, there is the miracle (*Wunder*) of constituting
rationality. What enables the familiarity and hominess of the world is
the primal, passive, associative syntheses by which we are enabled to
take the world as ordered. I take this (Y^2) as X because X is like Y^1,
which I have successfully taken as like X. I expect something (A) from
this event (Y^2) because I take it in a certain way; that is, it reminds me
of Y^1, which had such and such features and which I take to be like Y^2.
In short, the present experience is taken as being analogical to prior
ones. I expect A in regard to Y^2 because of (*propter*) the prior ex-

perience functioning now (*post*). The present necessity (or *propter*) of 'A because of Y²' is founded on the fact of the now functioning (*post*) prior experience (e.g., Y¹ in regard to A¹). This, Husserl notes, may look crazy, but it is the simple truth of the matter. All grounding of our rational motivations (e.g., our expecting A as the reasonable thing in this circumstance) is grounded on the prior factual experience of our retention and memory, that is, on what enables us to take this in precisely this way. The rational ordering of the world cannot occur without the fact of the appropriate past's functioning in the present. All apperceiving of the world, all meaning-giving, all 'taking it this way or that' is tied to the fact of the past's functioning appropriately now. All rationality and all necessity of 'this on account of that', 'if this, then that', and so forth is dependent on the fact of the appropriate functioning of prior experiences in the stream of primal presencings. Thus, our rational establishing of the cosmos is founded on the facticity of the past experiences working at appropriate times in the present presencing. Here we clearly have a sense in which the mind is a 'grace', that is, the responsible use of the mind itself is dependent on an a priori of genesis, which rides on a fact for which we are not responsible; all motivated, present experience refers to a prior consciousness factually and contingently functioning now as its essential ingredient. It is wonderful but true that consciousness is not a capricious flow of facts that could indifferently be something else. "The earlier consciousness motivates possibilities of later ones in such an a priori way that the later consciousness, in so far as it at least has the character of an empirical-transcendent apperception (thesis), in its facticity is motivated necessarily through a corresponding earlier consciousness."[48]

Such a discussion makes it clear that Husserl's *Wunder* is occasioned not by the fact of a mind's presencing but by the rational-teleological way in which primal presencing occurs. Dwelling on this enables what Husserl once called "the logic of metaphysical motivation," or the peculiar *monstrans* of a divine principle.[49] In this early text what is at issue is a single thread with two fibers: the teleological harmony and bond between and among the monads and the harmony and teleological bond within the phases of a single flow of consciousness. With respect to the latter, which enjoys a methodological priority, we can ask: Why does it flow in just this way? For what reason does it have this synthesizing, teleological rhythm? What we are looking for here is not an 'absolute thing' behind things or even an absolute thing behind this teleology. All thingliness is constituted. "What motivates a consciousness can only be a consciousness."[50] Here we have suggestions about the nature of the divine, that it is an analogous I or 'personal' consciousness, that it is the principle of perfection, and so forth. In section 8 we will briefly touch upon some of these matters. Of immediate interest is the context our discussion provides for passages in the *Cartesian Meditations*, which some have found puzzling. In these texts Husserl, in a remarkably condensed mode of description, writes of the transcendental I as an infinite, joined contextuality of connecting achievements in a universal genesis of levels that arrange themselves within the universal form of temporality. Thereby, the fixed form of the world is shaped and ultimately conserved.

> In all that the particular fact (*jeweilige Faktum*) is irrational; but it is possible only in the apriori form-system pertaining to it as an egological fact. Nor should it be overlooked here that the *fact* and its irrationality is itself a structural concept within the system of the concrete apriori.[51]

In our interpretation we take this text to state, first of all, that the world's noematic order is a contingency to be understood only in reference to the transcendental I. Further, that the examination of the I in terms of the primal presencing or passive genesis, as the concrete, 'innate', a priori, and ultimate principle, shows facticity to be a basic feature. Therefore, the ultimate transcendental phenomenological account uncovers contingency or, in some sense, irrationality at the ultimate explanatory level.

Here we move into the deeps of theological metaphysical waters. Husserl's founding of the *propter hoc* on a *post hoc* is not a reduction of rationality to a *Faktum*, and thereby what he basically regards as a denial of genuine rationality.[52] When Hume refrains from his tendency to dogmatic skepticism and attempts to describe the features of the "kind of *attraction* which in the mental world will be found to have as extraordinary effects as in the natural, and to show itself in as many and as various forms," whose causes "must be resolved into *original* qualities of human nature," he draws near to transcendental phenomenology.[53] And when Kant, instead of constructing the a priori forms as explanatory of the laws of experience, studies in his transcendental aesthetics the essential features of the passive-associative-generative syntheses, he approaches the *eidos* of transcendental subjectivity. The facticity (contingency, *post hoc*, etc.) is seen to be truly ultimate yet in need of a *logos*, which is manifest in the *Faktum*. This has profound implications for a transcendental phenomenological theology, and in the next section we wish to indicate some of them briefly.

7. The Necessity and Facticity of and within 'the Absolute Substance'

In Eugen Fink's essay on Husserl's thought during the later years at Freiburg, he notes that the distinction between "the timeless source (*Quellgrund*) of time and the flow of time" provided Husserl with a stimulating circle of problems, which he pursued with the technique of essence-analysis, or free imaginative variation. In these late eidetic analyses of transcendental subjectivity, Husserl was led to the 'peculiar' (*merkwuerdige*) consideration that

> the most original depth of the life of consciousness is no longer touched by the distinction between *essentia* and *existentia*. Rather here is the primal ground out of which first originates the bifurcation of *Faktum* and essence, reality and possibility, examplar and species, one and many.[54]

Husserl was led to modify the position in the fifth Cartesian meditation, Fink further notes, that the constitution of transcendent worldly being must be traced back to the prior constitution of intersubjectivity. Fink also notes that Husserl did not give up this position but envisaged the primal I as prior to the distinction between *ego* and *alter ego*, and that there is a sense of one-and-onlyness from which plurality emerges (cf. our discussions in section 1.4 above). In sum, Husserl's late position, according to Fink, is:

> Time is founded on a time-creating present which is not in time; the disunion of all being (*essentia-existentia*) in a primal unity, which is neither "factual," nor "possible," neither one nor many, neither an exemplar nor a genus. The plural of subjects is founded in a depth of life which is prior to any individuation of selves. . . . Husserl wants to think back to the formless ground, out of which formations come to light. He wants to grasp the *Apeiron*, the unlimited. But he is not in search of a mystical trance in the night in which "all cows are black" to use Hegel's mocking expression. He wants to grasp it as the primal

source (*Ur-Sprung*), as the breach, which dismembers the basis of life, as the negativity in the most primal being. That is, he wants to grasp time in its emergence out of the timeless-eternal, the world-texture of *Faktum* and essence in its fashioning (*Fuegung*), and the selves, the subjects, in the selving (*Selbstung*) of absolute being.[55]

Regarding this effort of Husserl's to catch the achievement of life by transcendental consciousness 'red handed', Fink cautions against a speculative and theological reading of the primal I. Even though Husserl uses the vocabulary of 'absolute metaphysics', he is quite removed from it in terms of the issue (*der Sache*). It is the view of this writer that it is less 'die Sache' that separates Husserl from German idealism than the method, and even this, on occasion, is not always so remote.[56] The more specific sense of Fink's remark seems to derive from a similar view, because he follows up his strong *caveat* with an observation on the manner in which Husserl arrived at these 'ominous concepts': They were generated by embarassment in the face of philosophical limit-situations, not through speculative thought.[57] This is not the occasion for a detailed pursuit of the topics listed by Fink in the above-quoted texts. In our view, Husserl's position leads more to an ultimate, unified whole, with essential irreducible moments, than to an original unity out of which these moments are generated. It is this tension that we shall briefly study in a doctrinal fashion.

We have stated, but not argued, that primal presencing cannot be mentally eliminated in favor of more ultimate concerns. Because of this ultimacy, primal presencing is 'the absolute substance'. This is not a well-developed concept in Husserl, but it is that toward which all transcendental phenomenological analyses converge. Primal presencing, as the principle of all principles, "has its ground in itself and has in its groundless being its absolute necessity as 'absolute substance.' "[58] As the absolute ultimate to which philosophical reflection reaches, the ultimate *Faktum* is also the ultimate necessity. It is a *concretum*, with respect to which everything else is abstract; it is that within which all other considerations 'inhere', a 'substrate' whose moments or modes must be explicated not only in relation to its peculiar and insurmountable facticity but also, of course, in relation to its founding necessity. The primal presencing, therefore, is not the fact of a maker or of a *facere*, nor the *Tatsache* of a *Taeter* or of a *Tat*, as if we were entitled to move from contingent effects or products to transcendent necessary causes, or as if we could remain content with the primal presencing, the primal *fieri* or *facere*, and declare it by the wave of a wand to be an explanatory principle, the *Ur-Tat!* All contingency and accidentality presuppose a horizon of essential possibilities in which that which is accidental is one of the possibilities, that is, the one that becomes actual. But this horizon of essential possibilities is ultimately constituted in the primal facticity. Therefore, in the case of the 'absolute substance', the fact is prior to the eidetic realm of necessities and is always presupposed by the necessities to be what constitutes them. Still, the necessity of this *Faktum* cannot be readily considered as necessary in a familiar sense. Not only is it a *Faktum*, but it necessarily founds the familiar senses of necessities, possibilities, conditions, and causes that give being and meaning to the eidetic realm of necessities.[59]

In the light of these considerations and of those in the last sections, we may appreciate the relative merit of Hans Wagner's critique of Husserl.[60] As we earlier saw, Wagner charges Husserl with the reduction of all theory to pretheory by reason of his locating the ultimate explanatory principle in the prepredicative experience of the originating primal presencing. If this primal streaming is the *origin*, the ultimate philosophical *principle*, notes Wagner, then we cannot distinguish the principle from that of which it is a principle. The primal pretheoretical evidence might well be a necessary condition for the evidence of the principle that accounts for the world, but it cannot be the sufficient condition or the ultimate explanatory dimension, that is, a principle. If we assume that Wagner has not moved out of the realm of the transcendental reduction (and imparted a sense of principle that derives from a constituted sense of *cause*), we can say that no one has better formulated the point of departure of Husserl's philosophical theology. Our considerations make it clear that for Husserl an ultimate and genuine explanatory principle cannot be found in the facticity of transcendental subjectivity as facticity, but as *Quelle*, as source (see the preceding discussion and *Ideas* I, sections 51 and 58). And, in this connection, Husserl considers 'the divine' as the necessary principle for the contingent rationality of the primal presencing and of the world it constitutes. Yet we have also seen that this necessity can be envisaged only within the ultimate primal presencing ('absolute substance'), which manifests both 'contingency' and 'necessity'—the inverted commas indicating that the meaning of these concepts cannot be considered on the same plane as, or univocal with, mundane or constituted senses.

The problem here is (granting the equivocal or, at best, analogical, character of 'founding', 'necessary', 'grounding', 'accounting for', etc.) how we are to envisage the way in which the divine necessary principle surmounts contingency. If we postulate a divine principle transcendent to transcendental subjectivity, and if we place it beyond the 'absolute substance' of the primal presencing, we then surmount the unsurmountable transcendental phenomenological ultimate. On the other hand, if we do not transcend the contingent rationality of primal presencing as the 'absolute substance', we seem to have no justification for a distinguishable (divine) explanatory *principle*, but rather are left with a contingent ultimate principle that, therefore, is not ultimate at all, and that leaves contingent rationality unaccounted for.

Or, in other words, if we do not transcend the contingent rationality of the 'absolute substance', when we reach the 'divine principle' we, in effect, have no reason to entertain this principle as divine, because we have as much explanatory power as we can get in the contingent rationality of the primal presencing. But if we do transcend the 'absolute substance', we have renounced the ultimacy of the 'absolute substance' and have arbitrarily undermined the transcendental phenomenological enterprise.[61]

On the one hand, we need to transcend the contingency because the *Faktum als Quelle*, the facticity as source, is such only if it is more than sheer contingent fact; but, on the other hand, *Quelle*, source, as essentially transcendent to facticity, as more than mere *Faktum* and as sheer necessity, is unwarranted by the ultimate absolute substance of transcendental reflection. The solution we are proposing as most Husserlian is one in which contingency is brought into the ultimate principle in such a manner as to preserve the contingency, the *Faktum*, and to secure a principle, *Quelle*, that is, ground and necessity. 'Absolute Substance' must contain within it a 'divine' principle that, on the one hand, accounts for the contingent rationality of the primal presencing but that itself is not contingent in the way the primal presencing is contingent. The problem, therefore, may be said to be: How are we to account for the contingency *of the divine* (i.e., within and belonging to the ultimate principle) in such a way as to avoid a contingent principle? We propose that it is possible to construe Husserl's position, therefore, in the following way: The ultimate principle ('absolute substance') involves contingency within itself in such a way that the divine's contingency in no way renders the divinity contingent or the ultimate principle of rationality contingent.

"The divine's contingency" thus stands for the essential correlate of divinity's agency; but both divinity and contingency are moments of the 'absolute substance'. This whole may then be envisaged as a *natura naturans, natura naturata* wherein the divine "does not create the world as a magician, but as an existing idea which as such presupposes a not-existing underground, the more or less dark consciousness" which is the *prote hyle*.[62] In this case the primal presencing as 'the absolute substance' is to be envisaged as a concrete whole made up of two parts, 'divinity' and the 'hyletic underground', which are abstract moments of the 'absolute substance'.[63]

This position enjoys symmetry with the ultimate 'dualism' or 'correlationism' in Husserl's final analyses of the living present, or what we are calling the primal presencing. What immediately follows is a doctrinal presentation of this most fundamental position for a Husserlian metaphysics (cf. section 1.3 above). We may distinguish the I-pole and the living-pole of primal presencing. The I-pole is a constituted unity achieved through acts, which becomes a theme through reflection. Prior to the reflective act that identifies the sameness of the source-pole of the reflected-on, transpired act with that of the source-pole of the reflection, there is the 'living-pole'. This is on occasion improperly named the I-pole. As the pure I-pole is not in the stream of acts and sensa, so *a fortiori* is the functioning living-pole not in the stream. And even though reflection always comes too late, this pole is known in its anonymity as the living-pole, which engenders the source-point of acts, including the act of reflection. This sourcing by the living-pole, then, is the standing-streaming primal presencing, which is prior to the I of acts because it generates the hyletic temporal unities that affect this I and that acts always presuppose. It is the preegological hyletic stream that engenders affecting unities 'automatically' (*vonstatten*), without the participation of any proper sense of I. Yet in the waking monad some sense of I is always 'present' (*dabei*), being affected and ready to come into play; in this sense a mode of active egological potentiality may be ascribed to it. Iso Kern has called attention to a key text asserting the irreducible egological and hyletic moments at the heart of the primal presencing and, therefore, at the heart of absolute substance:

> The constitution of beings at each level, the constitution of world and of times has two primal presuppositions, two primal sources which, speaking temporally (with respect to all these constituted tem-

poralities), always are at its foundation: (1) my primordial I as functioning primal I in its affections and actions with all the essential qualities belonging to the appropriate modalities; (2) my primordial not-I as primordial stream of temporalization and itself in the primal form of time, a time-field, constituting that of proto-rationality (*Ursachlichkeit*). But both primal grounds are united (*einig*), inseparable, and considered in themselves, abstract.[64]

On another occasion we hope to show the motives for this 'dualism' of moments (not pieces, i.e., not imaginatively nor conceptually separable parts) within 'the absolute substance' and to present the implications for a systematic philosophical theology. The systematic task requires 'somehow' joining the egological moment with the divine and the not-I with the *prote hyle* of nonawakened, nonactual monads. I believe that Plato, Aristotle, Leibniz, Fichte, Peirce, Whitehead, Brightman and, doubtless, numerous others struggled mightily with an analogous problem. And it is through studying Husserl's various efforts to get clear on the primal presencing in the context of this well-ploughed, analogical, hylomorphic field that we germinate the seed for a transcendental-phenomenological theology. Here we will let the matter stand as a promise and move on to what 'divinity' initially means for Husserl.

8. *The One Divine Principle of the Dipolarity of the Absolute Life or Substance*

When Husserl broaches theological themes in the sections of *Ideas* I and elsewhere, one is reminded of the famous ingenuous conclusion of Aquinas to his proofs for the existence of God: And this (the unmoved mover, the necessary, exemplary, final, and efficient principle of the universe, etc.) is what all men call God! Thomas's point, it would seem, is not that the nonphilosopher (the *rudes*) does in fact do this explicitly, but that if he or she were to study philosophy he or she would see that what faith and scripture teach about God (Savior, Lord, Spirit, Maker of heaven and earth, etc.) can be explicated in metaphysical terms. In other words, the proofs depend on a sense of divinity that is prior to the demonstration and that, it is assumed, will find a fit with the conclusions of the demonstration. Determining the nature of this fit is a notorious theological problem. Indeed, not the smallest reason for the problem is the doubt that there can be a fit.

Some believers and philosophers have, from their respective principles, urged that there can only be equivocation. Husserl's *Logos* theology empowers him to believe that there is a fit. When it comes to adjustments, however, the burden tends to be placed on the doctrines of faith. In section 51 of *Ideas* I, he refers to other ways of manifesting the transcendent divine principle "to which theorizing thought can adjust itself in a reasonable way." And, perhaps as an explication of this in section 58, religious consciousness is spoken of as able to lead to the *same* divine principle (as transcendental phenomenological reflection) "in the manner of rationally grounded motives." That is, the religious (and perhaps even mystical; see section 10 below) consciousness has a legitimacy in what Husserl regards as a *rational* motivation, which transcendental phenomenological reflection is capable of elucidating.

With these preliminary tangles noted but not unravelled, we wish in this section to offer a brief commentary on the important passages in *Ideas* I, sections 51 and 58. In spite of their terseness they may well be the best statements we have from Husserl on the sense of 'divine' and its allied notions, like 'religion', 'piety', and so on. The context for this exegesis is the mentioned, but not displayed, thesis that nothing at all, not even the divine, can be grasped in itself apart from and indifferent to transcendental subjectivity. Ultimately the reason is twofold. The first aspect regards the nature of transcendental phenomenology, and the second is a categorical development of this reflection. The first regards the ultimacy and insurmountability of the dative of manifestation. The second holds that the divine, as the principle of the rationality of this primal presencing, presupposes the primal presencing as a moment of its concretion and, in some sense not determined in this essay, of its self-realization. In each case the divine becomes a theme as the source of both the proto- and the developed rationality. As source it is apprehended 'through the effects known to us' (*per effectus nobis notos*) as Aquinas would put it. But the effect here is transcendental subjectivity and intersubjectivity in their primal and developed stages. We are not beginning and concluding with a consideration that is what it is regardless and independent of transcendental subjectivity. The divine principle is thus relative to the life of the mind both *quoad nos* and *quaod se*. This latter claim must remain a promise. We can best prepare for it by further examining it *quoad nos*.

The primal presencing of the dative of manifestation is to be studied in its most elemental and in its most developed stages. "The lower stages do not yet know anything of that future which becomes intentional by way of reason's intentionality; but their becoming is nevertheless a becoming in the direction of reason."[65] As we shall see in the discussion of the intentionality of prayer (see section 10 below), this means that the reflection on the dative of appearing is a consideration of that which is always tilted or off balance; or, rather, it means that the 'balance' of the mind is found in its pointing toward the not-yet-achieved accomplishments. The *noema* of the reflection is necessarily *also* the *sensus plenior* of the primal *hyle*; that is, it must also take account of the developing and mature reason (which is always developing!). Thus the meant or material for theological reflection is the constituting connatural *telos* of the mind, which is profiled and apperceived at all stages of achieving and achievement. Yet it would be one-sided to regard this divine principle as simply the ideal of all objects, the embracing horizon of all contexts, the final region of all regions—as if it were only and always over-against (an *ob-iectum; Gegen-stand*) by way of being ever in advance, out of reach, and the frame of the definite goals of the mind's striving. This would be to forget the divine as the principle of the rationality found in the contingent primal presencing of the dative of manifestation and its developing life. What this divine, entelelchial principle accounts for is the single, absolute, intersubjective intentional life with its dual aspects of ego-pole/world-pole, constituting/constituted, reason/being, appearings of what appears and what appears, immanent being and transcendent being, and so forth. That there is but one principle which accounts for intentional life's two aspects may be seen only in the transcendental attitude that has attained the source, the primal presencing. The sense of this sourcing is that it is the principle of the developed act-life; its streaming hyletic intentionalities have their fuller sense in the *terminus ad quem* of the ever-expanding act-life, just as the act-life has its *principium a quo* in the primal-instinctual presencing of the ultimate dative of manifestation. In the transcendental attitude we do not therefore have a realm of transcendence as a whole and adjacent to it a realm of immanence. These are both necessary moments of the intentionality of the absolute life or substance. This life is characterized as teleological, rational, cohesive, developing, and so forth by reference to these two moments. We may not therefore achieve a thematization of the *telos* of the world nor of the ultimate horizon of 'absolute oughts' as something separate or independent of the functioning teleology immanent in the primal presencing and in the subsequent stages of intentionality. Nor may we treat the source of the dative of appearing's protorationality or of the speculated 'I of I's' (cf. Steven Laycock's essay in this volume) as an exclusively transcendental 'subjective' principle, which is in no way transcendent and 'objective'. At the ultimate stage of transcendental phenomenological elucidation, we have together, as one, the infinite transcendent 'objective' dimensions, the whither of the life of the mind, as well as the irreducibly nonobjectifiable whence of all intentionality. A kind of zigzag might seem necessary here, but only if we relapse into the natural attitude and become unmindful of the mind's constituting, or if we objectify the constituting primal presencing (which similarly would be a form of the natural attitude), thereby concealing its vectorial, self-transcending, proto-intentionality, and regard the time phases which it constitutes as separable from it. Thus the divine entelechial principle, as the source of the teleology of the absolute life, affects this life in the unity of the dual features of intentional life as constituting and constituted, reason and being, immanent and transcendent, and thus, in a general sense, as subject and object.

In a late text (1930), Husserl expressed this unity in terms of the "achieved absolute teleology," which is itself a correlate of the absolute life. This absolute life comprises

the inseparable unity of all finite beings as mere non-autonomous (*unselbstaendiger*) moments in the "infinite" unity of a meaning derivative from a meaning-giving movement toward infinity; or, again, this teleology is understood in its relationship to absolute subjectivity as the infinite way to develop itself into true being; or, it may be understood as the infinite accomplishment (proper to subjectivity in its absolute and ultimate sense) of the constitution of a world as nature and as cultural world of human and personal communities (uppermostly, generative societies of nations) ascending into infinity of relative accord and relative truth. And, corresponding to this accomplishment of constitution, there is an absolute supreme idea as the ultimate total meaning-giving principle for truth and being, yes, even for the being of the absolute subject and the totality of subjects, which itself as absolute subjectivity, consists in the mutual implication of the universe of subjects.

Corresponding to the world which has its validity in the flux of validations and in the relativity of a stream of experience, thought and valuation; corresponding to a world which enjoys necessarily a unity in the flux of world appearances which mounts unto infinity in its

validation and unity of verification; furthermore, corresponding to
the transcendental all-subjectivity which in its streaming changes unto infinity within the infinite stream of the socialized constitution of
the world-validation and thereby of the infinite constitution of "the
true world" by way of the unification of the verified relative pieces of
evidence—corresponding to these is the absolute *ideal pole-idea*.
This ideal pole-idea is of an absolute in a new transworldly, trans-
human, supra-transcendental-subjective sense. It is the absolute
logos, the absolute truth in the complete and full sense, as the *unum,
verum* and *bonum* toward which each being is bound, and toward
which all transcendental subjective life, as vital being living toward
constituting truth, tends. This idea is borne by every transcendental I,
and in a socialized way by every transcendental We, in its transcendental
personality as an ideal norm for all relative norms. Thereby does the
individual and comunalized transcendental subjectivity bear in itself
an ideal of its true being toward which it is predisposed in its factual
personal being. However, this ideal is but a ray of the absolute ideal,
of the idea of an all-personality which is infinitely superior to
everything actual, to all becoming and to all development toward the
ideal by what is factual. The idea stands over all development toward
it as a pole which lies infinitely removed. This pole-idea is the idea of
an absolutely perfect transcendental universal community.[66]

Here we see that the divine principle emerges as one absolute supreme
'idea', which is 'constituting' in the sense of ultimate 'meaning-giving'
for the whole of absolute life, that is, it is both absolute subjective as
noetic meaning-giving principle and it is noematic objective 'meaning-
giving' horizon and goal.

This 'ideal pole-idea' (what in another context we shall call a
"divine personality of a higher order") must here be passed over in
order to consider the basic claim of Husserl: We reach the divine ideal
pole-idea as a unifying *Logos*, which constitutes both (1) the constituting transcendental subjectivity by holding sway over its facticity
and establishing the 'ABC's of constitution' of the world in terms of
protorationality and a burgeoning, incessant teleology, and (2) the
ideal of the developed and constituted realm of 'nature with a human
face' and the intersubjective coconstituting community as an infinite
ideal community. Thus the divine principle is, at least *quoad nos*,
dipolar.

We find this basic claim already stated in *Ideas* I. In section 51 we
read that the theological principle accounting for the teleology immanent in the facticity of the stream of consciousness "cannot be accepted as transcendent in the way the world is transcendent" because

this would be an absurd circle. But, at the same time, this divine governing principle of the absolute life *can be found only through absolute reflection.* And

> since a mundane God is evidently impossible, and since, on the other hand, the immanence of God in the absolute consciousness cannot be grasped as immanence in the sense of being as experience (*Eriebnis*) (which would be no less absurd) there must be in the stream of absolute consciousness and its infinities other modes of disclosure of transcendence than that of the constitution of thingly realities (as unities of consistent manifestations). . . .

This is picked up again in section 58, where we find that the divine transcendence is not like the transcendence of the 'pure I', which is immediately united to consciousness in its reduced state; rather, the divine transcendence "comes to knowledge in a highly mediated form, standing over against the transcendence of the world as if it were its polar opposite." Further, the divine principle of the facticity, which is the source of the possible and real constituted values, transcends not only the world

> but obviously also the "absolute" consciousness. It would thus be an "absolute" in a totally different sense from the absolute of consciousness as, on the other hand, it would be a transcendent in a totally different sense than that of the word.[67]

We can profitably dwell on the less obvious aspects of the claims in these passages from *Ideas* I.

1. Note that the entire discussion has for its point of departure the transcendental reduction and the absolute life. Thus the sense of the divine is anchored in this life with its two poles: the dative of appearing and the world as an ideal-pole.

2. The divine cannot be transcendent in the way the world is transcendent because this would be an absurd circle, or nonsense. Why? Apparently because worldly being is relative being and therefore looks to that to which it is related, absolute being, for its constitution. To explain what constitutes absolute being by what absolute being constitutes would be nonsensical. Therefore we must look to the absolute life itself for the governing principle of the absolute.

3. The notion of the divine's transcendence as other than the

world's transcendence, and the later mention of the I's transcendence, recalls the analogy and hierarchy of immanence and transcendence. The living-pole and primal presencing's phases are immanent to the I-pole as what is transcendent to them; the living-pole and the phases of primal presencing are immanent to the acts and the sensa, which are transcendent to them; the things are immanent to the constituted world which is transcendent to them. Persons, and the world and its things are immanent to the godly personality of a higher order (as the name of the essential approximation of the ideal pole-idea), which they constitute but which is transcendent to them. (Note however that this ideal transcendent pole is *not* constituted in its dipolar aspect as the divine principle of the *Faktum* as source nor as the entelechial ideal pole-idea; only the realization or concretion of this entelechy, as the *telos* of *logos*, in the godly person of a higher order is constituted.)

4. No less absurd than envisaging the divine as transcendent in the way the world is transcendent would be envisaging the divine as immanent, in the sense of its being an experience. It would be absurd to regard the divine as an experience because *Erlebnisse*, first of all, are passing and are accordingly constituted from out of the primal presencing and the general motivational context ('world'); the divine must be a principle adequate to account for the constitution of both the rationality of the world (as it is constituted in transcendental subjectivity) and the rationality of the life of this subjectivity (*Erlebnisse*) in its ultimate facticity as the source of meaning and value.

5. The divine transcendence is different from the transcendence of the pure I-pole (and with difficulty distinguishable from the living-pole). The transcendence of the I-pole is a transcendence in immanence, or a transcendence of the immanent dimension, that is, of acts and sensa (see *Ideas* I, section 58). This is the first sense in which we can understand what it means to stand "over against the transcendence of the world as if it were its polar opposite." The polar opposite of the world's transcendence must be the pole that is opposite to the pole of transcendent unities; this can only be that radically subjective, immanent pole of the 'pure I', or I-pole. Yet the divine's immanent transcendence is not the immanent

transcendence of the pure I-pole, because the I-pole, as the in-eluctable, nonobjective whence of acts and sensa, around which the acts and sensa gather, is intuitively evident in the acts and sensa; that is, it is 'given' as the same unifying whence, or source of the stream of acts and sensa. Its 'giveness' or evidence can thereby claim a kind of immediacy. The divine transcendence in immanence, however, is not im-mediately given but "comes to light in a highly mediated form." As we have seen, this is the speculated ground of ra-tionality in the facticity, or the principle that accounts for the contingent rationality of the primal presencing as source. Yet the sense of the divine "standing over against the transcendence of the world as if it were its polar opposite" seems to have *another* sense, because what is clearly the polar opposite is the I-pole. This other sense must refer to the divine as at once polar opposite to both the polar oppositeness of the 'pure I' *and* that of the world-pole.

6. This last consideration lends force to our dipolar assertion: the divine is an 'absolute'; that is, it is a kind of immanence totally different from the absolute of consciousness and totally dif-ferent from the transcendence in immanence of the pure I-pole; but, at the same time, it is transcendent in a totally dif-ferent sense from the world's transcendence. Yet the divine is not two principles but one 'governing' principle, which 'holds sway' (*waltet*) over the absolute life in its dipolar, that is, im-manent and transcendent, aspects.

As a conclusion to this section we may note that our interpreta-tion avoids the opposition that Klaus Held finds between the divine as objective, pole-ideal principle of constituted objects and as the "inner ground of self-communalization . . . the pre-form of the teleological primal fact which reflection uncovers."[68] In Held's view we apparent-ly have two incompatible philosophical and religious claims: God as the whither of the absolute ought, or pole of the ideal intersubjective world, and God as inner ground of the primal, protorational, teleological facticity. In this view either God must be the nonegological final goal of the tendencies of the life of the mind or God is 'person', 'I of I's', as ground of the anonymous self-communalization. Despite Held's rich and suggestive discussion, we urge that the texts reviewed require an acknowledgement: Husserl's concept of the divine entelechy deliberately includes the opposition between a primal, egological, nonobjectifiable principle and one that is the absolute final horizonal lure—which, it turns out, also has quasi-'egological' features as a personality of a higher order. This opposition is a correlate of the dipolarity of 'absolute life', *quoad nos et quoad se*; it is not an inadvertency in Husserl's meditations. We further suggest that the texts in *Ideas* I as well as the often-used notion of divine 'entelechy' point toward a unifying consideration (*Idee*), which is possible only in the transcendental attitude and which urges that we avoid seeking to conceive the divine exclusively in terms of either the absolute life's transcendence or its immanence. Independent of the transcendental reduction, this position is one which has, through the influence of Plotinus and Augustine, become embedded in the Western mystical tradition. Here the divine is the center of all conscious centers, the soul of souls, as well as the horizon of the most beatifying and utopian projects. Nevertheless, in spite of our circumvention of what appeared to be a difficulty for Held, we must affirm with him that the divine principle can never be other than an egological principle—but not only that. As essentially entelechy, the divine ego/mind is also facing the ideal pole-idea which is itself as mediated through the infinite potentiality of the monadological *prote hyle*. This ideal is the *telos* of *logos*, the infinitude to be realized through the reciprocal divine-monadic creativity. This is a personalization of the monadic universe in the direction of a (constituted) godly person of a higher order.

We may summarize much that has been discussed by turning to some views of Paul Natorp.

9. *Some Affinities with Natorp*

Both Rudolf Boehm and Iso Kern have called attention to the spiritual kinship that obtained between Husserl and Paul Natorp. In this particular issue of the divine principle there are some parallels and differences that illuminate and enrich the basic issues and their implications in such matters as the meaning of evil, tragedy, history, and divinity. For Natorp, as for Husserl, the ultimate task of human life is the pursuit of 'origins' by way of a reflection which results in praxis,

a return to the necessary, one, ultimate and pure origin (*Ursprung*) out of which all content of life is produced, intellectually as well as ethically and aesthetically, each equally and inseparably required in connection with one another: That cannot be "purely" understood, "purely" willed, "purely" formed which is not grasped in the radical generation from out of the origin. Only thereby is there complete light and complete life, for life desires light and light life.[69]

This commitment to radicality results in a twofold, infinite labor of the spirit: a return back to the central ground and origin, and a passage forward to infinitely expanding horizons. The detailed philosophical investigation of this twofold field of work involves a lower and an upper limit. This clearly parallels Husserl's requirement for the ultimate philosophical-theological task: that we immerse ourselves in the ultimate *Faktum's* irrational and rational ingredients, with their undifferentiated material, as well as in the development that is permeated by guiding ideas.

In his *Allgemeine Psychologie* (1912), Natorp envisages the life of the mind as an ongoing determining or objectifying from out of a nonobjectifiable source. Each higher level of objectification (e.g., considering the 'Big Mac' as a product peculiar to the American social-economic fabric), builds on lower-order determinations which stand in a relation of potentiality and determinability to the higher-order ones. Thus the 'Big Mac' as a cultural product, reaching into a 'service economy', into marginalization, multinationals, plastics, and so on, builds on the perception of 'fast food', 'hamburger', and the like. Each lower level is itself a higher level with respect to its founding strata, just as multinational 'fast food' builds on 'hamburger' which builds on 'food' and 'food' on 'that-edible-something' (as an identity in a manifold), and so forth. In the analysis of the genesis of constitution, one moves toward an ideal limit of a founding layer of something absolutely not-determined or objectified, something purely determinable and to-be-determined, approaching the Aristotelian *prote hyle*, or a chaos out of which the entire world-creation by consciousness emerges. For Natorp this is an infinite task, and to expect to presence such an ultimate, founding potential layer in an actual datum is clearly nonsense: One cannot presence what is without any determination whatsoever. Rather, Natorp holds, we can only *reconstruct* and postulate this founding layer. Here we can merely refer to Husserl's efforts at an appropriate presencing of the nonpresent primal presencing and point to the differences between him and Natorp over the possibility of a phenomenological *Ursprungsanalyse*.[70]

In addition to the lower limit of investigation there is also an upper ideal limit. Whereas the former is in some sense an implicit or preobjective 'subconsciousness', the latter is a higher transconsciousness. In this case we similarly do not have any object for consciousness, any determination that is presenced. We do not have any determinate, actualized product over against the actualizing determining. This nonobjectifiability is not so through a lack of determination but rather by way of an excess, inasmuch as it is the comprehensive determining for all determinings. As the Idea it embraces all determinations of the mind; all explications are within its scope; all research is a determination of it. Here we have all determinations actually and none potentially; here we have full determination and no further determinable background. Aristotle again provides the key formulation for this ideal upper limit of philosophical investigation: self-thinking thought, pure mind self-aware, *noesis noeseos*.[71]

In Natorp's later writings (after 1917), there are considerations that unite these two limits and that draw his thought close to Husserl's 'divine principle' of primal presencing, that is, to the ultimate fact as source—and yet in such a formulation that a fundamental opposition in theological matters comes to light.

> An ultimate not understood sensibility remains as lower level, an ultimate transintelligible, transsensible remains the upper level. Neither of which are absolutely irrational, but rather are to be regarded as X = the never completely rationalized. And this is not ultimately to be regarded as something twofold but as the transfinite which is in itself and which, on the one hand, is lived only from moment to moment, and, on the other, is illuminated by the light of thought in the presence of an eternal eye . . . as if seen in an eternal unifying glance. . . . Nothing is so transient, so "accidental," so momentary that it can escape the ultimate limit-relation to the eternal.[72]

In philosophical terms this means that there is no *prote hyle*, no formless stuff, no alogicality, no amorphous dimensions; rather all is 'aperimorphous', that is, infinitely and thoroughly informed by *Logos*. This means that the ultimate is what Natorp calls "the individual." This individuality is not the particular, such as that composed of a not-universal, not-rational 'principle of individuation' as well as of a rational, formal principle. The ultimate as individual is soaked with rationality and there is no ontological residue of irrationality. If we take the factual primal presencing and the concrete monad as instances of ultimate individuals, we do not find any residue of irrationality; rather, each is fully determinate in the continuum of what is. Of course, the ultimate individual is not determinate in the sense, for example, that the primal presencing is rational fact, abstractly in itself, or that the monad is exhaustively determined or known. But if one considers the matter less in the light of an achieved goal than as a function, a way, to unrestrained progress of determination, then we may appreciate the full determinateness of the individual. The idea of infinite determinability entails the presupposition of total determinateness of the individual and thereby of the full logicality of the amorphic *apeiron*.[73] We will have another occasion to discuss Husserl's theory of history and tragedy. Here we may merely note that if Husserl holds to a doctrine of *prote hyle* as a constitutive moment, with the divine, of absolute substance, then there is a basic theological difference between this view and that of the late Natorp, for whom there is an ultimate *coincidentia oppositorum* and for whom tragedies are mere moments in the higher divine *logos*, which permeates completely all aspects of life and being.

10. *A Husserlian Theory of Prayer*

We would expect the most basic sense of prayer to mirror or retrieve the ultimate metaphysical situation. For transcendental phenomenology we believe that to be the following: The divine entelechy, that is, the infinite ideal of perfection and the good, immanent within the monadic universe in a way that establishes an *eros* for realization (a *vis a tergo et a fronte*), constitutes wakeful monads by a 'trusting persuasion' of the *prote hyle*, which even in its dormancy is a principle of creativity. The preoccupying sense of the divine is the infinite *telos*, the idea of absolute perfection of the monadic community, which can be envisaged as a higher-order person constituted by this community. This sense is preoccupying, most fundamentally, not only because the divine is the entelechy for the monadic *prote hyle* but because being the entelechy (or formal and final cause) of the monadic universe is the essence of the divine. For transcendental phenomenology (cf. Thomas Prufer's essay in this volume), it is *not* true that God and the world are not greater than God alone. (Another reason why the infinite *telos* is the preoccupying sense is because being preoccupied naturally means being taken up with a *telos* of intentionality; in this case, of course, it is not ''transcendent in the way the

world is transcendent.'') The 'idea of God' is an objective and subjective genitive for God and monads in a mutually constitutive way (cf.
Steven Laycock's essay in this volume). Divinity also lives in the face
of the Good, or itself as an infinite ideal. This pole is not another being
or cause apart from the divine as egological-intellectual moment of absolute substance. But this *logos*, or infinite frame of compossibility,
takes its bearing from the Good; the Good is not derivative from a
finished articulation of compossibility. The 'love of God' of divinity is
not only the unmediated *quies* or complacency with itself; it is also
eros because divinity is actual only through the mediation of the
monadic universe as the eternal product of divinity's informing its
Other, the *prote hyle*. The divine essence is therefore at once infinite,
productive subjectivity (mind and will) *and* the Good; and the divine
Good is not only itself as the Good of the world but also *for* itself as
the Good of the world. Divinity is not only in process but is also the
world's process—most manifestly when 'things are going right', that
is, when monads are doing what they ought to be doing, when the
divine persuasion is working, and when the dormancy, opacity, and
recalcitrancy of the *prote hyle* (wherein lies *acedia* as the root of sin)
are penetrated by light and rational will. *Acedia*, that is, inertia, *quies
indebita*, melancholy listlessness in the face of the Good, is the radical
evil of the monadic universe. The institutionalization of cynicism and
mediocrity is its victory over the divine power of persuasion.

In lieu of an extended case that these claims are Husserlian, we offer the following text:

> The ultimate meaning of being (*Sinn des Seins*) is the Good and that is
> the divine activity toward which the All of divine action is directed.
> But divine activity is the willing-to-be-real of God (*das Reale-sein-
> wollen Gottes*). God as will of the Good is the ultimate reality. It
> receives ultimate realization when the Good is, and so the realized
> Good is the fulfilled will of God, the fulfilled realization of God.
> Everything else is good as action towards this goal. In everything
> noble and good, which I realize in me, I am therefore realized God,
> fulfilled will of God, mere nature has become God, a fulfilled God.
> God as entelechy, God as energy (*Energie*).[74]

The task of human monads or persons is hinted at in their ongoing
establishment of a world, and correlatively of themselves, through
position-taking acts, that is, acts like existential judgments, predicative
ties, essential insights, resolutions, decisions, promises, and so forth.

These acts, though lasting merely so long, endure indefinitely until 'modalized', revoked, and so on. They establish the abiding contours of the world and the more or less permanent *hexis* of personhood. Immanent in this ongoing adventure of persons taking positions that sometimes bear fruit, are sometimes unlucky, sometimes crumble because the necessary worldly conditions shatter, are sometimes fulfilling, are often disappointing, and so forth is the *telos* of 'the blessed life' within 'the beloved community'. Thus, what is immanent to the adventure of being a person is the quest for a position-taking that is categorically required, unregrettable, and irrevocable. Husserl calls this generically "the absolute ought." There is much to say about this overriding, unconditional ought and about why Husserl seems to settle on 'universal ethical love' as the solution to the task of its identification and the quest of being a person. Here we merely state that it fulfills the conditions of being the kind of categorical imperative with the material content by which the

> will to realize my genuine humanity . . . is absolutely motivated. Or when I consider the possibility of a life such as I would love absolutely and unsurpassibly then I cannot help but decide to will such a life—even if it is true that I become weak in seeking, loving and willing.[75]

With these sketchy general remarks as background, we may turn to a Husserlian theory of prayer. It would seem that prayer, on the one hand, is inseparable from the absolute ought; on the other hand, it must be distinguishable from the action that is faithful to the ideal: *orare est non solum laborare et agere.* If we take prayer to be the mode of intentionality that most properly appreciates, that is, worshipfully presences, the divine, then surely making evident the goodness and beauty of the divine as the motor of our wills would be a form of prayer. Prayer in this sense would be the mode of meditation, that is, of self-gathering, nourishment, and edification, by which the absolute ought is enabled to appear in such a manner that it solicits our unconditional engagement of universal, ethical love. Prayer would thus be the employment of the best available means for fostering both the will to believe and the ethical as-if. Here prayer is meditation tilted toward action. In accord with the fuller doctrine of the *telos* of the world as a divine personality of a higher order, prayer is necessarily an attunement to the idealizing drift of the mind. It is being awake to the lure of the absolute ought. In effect, it is placing oneself in the presence of that than which nothing more morally edifying nor energizing can be conceived. As Husserl once put it:

> God can be no object of experience (as in the sense of a thing or a human). But God would be "experienced" in each belief that believes originally-teleologically in the perpetual value of that which lies in the direction of each absolute ought and which engages itself for this perpetual meaning.[76]

Prayer in this sense is a form of what we elsewhere call "utopian poetics." But do we thereby exclude more quietistic senses of prayer and worship? Before we deal with this question directly we must remind ourselves of an earlier discussion (see section 8 above). There we noted that the divine is dipolar, *quoad nos* and *quoad se*. And *quoad nos*, the dipolarity (of the transcendence in a totally different sense from that of the world as well as of the transcendence in immanence to the I-pole) is understandable only within the transcendental reduction. Only in the transcendental attitude can the dipolarity appear as two aspects of the one divine principle rather than as two divine principles. With these considerations in mind, it is clear that a Husserlian theory of prayer must be attentive to this dipolarity, as disclosed through the 'turn within'. Husserl's occasional recourse to the Plotinian-Augustinian refrain, "Do not go outside yourself, but turn within. Truth dwells within," cautions that the language of immanence as well as that of transcendence is to be understood within the transcendental reduction.[77] In a brief meditation on prayer we find: "In real genuine prayer, the praying I is not directed outwardly but inwardly."[78] Prayer is not directed toward something within the world of the natural attitude. "All cultic pictures are pictures but then again not pictures."[79] Divine significations have an odd form of reference; clearly they are not a form of picturing: "If God as 'father' is represented in a worldly real fashion with the form of a real father, God is no longer God." The intentionality of prayer is 'within' to "the inkling of the interiority (*Innensein*) of God which founds every real relating"[80]—most elementally that of the primal passivities and instincts. That 'within' to which we are directed is 'the divine', but this is to be understood as both the whence and the whither poles of the mind's life. Authentic prayer resembles the reduction in that its turning within is not to a private realm but to that which is inextricably intersubjective and transsubjective. In another meditation on the meaning of life as 'the way' from the standpoint of transcendental subjectivity we find:

> From each I (from me as I and from the other I who is Other as I to him) the way leads as the way proper to each; but all ways lead to the same trans-worldy and trans-human pole which is God. But these ways do not lead as separate ways converging together at a point. Rather the ways mutually penetrate one another in an indescribably spiralling fashion. This means the way of the neighbor, in so far as the way is the right way, belongs essentially, to an extent, to my way; the way is the way of love of neighbor.[81]

Authentic prayer (like universal ethical love) thus has features symmetrical with the transcendental attitude. Authentic prayer breaks the bondage of the natural attitude by reason of its apperception of the divine's transcendence of and immanence to all significations. This awareness of the inadequacy of the religious representations converts them into essentially empty intentions because, for one thing, they become referents to an infinite horizon. This latter situation is thus an awareness of the infinity of the intentionality of the mind, and this awareness is a sense in which we may understand Husserl's claim that authentic prayer is directed within.[82] Its excess (*Ueberschuss*) of all significations is apperceived; the mind is thereby attentive to itself as infinitely transcending its achievements. Furthermore, there is a sense in which prayer can be said to be what founds the awareness of the inadequacy of religious symbolism. Husserl can hold this because he ties prayer to instincts, as the elemental inklings of unfilled horizons characteristic of our being human monads. If we consider instinct to mean basically the original inkling of what fulfills the conditions of monadic life, prayer may be called the original instinct, or original inkling, of the divine within, beckoning the mind and constituting its infinite *eros* to fill empty intentions. But the intentionality of this infinite *telos* has a whence-pole. Unless we have a way of attunement to the whence, it seems that the life of the spirit is in danger of misconstruing its task and faltering in its adventure. If it is not empowered to cherish the primal receptivity or to appreciate what we may call transcendental self-trust, an essential moment of action will be ignored. *Orare est non solum laborare sed etiam quiescere.* In our view the establishing of a transcendental phenomenological *quies debita*, an appropriate quietism, is indispensable to the theory of prayer. What follows is a brief review of some of the possibilities.

Both Held and Kern called attention to the 'first grace' of the primal presencing. Strictly considered, the anonymous functioning of primal presencing is not, without distinction, a creation. Indeed, the anonymous functioning is not an egological achievement in any sense, and therefore, because the functioning living-pole is the necessary condition for egological achievement, neither the personal I nor the I-pole may be regarded as self-creative. Further, even though the anonymous functioning is not an achievement to which I can lay claim, its coming to be is still inconceivable for transcendental phenomenology. In this respect the transcendental subjectivity is un-created and unbegun. But the awakening of I, that is, this self-presence of the hyletic creativity or the wakefulness of the I to itself and to its anonymous passage, retention, and protention, may indeed be regard-ed as the first grace. One is never aware of this pregiven contingency and facticity (cf. our earlier discussion in sections 4 and 5) as a certain possession, and therefore, as Held has put it, the I of acts must ever again 'accept' itself in the form of anonymous pregivenness.[83] Even though the coming to be of this anonymous primal presencing is in-conceivable, *that* I am, or, that this anonymous functioning of the living-pole is awake to itself, is not my (as the I of acts) doing. (It is a 'contingent fact' but not to be measured by the necessities and non-necessities of constituted or constituting being.) I am this wakefulness and yet 'receive' it. This receptiveness does not mean, on the one hand, that I am antecedent to the 'gift'; on the other hand, it does not mean that the 'giving' or the extrinsic conditions of the wakefulness are absolutely prior to it, as if primal presencing's coming to be were conceivable.

Granting these distinctions, however, it is interesting to see Husserl occasionally using the metaphors of 'source' or wellspring (*Quelle*) and 'pulse' in ways that would seem to sacralize the primal presencing. Thus we find the following lyrics jotted down, echoing perhaps Goethe:

The pulse beats with vitality
From new streams of power.
The heart beats forth clearer streams.
The heartbeat becomes livelier
Spreading new power streams.[84]

Husserl uses the wellspring and pulse metaphors to highlight the way in which the standing-streaming primal presencing is a self-identical source but not a source self-identical through any act of identifying or of active identity synthesis. Rather, the pulsing and jetting emphasize that its primal *pre*-being is an *originary* 'gushing' *self*-sourcing 'source-point'. This 'living pulsebeat of the present' is, on the one hand 'for me' insofar as it is irrepressibly self-objectifying, ontifying, and being-constituting; but it is always, on the other hand, also 'me' in advance or prior to my being for myself.[85] William James makes a remarkable statement concerning how the whence of the primal presencing may be regarded as the focus of the piety of experiencing:

> The living moments—some living moments, at any rate—have somewhat of [an] absolute that needs no lateral support. Their meaning seems to well up from out of their very centre, in a way impossible verbally to describe. If you take a disk painted with a concentric spiral pattern, and make it revolve, it will seem to be growing continuously and indefinitely, and yet to take in nothing from without; and to remain, if you pay attention to its actual size, always of the *same* size. Something as paradoxical as this lies in every present moment of life. Here or nowhere, as Emerson says, is the whole fact. The moment stands and contains and sums up all things; and all change is within it, much as the developing landscape with all its growth falls forever within the rear windowpane of the last car of a train that is speeding on its headlong way. The self-sustaining in the midst of self-removal, which characterizes all reality and fact, is something absolutely foreign to the nature of language and even to the nature of logic, commonly so-called.[86]

This would seem to be for James an apodictic phenomenological fact, which religion retrieves by way of beliefs that are historically and culturally mediated:

> Remember that the whole point lies in really *believing* that through a certain point or part in you you coalesce and are identical with the Eternal. This seems to be the saving belief both in Christianity and in Vedantism. . . . It comes *home* to one only at particular times. . . .[87]

Both the phenomenological consideration and the religious interpretations assign a priority to a *quies debita*, a silence, which, of course, is not the mere absence of noise, thoughts, and conversation. For the religious interpretation, rather, it in some odd sense qualifies as the 'primal word', the 'inner light', and so on, to be met only by a 'waiting', 'trust', 'abandonment', and the like (cf. Husserl's fondness for Isaiah 40:13; see *Chronik* 22, 489). The inverted commas render the difficulty of finding terms to name that which retrieves what we originarily are and which all attitudes, passive and active, presuppose.[88] For Husserl, as we have already seen, the response of the phenomenologist to the *Faktum* of the primal teleology and rationality characterizing primal presencing is astonishment (*Wunder*), that is, spontaneous acknowledgement of the unpreparedness of one's passive synthetic ability to manage conceptually what is transpiring. But this, of course, does not of itself equate with anything like 'worship of the Inner Light'. The efficaciousness of the *Gelassenheit*, the quiet or wonder, which retrieves the elemental receptivity that originates mind, is a commonplace in mystical literature. It is a quietism in the sense that it is attentive to and trusting toward the passivity that founds agency. Agency is not understood, and it is oblivious to its essential nourishment if there is not attunement to the gracious passive centering. Here, as elsewhere, rest is the energizing of activity.[89]

Husserl was indirectly confronted with an attempt to focus the piety of experiencing in the whence of the primal presencing when his student, Gerda Walther, submitted an early version of her phenomenology of mysticism.[90] In Walther's letter to Husserl (in response to an earlier stenographic and therefore scarcely understood letter from him), she related Pfaender's view of the I's structure: On the one hand there is a punctual vital center and on the other a periphery, composed of "source-points," i.e., what Husserl calls attitudes, character-building experiences, and so on which comprise the 'voluminous self'. Walther describes 'source-points' as "not tight, self-contained, graspable 'points' in the background of consciousness, but rather 'points' in an improper sense; perhaps one can say 'directions' in the background." They form the core-point of the personality and have their root in God. She appeals to the "deep understanding" that characterizes mystical claims. Such may be said to come from beyond or behind the I, to bathe it in light, and the like. Walther cautions that this is not a noematic reflection 'forwards' on the content of experience, but 'backwards' toward the source of experience. Thus it is a species of noetic reflection.[91]

Husserl's drafted letter (in stenograph), perhaps in direct response to Walther's, is of great interest for what it does not say, as well as for what it explicitly discusses. For example, it does not convey Husserl's fondness for German mysticism.[92] It does not pick up the obvious topics of *Quelle, Pulse, Quellpunkt*, and so on, nor the passivity at the heart of all being and finite mind. There would seem to be two reasons. The first has to do with Husserl's view that mysticism, understood as quietism, is inadequate and incomplete piety.[93] The second concerns his view that Walther and Pfaender never appreciated the transcendental reduction. For Husserl, Walther's discussion was oblivious of the transcendental senses to be given such expressions as 'source-point', 'I', and even 'God'.[94] Perhaps it was because Walther tied the issue of source-points to the occasional experiences of fervor, light, overwhelming tenderness, and 'deep' understanding and because she used conventional religious terminology that Husserl wrote a rather demystifying response. Thus his response to her does not pick up the topic (of *Ideas* I) of how the source of transcendental subjectivity may become a religious theme; he chooses rather to discuss the experiences that Walther highlights, that is, those that come from the 'deepest deep'.

Husserl prefaces the discussion with the significant remark that he can accept the description of "source-points as the residence of the quality of the subject." But he adds that Walther's phenomenological analysis is a static, ontological one. What is called for is an understanding of the constitutive coming-to-be of the 'phenomenological data'. Just as for the archaeologist, the great task for transcendental phenomenology is not a description of the findings of the 'dig' but is the reconstructing or constitutive uncovering of their genesis out of the source.[95] Husserl then goes on to give an elegant condensation of his theory of the personal I as constituted by position-taking acts. These abiding validities have a hierarchy of relevance, which functions in a habitual way as the background of the person's life. On occasion 'sleeping' or 'unconscious' position-takings, which have long been mere empty intentions, are brought into play by something that organizes habitual directions in a novel way. There now occurs a new unity of what before functioned as disparate, unrelated motives in the passive underground, and this permits the opening of endless landscapes and an infinity of possibilities. This is the sense in which Husserl understands Walther's remarks on the surfacing of illuminating thoughts that touch us in 'the deepest depths'. In other words, Husserl is here prepared to treat the mystical experiences cited by Walther as instances of (what Scheler calls) "*Sammlung*," those passive, synthetic gatherings, or concentrations of the whole of one's constitutive position-takings that occasionally grace us, for example, in times of decision and recollection, through the power of great works of art, and at moments of nostalgia and reverie. That which is present calls forth or reactivates the acquired values of the heart, of which we might typically be oblivious.[96]

We may here ask, why do these gatherings, these *Gestalten*, so important for the absolute ought, occur? Doubtless because we want them. Without hope keeping alive the validity of the past position-takings, whereby they still demand filled intentions, there could be no such poignant concentration within a present experience of our strewn-out lives. Still, we do not seem to have the unique apperceptions which occasion these reorganizations of experience at our ready disposal. Doubtless poets, religious masters of novices, and even friends and teachers have the task of developing techniques by which human beings are enabled to 'get it all together'. And physicians of the soul must strive for the syncopation that can deconstruct damaging associations and establish fulfilling rhythms. Husserl never pursued these themes (so dear to G. Bachelard and his friend Natorp). But the analyses of passive synthesis would seem to provide the foundational and formal framework for such practical considerations. The concepts religious retreat, revival, Ignatian exercises, and so forth testify to senses of prayer (in solitude or in the company of others) that take the form of fashioning these unique reorganizations of experience.

This mode of prayer is obviously not that of the silence or quiet enjoined by the mystical tradition or by our reflections on what we are calling transcendental self-trust. The problem with conceptualizing transcendental-phenomenological prayer of quiet is that the whence-pole is precisely what is absent and anonymous and that the mind only 'dwells' on what it presences—and presencing is what it does irrepressibly. Furthermore the primal presencing's 'streaming' is manifest only in the elemental, temporal phases of the inner objects of the stream of consciousness. This is being-conscious and wanting to dwell worshipfully on it does not make obvious sense. Here, in these phases, the protorationality is manifested. By no means is the ultimate reduction an uncovering of an exemplary ground of being or of *veritas divina ipsa*. Rather, what we 'come upon' is a feeble pulsating, which is not itself the divine ground; rather this feeble 'event' is manifest only in the phases of the elementary ingredients of life, that is, in acts and *sensa*, themselves obviously not objects of worship! And yet here is the 'absolute actuality', the primal generation and protorationality! The transcendental phenomenological reduction leads us back to ourselves, not ourselves as divine abundance but as humble quivering, begun-beginnings.

Yet there is still something very Augustinian about this turning within, inasmuch as mind not only turns from the world of the natural attitude but must also transcend itself in a twofold way. I transcend myself in the sense that I must leave behind, or renounce, the agency of the turning within that discloses me to myself; what I am in search of is what is prior to, presupposed by, and not a result of this agency. Further, I must transcend myself in the sense that I, as wakeful living-pole and eventual I-pole, cannot account for myself unless I acknowledge that the quickening rational-teleological *Walten* is beyond my wakeful facticity. That I can indirectly become aware of myself as the feeble protorationality means that I come upon a wakefulness prior to that of my egological act-life and for which *I* in a proper sense am not responsible: *Here* I am, 'graciously'; 'there', already begun. This is not I as trustworthy and so proven on the basis of achievements. This is not I as trusting and in need of a trusting disposition toward what exists, independent of me. This is not the divine in whose power and goodness I may place my trust on the basis of a prior, evident power and goodness. Here I do not come upon the divine itself; I come upon a godly medium, which I am and which (with the others) knows all things. I 'come upon' (i.e., there is a proper mode of evidence for) the holding sway of a principle of my rationality and my teleology, that is, my wakefulness. This holding sway (*Walten*), this beginning (*principium*) or rationality, is me, is 'my' wakefulness; but it is, at the same time, my acceptance or reception of myself. I exist through this holding sway, this gracious wakefulness; yet it is not my achievement. It is not my possession in the sense that I, as living-pole or as the I of acts, account for it or have it. The contingency of this 'self-acceptance' is 'always', and there is no assurance that the good service of the retention of former presencings will continue, nor is there a guarantee of the imminent, hoped-for future. Sickness, death, decline, weariness, sleeping, and waking are ubiquitous signs of the more fundamental contingency that is holding sway in wakefulness. This self-presence and self-acceptance comprise the protorationality, the passive synthesizing, by which I am alive to myself, to Others, and to the world. Transcendental self-trust is fundamentally this constitutive self-accepting of passive synthesizing; but it can be actively appreciated; that is, one can appropriately esteem oneself under the sway of the principle that quickens the hyletic creativity, which one is and to which one is awake. This fundamental 'self-trust' is constitutionally prior to all senses of confidence in oneself, prior to proper senses of trust and belief-in, and prior to all objects worthy of trust and belief-in. It 'happens' apart from the appreciative acknowledgments; yet without appreciation, all versions of 'I', 'trust', and even 'appreciation' are incomplete, if not askew.

If we understand wakeful experience as the passive and active gathering of position-taking, we can, with Wolfgang Cramer, say that wakeful experiencing is 'taking time', or, that time (primal presencing) is taking the times taken, that is, retaining what has already been presenced. Experiencing as the ongoing, originary primal presencing saves what it has presenced and, 'at the same time', is in pursuit of what it has presenced as having gone before. And 'at the same time', it, as the originating streaming, is also ahead of itself not only inasmuch as it is in pursuit of what it has already originated but also in its anticipating of what it has not yet actually originated. In order for primal presencing to posit passively and actively what it wants to be, ought to be, and desires to realize, it must 'count on itself' to take time, to take the right times, and to remain the same in its time-taking throughout the future—to remain the same originary primal presencing, which is the originary preservation of the same presented presencings and the originary protention of the anticipated presents of the same. This 'counting on itself', or self-trust, is not however something that the self may be said to depend on itself to do, in the sense that an achievement exists that might break down, thereby causing a calamity *for* the self. (Awareness of such a 'failure' would be as inconceivable as the awareness of its own cessation.) The originating self-trust, rather, involves precisely the awareness that to be able to be aware of anything it has to be self-trusting in its 'taking time'. The basic *Angst*, which is a moment of *acedia*, is founded in the awareness that at the most basic level, wakeful mind is not responsible for its wakefulness or for taking time, that is, for its abiding as this retentional-protentional primal presencing; and in this sense it is not responsible for its self-trust. The explicit acts of self-trust, as the quiet acknowledgment of the original self-trusting, lead to what we on another occasion will call the "ethical as-if" and "utopian poetics." These are ways in which active trust and belief wrestle with the prototrust and belief that are at the heart of wakeful life. Monadic history has provided the universal, concrete arena for this wrestle. If we take this passive primal trust of wakeful mind as coincident with God's trust in the monadic community, we may take the active life of faith and utopian poetics as trust in this divine trust.[97]

Transcendental self-trust is thus an appreciation of the divine as the *Walten* by which I am and know all things; but it is not of the divine as a *principium quo* apart from that gracious self-acceptance which I am.[98] This transcendental self-trust approximates traditional senses of worship if the 'turn within' does justice to both the anonymity of the reflecting I-pole and the absence of that which is worshipped. Clearly the feeble pulsing is not a topic or theme upon which one dwells or meditates. Furthermore, the apperception of primal presencing's phases in the time-stream as such is not worship. The appreciative silence of transcendental self-trust involves the delicate, balanced activity-passivity of taking the *Walten* as tied to a transcendent principle. Yet I do not come upon the gracious whence initiating my being, but I come only indirectly upon my anonymous prebeing, to which I as living-pole and I as agency and reflection am indebted. And I come upon this anonymous prebeing (i.e., this primal streaming-presencing is awake to itself) by reason of the *Walten*. This holding sway is more immanent to me than is the living-pole and the I-pole because it frames the anonymous streaming; that is, it quickens the primal presencings to protoreflections, to self-trustings, through which emerge 'I can' and 'I am.'

In this respect Husserl could also say *"Cogito ergo cogitor"*; that is, because the fact of being an ego entails the existence of rationality in the facticity, it displays the divine principle holding sway over the hyletic creativity. However, the attempt *to take* the passive streaming *as* 'I am thought by God' (*cogitor a deo*) threatens to distort the wakeful receptivity (*Gelassenheit*) by way of an active apperceiving or interpreting. Furthermore, the 'divine *cognito*' itself is on the verge of sliding into the grasp of a thematizing consciousness. Appreciating the divine holding sway over the anonymous primal streaming requires not only a renunciation of all efforts to objectify the anonymous *Walten* but *a fortiori* it demands acceptance of the essential necessity of the divine absence.[99] And this involves not only *not* transforming the absence itself into a presence but also resisting the pull to reduce the absence to nothing. The absence must be regarded as necessary to the meaning of divinity for the human monad. The absence is dipolar; that is, it includes both the ideal personality of a higher order and the principle of the anonymous *Walten*. A proper understanding of the formulation of prayer as transcendental self-trust prevents the pull toward making the divine present as well as the arrogation of 'self-confidence'—as if human agency were not indebted to a divine principle.

A good symbolic approximation of transcendental self-trust as the appropriate appreciation of the divine entelechy's holding sway is meditation involving breathing exercises. We are born with our first breath and die with our last. For these exercises one must actively turn away from involvement with the world and turn to one's 'vital signs' as the condition for this involvement. Although we are concerned about food and are almost always thinking about it, air is a more immediate need than food—yet it is rarely thought about. Perhaps because, at least at the present, it costs nothing. Turning to it is turning to what is most obvious. This turning-to is a letting-be of the ongoing, functioning condition of life, breathing. This condition is not separable from one's self. Indeed, there is a clear sense in which I and I alone breathe. Nevertheless it is also as true that I am breathed, that 'it' breathes, as much as that I breathe; it is the 'gift' that makes giving possible, and so on. But this is only an approximation because, after all, breathing comprises kinesthetic, spatial-temporal syntheses.[100]

In spite of these and other difficulties, it must be said that the effort to be still, to be trusting, to 'wait' upon that which is necessarily always absent, already under way, and is yet the 'wind at our backs', will not appear empty if it is understood as the gracious passivity to required agency; if the demand of the absolute ought as the whither-pole of the mind's life is kept alive as the other pole of prayer, resting in the gracious silence will be welcomed. The absoluteness of the claims of the absolute ought, the infinity of its heights, the incessancy of its demands, can be properly met only if the energizing rest and strengthening quiet, which the active transcendental self-trust explicates, is there. Such is the sense we give to the following collection of lyrical sketches by Husserl.

> We find a way to God. The unsearchable Within.[101]
> The absolute world and God as the *one* 'substance',
> As the source of all being,
> As the principle of all development in the world,
> As the world-ordering power, as world-creator,
> As the principle of the constitution of a world that has laws
> and is oriented toward values and the realization of values.

The divine life passes through my heart, through the
pulsebeat of my life.
The love of God and the love of the world.[102]
The I-All is born in the free creation of a best world,
But in the divine drive, and on the basis of the divine
creation of
An undisclosed true world.[103]

The exhortation to rest in the holding-sway (*Walten*) of the divine
over the whence-pole is not an invitation to an indefinite vacation in a
sacred spa; its sense of receptivity and silence are correlated to the infinite and precarious task of being cocreators of 'the world of God'.
With the rhythmic acknowledgment of this primal grace, the infinity
and danger of this task can be courageously faced.

Notes

1. This work is indebted to numerous path-breaking researchers in the
Husserl Archives, especially Boehm, Kern, Held, Toulemont, and Diemer,
whose works will be cited later. The precis is *a* Husserlian philosophical
theology; there are already philosophical theologies indebted to Husserl,
which stand at a considerable distance to Husserl's own positions. Thus, e.g.,
we have Heidegger's and Fink's agnostic or negative theologies, Levinas's
Hebraic personalism, Findlay's neoplatonism (see the lovely essay in this
volume), and Sokolowski's elegant and novel Neo-Thomism (cf. Thomas
Prufer's essay in this volume). Henry Duméry, without being an expert in
Husserl's thought, has perhaps come closest to Husserl's own positions (see
Charles Courtney's essay in this volume). Without the *Nachlass* MSS there is
little encouragement to attempt a Husserlian theology. I am indebted to the
Husserl Archives in New York, Cologne, and Louvain. I am especially grateful
to Guy Van Kerckhoven of the Louvain Archives for taking me through important untranscribed texts, expecially A V 21. This kindness had the effect of
convincing me that whatever *the* Husserlian position is (and I hope this work
contributes to the issue), my effort is at least Husserlian. My thanks also to Professor Samuel IJsseling, Director of the Husserl Archives, for permission to use
and quote from the *Nachlass*.

2. See Husserl, *Erste Philosophie* II (The Hague: Nijhoff, 1959),
410–412. The literature, and therefore the debates, around the primal presencing are beginning to grow. For this précis I confine my references to what have
been helpful secondary texts providing expositions of Husserl's writings on
inner-time consciousness, i.e., especially *Husserliana* X, the C- and L-MSS. See
Klaus Held, *Lebendige Gegenwart* (The Hague: Nijhoff, 1966); Robert

Sokolowski, *Husserlian Meditations* (Evanston: Northwestern University Press, 1974), 124–168; and John Brough "The Emergence of an Absolute Consciousness in Husserl's Early Writings on Time-Consciousness," *Man and World*, V (1972), 298–326; Thomas Prufer, "An Outline of Some Husserlian Distinctions and Strategies, Especially in 'The Crisis'," *Phaenomenologische Forschungen* I (1975), 89–104; Rudolf Bernet, "Die ungegenwaertige Gegenwart. Anwesenheit und Abwesenheit in Husserls Analyse des Zeitbewusstseins,"*Phaenomenologische Forschungen*, 14 (1984), 16–57.

3. See the MS. L I, 21, pp. 16, 22, and 30.

4. See K. Held, *Lebendige Gegenwart*. Iso Kern in his fine *Idee und Methode der Philosophie* (Berlin: de Gruyter, 1975), 155, has an excerpt from the important C MS; see section 7 below.

5. I believe these conclusions are warranted by texts to be found in *Zur Phaenomenologie der Intersubjectivitaet* (The Hague: Nijhoff, 1973), I, 244–247; II, 170–171, 210–212; III, 204.

6. Held, *Legendige Gegenwart*, 162–163.

7. See B I 14 XI, 24; also, R. Sokolowski, *Husserlian Meditations*, 258, note 18. For the problem of the indexicality of the transcendental I, see Thomas Prufer, "Welt, Ich, und Zeit in der Sprache," *Philosophische Rundschau*, 20 (1974), 224–240.

8. C 17 V is perhaps the most important text for this speculation, although various texts on teleology, instinct, will, etc., in the *Intersubjektivitaet* volumes may be taken as supports. See v. III, 586–588 and *Krisis der Europaeischen Wissenschaften und die Transzendentale Phaenomenologie* (The Hague: Nijhoff, 1962, sections 54b–55 for some mighty wrestling with this topic. Although it bears frequent mention, I will only here observe that the speculative contours of Husserl's thought seem to have a predelineation with Fichte's wrestling with *Wissen* (cf. immanent awareness) in the later *Wissenschaftslehre(n)* and *Die Anweisung zum Seligen Leben*.

9. Husserl, *Zur Phaenomenologie des innern Zeitbewusstseins* (The Hague: Nijhoff, 1966), sections 7 and 20. For the first problem of the problematic 'streaming' as not being 'in time', see note 2 above, the discussions of Brough, Sokolowski, and Prufer.

10. See section 5 below. Held wrestles with the problem of how the living-pole as the abiding *nunc stans* and present of the ongoing functioning 'now' may be said to be constituted in reflection; see *Lebendige Gegenwart*, 123–140. My problem: Is not its 'being there' prior to reflection and as egological moment nontemporal in a sense prior to constituting reflective acts? The theological question requires the integration of the issue of the temporality of the divine *intellectus agens* or *intellectus ipse*. If this informs or actuates the egological principle, i.e., this monad's wakefulness, in what sense is the

egological moment temporal and constituted as all-temporal through reflection? Here in this précis we can merely mention this important but serious difficulty.

11. Dieter Henrich, "Self-Consciousness, a Critical Introduction to a Theory," *Man and World*, IV (1971), 13. Cf. Fichte, *Nachlass* I (Bonn: Marcus, 1834), 178–179.

12. Husserl, *Zur Phaenomenologie der Intersubjektivitaet* II, 45; cf. 301.

13. See Husserl, *Erste Philosophie* I (The Hague: Nijhoff, 1956), 366, where these three aspects are given implicitly a unified perspective.

14. See F I 14, excerpts from which are to be found in A. Diemer, *Edmund Husserl* (Meisenheim am Glan: Hain, 1965), 314 ff; see also A V 21. In our interpretation, this kind of meditation for the later Husserl also took the form of 'utopian eidetics', i.e., conceiving the ideal monadic community as a godly person of a higher order.

15. Husserl, along with his colleagues and students, made an appreciable run at a comprehensive investigation of regional ontologies. For efforts in the phenomenology of religion, see the bibliography to the *Encyclopedia Britannica* essay in *Phaenomenologische Psychologie* 255.

16. "Correspondencia entre Dilthey y Husserl," Walter Biemel, ed., *Revista Filosofia de la Universidad de Costa Rica*, I (1957), 101 ff; translation in *Husserl: Shorter Works* (South Bend: Notre Dame, 1981), 203–208.

17. This is a theme in various places that finds special relevance to religion in the letter to Dilthey and in the notes of Sister Adelgundis, O.S.B., "Gespraeche mit Edmund Husserl: 1931–1936/1936–1938," *Stimmen*, 199 (1981), 48–58, 129–138.

18. Cf. the discussion of eidetic and hermeneutical phenomenologies of religion in *The Piety of Thinking: Essays by Martin Heidegger*, translation, notes, and commentary by James G. Hart and John C. Maraldo (Bloomington: Indiana University Press, 1976), 75–124, 184–198. Heidegger's surmounting of regional ontologies parallels, and yet is intended as a critique of, Husserl's transcendental surmounting of them. Whether this critique holds cannot be addressed explicitly here.

19. See the letter to Otto dated March 5, 1919.

20. Dorion Cairns, *Conversations with Husserl and Fink* (The Hague: Nijhoff, 1976), 46.

21. On another occasion I hope to do more justice to this important topic in Husserl's philosophical theology. See, e.g., Husserl, *Analysen zur passiven Synthesis* (The Hague: Nijhoff, 1966), 377–381.

22. Good examples of Husserl's reconstructive metaphysics can be found in *Zur Phaenomenologie der Intersubjektivitaet* III, 593–596, 608–610 and

666 ff. For reservations on this aspect of Husserl's thought, see Iso Kern's essay in this volume.

23. See A. N. Whitehead, *The Function of Reason* (Boston: Beacon Press, 1958), 60. Yet for Whitehead himself, nature is derivative of a universal quasi-monadological agency. Among Husserl's students, Hedwig Conrad-Martius alone developed an elaborate philosophy of nature, which was an exemplary metaphysics in the first Husserlian sense, i.e., it applied to contemporary biology and physics a developed regional ontology of nature. In the light of her acknowledgment of the significance of transcendental phenomenology at the end of her life, it is an open question whether she would find the task of reconstruction a 'category mistake' and wish to insist on the need to respect the essential differences in the order of being.

24. *Ibid.*, 58 ff.

25. *Ibid*, 15 and *Process and Reality* (New York: MacMillan, 1936), 252. See Kant's appreciation of the heuristic value of monadological reconstruction in the *Critique of Pure Reason*, B696. Also see the rich dialogue often touching on this matter between Hegel and Whitehead found in the numerous writings of Darrel Christensen.

26. See Kern, *Idee und Methode der Philosophie*, 333 ff.

27. *Ideas* I, no. 49.

28. See Husserl's glosses to *Sein und Zeit*.

29. See, e.g., *Erste Philosophie* I, 220, 392–394 and pass., and *Ideas* I, no. 58.

30. E III 4, 7; cf. A V 22, 10.

31. *Zur Phaenomenologie der Intersubjektivitaet* III, 210–214; these are good 'metaphysical' pages.

32. See Kern, *Idee und Methode der Philosophie*, 342.

33. *Erste Philosophie* I, 189–190, 392–395; B IV 9, 19–21; also Iso Kern, *Husserl und Kant* (The Hague: Nijhoff, 1964), 297.

34. See Hans Wagner, "Husserl's Posthumous Writings," in R. O. Evelton, ed. *The Phenomenology of Husserl* (Chicago: Quadrangle, 1970), 244–255; also Wagner's insufficiently appreciated *Philosophie und Reflexion* (Basel: Reinhardt, 1959/1967), 331–338 and my study of this work, "Constitution of the Being of Mind," in *Contemporary German Philosophy* IV (1984).

35. J. -P. Sartre, *Transcendence of the Ego* (New York: Noonday, 1964), 98 ff.

36. See E. Fink, *Studien zur Phaenomenologie: 1930–1939* (The Hague: Nijhoff, 1966), 117; this summarizes such texts as A VI 14 and B III 9. See also Heidegger, *Sein und Zeit*, 363 n.; see also Heidegger, *Metaphysische Anfangsgruende der Logik* GW, 26 (Frankfurt am Main: Klostermann, 1978), 215;

and *The Basic Problems of Phenomenology*, trans. A. Hofstadter (Bloomington: Indiana University Press, 1982), 162, 268, 313 ff.

37. The text is not clear here whether the differentiations or separations into individuals (*Sonderungen nach Individuen*) refer to the discernible individual meaning-units or to something like the Fichtean speculation on the divine mind differentiating itself into a plurality of minds. Although this Fichtean theme is also a problem for Husserl, the following text, from *Ideas* I, section 58, urges the former possibility as the more correct one.

38. B I 4, 2 ff.

39. See Schumann's edition of *Ideen* I, 563–564.

40. *Chronik*, 295.

41. Cairns, *Conversations*, 23.

42. F I 24, 41b; the transcriber notes that the larger part of this page is crossed with a big penciled cross next to which stands: 1920.

43. K III 1, VIII, 4; E III4, 7.

44. Franz Brentano, *The Foundation and Construction of Ethics* (New York: Humanities, 1973), 266.

45. *Ibid.*, 267.

46. See, e.g., *Zur Phaenomenologie der Intersubjektivitaet* I, 14 ff and II, 151–160; *Erste Philosophie* II, 410 ff., 480–482.

47. Rudolf Boehm has made this point in his important "Husserl's Concept of the Absolute," in Evelton, 198–199.

48. *Zur Phaenomenologie der Intersubjektivitaet* I, 357; see this entire discussion (351–357) devoted to the phenomenological problem of origin.

49. See the MS. from 1907–08, B II 2, 46 ff., and B I 4, 2–3. See Kern, *Husserl und Kant*, no. 27.

50. B II 2, 46 ff.

51. *Cartesianische Meditationen* (The Hague: Nijhoff, 1960), 114; Cartesian Meditations, trans. by Dorion Cairns (The Hague: Nijhoff, 1973), 81.

52. This is a move Husserl attributes, with some qualifications, to both Hume and Kant. See *Erste Philosophie* I, 404.

53. David Hume, A *Treatise of Human Nature* (Oxford: Clarendon Press, 1949), 12–13.

54. Eugen Fink, *Naehe und Distanz* (Freiburg/Munich: Karl Alber, 1976), 223.

55. *Ibid.*, 223–224; cf. section 1 above.

56. For the relation of Husserl to German idealism, see the fine pioneer-

ing essays by Rudolf Boehm in *Vom Gesichtspunkt der Phaenomenoimlogie* (The Hague: Nijhoff, 1968), 18–71 and Iso Kern, *Husserl und Kant*, pass.

57. Fink, *Naehe und Distanz*, 224.

58. *Zur Phaenomenologie der Intersubjektivitaet* III, 386.

59. *Ibid.*, 668–669.

60. See note 34.

61. I am indebted to Thomas Prufer for helping me think through the issues here.

62. B IV 6, 105–106.

63. Basic here are Husserl's distinctions in the third of the *Logical Investigations*; See also Sokolowski, *Husserlian Meditations*, chap. I.

64. C 10, 24. See for an excerpt of the text, Iso Kern, *Idee und Methode der Philosophie*, 155. This is not an isolated text; i.e., there are several published texts and places in the *Nachlass* that point to this ultimate 'dualism' of moments of the whole, which the absolute substance is.

65. E III 4, 29.

66. E III 4, 60–61; See Diemer, 313–314 for most of this text. The translation is in need of polish and the text begs for an extensive commentary. We believe that the present précis indicates a sense of how this *logos* is, vis-à-vis the world, entelechy; the social utopian teleology we shall discuss in a forthcoming work. The text also indicates how the divine is the polar opposite of the transcendence of the world *and* that of the transcendence in immanence of the I-pole. See our discussion below.

67. *Ideas* I, no. 58.

68. Held, *Lebendige Gegenwart*, 180.

69. Paul Natorp, *Deutscher Weltberuf* (Jena: Diedrichs, 1918) II, 124.

70. See *Allgemeine Psychologie* (Tuebingen: Mohr, 1912) 232–234 for the discussion of the lower level, idea-limit of investigation.

71. *Ibid.*, 239–240.

72. *Deutscher Weltberuf*, II, 127.

73. See Paul Natorp, "Bruno Bauchs 'Immanuel Kant' und die Fortbildung des Systems des Kritischen Idealismus," *Kantstudien* (1918), 453–454; see also H.-G. Gadamer's introductory essay in Natorp's *Philosophische Systematik* (Hamburg: Meiner, 1958), xiv–xv.

74. B II 2, 54. Again, this is not an isolated text.

75. E III 4, 20; see also E III 1, 4–9; cf. Roth, *Edmund Husserl's Ethische*

Untersuchungen (The Hague: Nijhoff, 1960), 119. I address these matters at length in a forthcoming work tentatively titled, *The Godly Person of a Higher Order: A Husserlian Social Philosophy.*

76. A V 21, 128a. See Kant, *Religion Within the Limits of Reason Alone* (New York: Harper and Row), 182 ff.

77. See the conclusion to CM as well as that of the *Paris Lectures*; the text is from St. Augustine, *de vera religione*, xxix, 72.

78. E III 9, 30.

79. *Ibid.*

80. *Ibid.*

81. K III 2, 54 ff; cf E III 9, 30–31.

82. E III 8, 30.

83. Held, *Lebendige Gegenwart*, 165.

84. K III 28; cf. Goethe, *Faust* II/1, 148:
> Pulse of life beating with fresh vitality
> Greeting softly the aetherial dawn
> You, Earth, were also constant this evening
> And are breathing responsively to the tread of my feet,
> Already you begin to surround me with desire
> And inspire and instill a powerful resolve
> To strive continuously toward the highest life.

This text indicates the point where this Husserlian interpretation of prayer, or the piety of experience, is to be focused: between the I-pole's genesis and that of the ideal of the world-pole or the absolute ought.

85. For these metaphors see, e.g., C II 1, 3; Int. II, 359; n. 1: A V 5, 5; LI 21, 14a.

86. This is from the original paragraph which James wrote for the opening of *The Varieties of Religious Experience*. See R. B. Perry, *The Thought and Character of William James* (Briefer Version) (New York: Braziller, 1954), 258. Why James says "some living moments, at any rate," instead of speaking of the living present as such, will be discussed below.

87. *Ibid.*, 259. The Christianity of which James speaks is exemplarily to be found in the Rhineland Mystics, Anabaptists, and Quakers.

88. Paul Natorp, Husserl's dear *Gespraechspartner* in the development of an idealistic world-view and a philosophical theology, culminated his philosophical efforts in a celebration of the *Quelle* or creative sourcing which, Natorp argued, was prior to the distinction of subject and object, mind and beings, for-itself and in-itself. This primal ontological *Ereignis* correlates with a quiet receptivity and stillness which Natorp found at the heart of Lao Tse, Dostoevsky, the Quakers, and Eckhart. Although this theme is systematically

worked out in the later writings of Natorp, which Husserl most probably did not read, one finds lovely discussions of it from a more transcendental viewpoint in Natorp's presentation of Eckhart and Luther in *Deutscher Weltberuf*, II (Jena: Diederichs, 1918). This work provoked in Husserl an outpouring of love and admiration for Natorp as a human being and thinker and an acknowledgment of basic agreement in the conception of the meaning of the development of the world as the true development of God and the creation of the world in subjectivity. See the letter to Natorp dated June 29, 1918. Cf. Kern, *Husserl und Kant*, 29–33.

89. A remark of Teilhard de Chardin to an anguished friend dramatizes the conflation of the senses of rest. Teilhard states that "the true and great prayer in moments of great sickness" is to be able to go to sleep with an active confidence and trust. See P. Teilhard de Chardin, *Letters to Two Friends*: 1926–1952 (New York: New American Library: N.D.), 103–104.

90. Cf. Gerda Walther, *Phaenomenologie der Mystik* (Halle: Niemeyer, 1923/1970). Walther was dependent on A. Pfaender's work, especially his *Psychologie der Gesinnungen*, II in *Jahrbuch fuer Philosophie und phaenomenologische Forschung* Bd. II (1916), 67 ff., and early versions of his *Die Seele* (Halle: Niemeyer, 1933). In the latter work (226) we find a statement of the basic position Walther proposes as well as overtones of Husserlian themes: "The human soul is ultimately in its essence of a religious nature. It is a living being which doesn't create itself. Its animated life and being does not come to it from without. Neither the body nor anything in the external world forms the ground and source of its being and its life. If it pursues its being and its life to the point of the source's origin it is indeed led to its own interior but here gushes up its life and being in an abiding manner without any agency from the side of the soul itself. Its life and being are continuously given to it. It is essentially creature and not creator of itself. It doesn't produce (*erzeugen*) itself but it can constitute (*auszeugen*) itself from out of itself. At the deepest point of itself it is bound in a reverse direction with the abiding creative point of itself. It can, therefore, only fully generate itself in that it abides in contact with the abiding creative ground. . . ." Husserl's dilemma is clearly delineated here: Even though such regional ontological analyses have symmetry with his mode of expression, can they be said to be speaking of the same thing if there is no transcendental reduction?

91. Walther's letter is in the convolute A V 21, dated May 18, 1920. Husserl's letter finds the archive notation A V 21, 61a ff. Whether it was ever sent is not clear. In the later edition of *Phaenomenologie der Mystik* (Olten: Walter-Verlag, 1970), 16–17, Walter expresses her regret that Husserl saw in her discussions not descriptions of realities but, at best, "ideal possibilities." Husserl, she says, was of the opinion that the only reality (*einzig Wirkliche*) in this matter is the experience of the mystics (*Erleben der Mystiker*), the fervor of love, not the 'object' of these experiences. This appraisal of Husserl is just if its only source is Husserl's drafted letter. It is unclear whether Husserl's un-

dated draft is of the letter that occasioned Walther's, or whether it is in response to her letter. She might well have mentioned the chief Pfaenderian themes on an earlier occasion.

92. In a 1917 listing in the *Chronik*, (215) we find: "I read often *Die Deutsche Theologie* and have it by me. I love it very much. I have, in general, a great attraction to German mysticism. I think I have access to mysticism. But I haven't lived enough therein." The *Theologia Deutsch* (composed in the late fourteenth century) is of course the text greatly esteemed by Luther for its doctrine of divine grace as prior to all human works. However, it was doubtless of interest to Husserl (and perhaps to Fichte) because of the way it synthesized themes of Rhineland mysticism. It conceives the divine as the best and the 'absolute ought' of human action as well as the source of subjectivity. The divine is properly presenced by a purifying, detaching 'reduction' from the manifold of the world and from the alienated, distracted, scattered self to a unifying, gathering selfhood, or I behind straightforward senses of I. The process of unification is a 'suffering of God' (understood both as an objective and subjective genitive).

93. Cf. the remarks in Cairns, *Conversations*, 91: "Every evidence has its right. The question is always of the scope (*Tragweite*) of any given evidence. This applies also to the particular evidences which the mystic has. Whole pages of Meister Eckhart, Husserl said, could be taken over by him unchanged. He · doubts, however, the practical sufficiency of mysticism. The 'awakening' from the mystical experience is likely to be a rude one. On the other hand, the insight into the rationality of the world which one gains through scientific investigation remains through all future experience. The difference is furthermore one between passive enjoyment and work. The mystic neglects work. Both are necessary."

94. Cf. Cairns, *Ibid.*, 46 and Husserl's view of the hopelessness of gaining a radical understanding of the meaning of God and God's existence "short of the phenomenological *Einstellung*." When one recovers from the *chutzpah* of this remark, one may recall that practically all the formative philosophers and mystics have made similar claims for their 'points of view'. Insofar as the reduction is isomorphic with the religious detachment and the letting-go, Husserl's position states nothing novel. See, e.g., the work of Lanza del Vasto referred to in note 100.

95. A similar, even though less directly expressed, point is made to Rudolf Otto. Here he seems to require more attention to the descriptive phenomenological analyses as a preparation for a *philosophical* theory of religious consciousness. Otto's work, *Das Heilige*, is hailed as original in the sense that it goes to the original phenomenological-noematic material. But the drift of the remarks seem to be that Otto has not reached the genuine *Ursprung* nor the essential necessities of religious consciousness. See the letter dated March 5, 1919.

96. See *Analysen zur Passiven Synthesis*, pass., but especially, 178–182, and James G. Hart, "Toward a Phenomenology of Nostalgia," *Man and World*, VI (1973).

97. For this discussion of transcendental self-trust I am indebted to Erick Frank, *Glauben, Wissen, Wollen*, (Zuerich and Stuttgart: Artemis, 1955), 378, and especially to Wolfgang Cramer, *Die Monade* (Stuttgart: Kohlhammer, 1954), 88–89. For the 'primal belief' of protention, see e.g. *Analysen zur passiven Synthesis*, 103.

98. Cf. St. Thomas Aquinas, *Summa Contra Gentiles*, I, 11.

99. Whether the testimony of those who were with Husserl at his last hours to his rapturous experiences contradicts this position must be decided by those with appropriate capacities. I find it not only endearing, and even amusing, but also philosophically suggestive that he wished to write down these experiencs. See *Chronik*, 488–489, and Sister Adelgundis' "Gespraeche."

100. Cf. Lanza del Vasto, *Make Straight the Way of the Lord* (New York: Alfred Knopf, 1974), 44 ff.

101. A V 21, 42a.

102. A V 21, 47a.

103. A V 21, 102a.

STEVEN W. LAYCOCK

8. The Intersubjective Dimension of Husserl's Theology

Edmund Husserl described himself as a "perpetual beginner" and devoted the major effort of his philosophical career to the project of establishing those foundational 'beginnings' of the phenomenological enterprise upon which others might build. Beginnings, however, are for the sake of endings, and, as in Husserl's case, this fact is rarely appreciated. Indeed, those few faint indications of Husserl's vision of the theological culmination of phenomenology are altogether too apt to be overlooked by those so immeasurably indebted to his astonishingly rich and nuanced contributions to foundational phenomenology. Yet Husserl was not, as it might at first appear, entirely innocent of theological motivation. A discernible piety is exhibited in his explicit avowal to Edith Stein that

> I have tried to arrive at the end without the help of [speculative] theology, its proofs, its methods. In other words, I wanted to reach God without God.[1]

One thing, at least, is patent: For Husserl, the *end* of phenomenology is the intuition of God.

Husserl's rare theological remarks have not, however, gone without some comment.[2] We know, for example, that Husserl's God is a God *in process*, a dipolar God: both *entelechy* and *telos* of the universal teleological process whereby consciousness is endlessly enriched with novel, synthetically identified world vistas.[3] Husserl's God is, as it were, a single, universal intentional act, spanning Absolute Subject and Absolute Object. This much, as least, has been noted. Yet

169

an intentional act is the appearing-of-something-to-someone, an appearing necessarily mediated by an *appearance*. And an altogether unremarked feature of Husserl's theological vision is that that appearance, which mediates the divine intentional act, is precisely the universal intersubjective community of finite minds. It is, then, the task of the present paper to exhibit this theme of Husserlian theology.

I

Dorion Cairns's playfully tautological remark that "whatever its sense, a theory is phenomenological if, and only if, it is produced phenomenologically"[4] sets in relief the fundamental fact that phenomenology is distinguished not so much by its *content* as by its *method*. The practice of phenomenology involves vigilant reflection upon the 'source' of philosophical knowledge—experience, understood in the broadest possible sense. Phenomenology is the reflective investigation of *phenomena*: objects *precisely as and only as they are given to us in experience*. It concerns itself neither with the discovery of empirical facts regarding the objects of our experience nor with the establishment of empirical generalizations embracing broad reaches of such facts, but rather, with the manners in which experienced objects are presented to us, with their *modes of givenness*.

Phenomenological method is emphatically *not* that of theorizing about experience. The data embraced by a given theory necessarily underdetermine the theory in much the same way that Wittgenstein's celebrated 'duck-rabbit' underdetermines the ways in which it is seen (i.e., as a duck-picture or as a rabbit-picture). The theory, or theoretical 'way of seeing', always, and necessarily, asserts more than its data. And this 'more' is extraneous to the rigorous discipline of phenomenology. Phenomenology is never an attempt to account for, to provide an explanation or theory of, the data of our experience—a procedure that, at best, establishes some determinate relationship between certain aspects of experience and the nonexperienced postulations in terms of which experience is said to be 'explained'. Again, phenomenology is nothing if not concern with phenomena. The task of phenomenology has nothing to do with the construction of theoretical superstructures from which the experiential substructure can be deduced. If more is seen in deductively elaborated theorems

than in their axioms, phenomenological attention turns toward the experience articulated through such theorems.

The intent of phenomenology is most emphatically that of
elucidating, of shedding light. Phenomenology is elucidation in the
sense that it is concerned to provide a 'standpoint'—that of reflection—from which its truths may be lucidly *seen*. Mists and obstruc-
tions must be cleared from the path of our vision, and this, ultimately,
is what phenomenological labor consists in.

A phenomenological investigation of God, no less than the
specific 'pheomenology' of any other region of experience, must be
'produced phenomenologically'. God cannot be invoked to explain
experience, but must be discovered through experience. The
phenomenology of God is the disclosure of the *God-phenomenon*:
God *precisely as and only as given to us in experience*. The
phenomenologist of God is concerned neither with proofs for God's
existence nor with the implications of God's existence, but solely with
God's 'manners of givenness'.

Speculative theological theories contradict one another. And their
mutual contradictoriness may be accounted for by the fact that
theories of necessity assert more than their data. Failure of unanimity
is inevitably due to a failure of adequation between God, as the 'Object' of religious experience, and the theoretical characterization of
this 'Object'. Phenomenological description, remaining within the
bounds of the experienced *as experienced*, cannot be affected by the
abstract segregation of experienced 'matter' from interpretive 'form'.
The God of the phenomenologists is God *as revealed through reflection upon concretely lived experience*. The plane of reflective consciousness in no way disturbs the primal flow of conscious life.[5] Strict
phenomenological method demands that nothing be attributed to God
that is not manifest within the experience of God. And this requires
that God be not only presented in lived experience, on the level of
'primal presencing', but also represented in the reflective apprehension of this experience, on the level of reflection. What cannot be apprehended through reflection cannot legitimately be attributed to
God.

The God of speculative theology is, from a phenomenological
standpoint, an already-constituted meaning. Husserl's effort to "reach
God without God" involved a description of the 'God-phenomenon'
without in any way importing theological assumptions or adding
'more' to the description than was there in the experience. Beliefs

concerning God and the divine nature must be 'bracketed', barred from modifying the phenomenological description of the God-phenomenon. Such beliefs and their implications are utterly inadmissible as phenomenological truths. The divine nature must be approached in a way that in no way presupposes the truth of already-operative beliefs concerning the divine nature, in a way that is theologically presuppositionless. Legitimate attributions are aspects of the phenomenological description of the God-phenomenon. All other attributions are 'suspended'.

To describe the God-phenomenon is to describe God *as experienced by me*. In this way, as Husserl maintains, "the I . . . bears its God in itself."[6] The reflective act, in virtue of which the first-order lived experience of God is apprehended, is *my* reflective act. Only what is revealed *to me* through *my* act of reflection is phenomenologically admissible. And nothing is revealed to me through reflection that is not itself a consciousness.

Through phenomenological reflection I *see*, in an immediate, intuitive, and self-evident way, the essential structural forms of consciousness as evidenced in each fleeting moment of conscious life. Were it possible for such phenomenological intuition to be mistaken, for experience to falsify reflection, phenomenological reflection would drop to the status of mere theorization *about* experience. Phenomenological description would become, at best, a hopeless ideal. If, however, phenomenological description is possible, then those features that I intuitively *see* to be essential to every consciousness and upon which I reflect are adamant and unshakable necessities.

If the divine consciousness is a consciousness upon which I can reflect, then not even the mind of God can escape those necessary structures of consciousness in general, revealed to me through phenomenological reflection. And if divine consciousness is in no way revealed through reflection upon *my own* lived experience, there is, for me, no God-phenomenon. Hence, if phenomenological intuition reveals that consciousness is necessarily intentional, then divine consciousness is intentional. If such intuition discloses that every act of consciousness revealed through reflection is a moment of a teleological process oriented toward the enjoyment of an ever more expansive vision, divine consciousness is likewise teleologically oriented.

This, it must be stressed, is an inescapable result of consistently applied phenomenological method and will undergird any description of the God-phenomenon. The reflective plane of consciousness, in contrast to the concrete acts of reflection that occur upon it, can be understood as the ensemble of necessary conditions for reflective experience. As such, the reflective plane is intersubjectively shared, common to the universal intersubjective community of finite minds. And we shall see that, for Husserl, the reflective plane itself refers to the divine consciousness, in the sense of comprising its field of consciousness. Intersubjectivity *is* the divine envisionment.

In the pages to follow this connection will be progressively elucidated. Our vision, however, is obstructed by the Sartrean contention that the universal intersubjective community comprises "a synthesis whose totality is inconceivable."[7] Should Sartre's contention prove true, all hopes of demonstrating the identity of intersubjectivity and the divine envisionment in strict conformity with phenomenological method would be dashed. We need first, then, to remove the obstruction.

II

In Sartre's view, individual subjects are internally related by means of *internal negation*, conceived as the distinctness of one aspect of a totality from another. Internal negation has served Sartre well in his treatment of the prereflective and reflective ek-stases as

> the negation which divides being into reflected and reflecting and in turn divides the dyad reflected-reflecting into (reflected-reflecting)-reflected and (reflected-reflecting)-reflecting.[8]

The *prereflective ekstasis* is consciousness's not-being the object that, in the favored Sartrean metaphor, it 'reflects', the primary division of being into reflected and reflecting. The *reflective ekstasis* is the second-order 'mirroring', the division of the first-order totality, *reflected-reflecting*, into reflected and reflecting aspects. The final, and most radical, ekstasis, the *intersubjective ekstasis*, is effected by one consciousness's *not-being* another.

> The negation is divided into two internal and opposed negations; each is an internal negation, but they are nevertheless separated from one another by an inapprehensible external nothingness. In fact since

each of them is exhausted in denying that one for-itself is the other and since each negation is wholly engaged in that being which it has to be, it is no longer in command of itself so as to deny concerning itself that it is the opposite negation.[9]

Sartre's hierarchial triplet of ekstases illustrates that the totality effected by ekstatic nihilation on one level can be thematized only on the next. The totality, *reflected-reflecting*, is not present to the first-order reflecting consciousness; nor is the totality, (*reflected-reflecting*)-(*reflected-reflecting*)-*reflecting*, present to the second-order reflecting consciousness.

The totality, *I-Other*, according to Sartre, is also "a synthesis whose totality is inconceivable" precisely because, as the final member of the sequence of ekstases, this totality cannot be brought to presence.

> Only a witness external both to myself and to the Other could compare the image with the model and decide whether it is a true one. Moreover this witness in order to be authorized could not in turn maintain a relation of exteriority with both the Other and myself, for otherwise he would know us only by images. Within the ekstatic unity of his being, he would have to be simultaneously *here* upon me as the *internal* negation of myself and *over there* upon the Other as the *internal* negation of the Other. Thus the recourse to God, which we find in Leibniz, is purely and simply a recourse to the negation of interiority. . . . He must of necessity *be* myself in order to apprehend my reality without intermediary and with apodictic evidence, and yet it is necessary that it not be me in order that he may preserve his impartiality as witness and be able over there both to be and not be the Other.[10]

The totality *God-(I-Other)* would require, as a condition of its being brought to presence as an internal negation, a 'God beyond God', which in turn would require, as a condition for the thematization of the totality, God_2-(God_1-(*I-Other*)), a 'God beyond the God beyond God', and so forth *ad infinitum*. Yet:

> No consciousness, not even God's can "see the underside"—that is, apprehend the totality as such. For if God is consciousness, he is integrated in the totality. And if by his nature, he is a being *beyond consciousness* (that is, an in-itself which would be its own foundation) still the totality can appear to him only as *object* (in that case he lacks the totality's internal disintegration as the subjective effort to reapprehend the self) or as *subject* (then since God *is not* this subject, he can only experience it without knowing it). Thus no point of view on the totality is conceivable; the totality has no "outside."[11]

Here Sartre parries the theist's anticipated thrust: Must there not be an end to the regression of 'Gods'? Must there not be a being capable of simultaneous nihilation and recovery, a being who can both *not-be* the intersubjective totality and at the same time thematize this totality? Sartre argues that the proposed arcing of divine intentionality upon itself, its circular closure, can at best provide an immanent 'experience' (*Erlebnis*), which itself cannot be reflected upon—an anomaly that would destroy the internal negation between divine Subject and intersubjective 'Object'.

III

Sartre's argument for 'detotalization', and its atheistic consequence, belies a neglect of the fundamental cooccurrence of *apperception* with every act of perception. Together with the sensuously filled presentation of an object as it confronts consciousness in perception there are more or less determinate, though clearly determinable, anticipations of what the object *would* look like *were* we to perceive it from other angles. And we may accordingly consider apperception as the *counterfactual mode of intentionality*. In perceiving an object this imaginal-anticipatory movement of consciousness presses beyond its sheer positive presence, beyond the locus of maximum perceptual givenness enclosed by the object's horizon. Only *our* side of an object is perceptually 'given'. We apperceptually 'take' its hither sides as well. Apperception is transhorizonal. To enjoy the apperception of an object's hither sides is to have certain expectations or anticipations regarding its 'look' as mediated by alternative profiles. Sartre fails to recognize that apperception is intrinsic to experience, as we shall see.

Our awareness of the possibility of other actual views of a given object contributes to the sense of objectivity that the object has for us. That I alone should be able to enjoy the object from a plurality of angles is not sufficient to differentiate it from any privately experienced denizen of my dream world. That there may be not merely alternative *views* of the object but other actual *viewers* wrenches the object away from mere private consideration. Objectivity rests, then, and crucially, upon our apperception of alternative viewings. We must be able to anticipate not only what the object would look like from 'over there' but also what it would be like thus to view the object. That is, we must not only be able to apperceive the object's 'look' as it would be given to a consciousness immersed in the straightforward, 'natural' attitude, but crucially more, we must be able to apperceive that very act of intentionality as it would be given through reflection. Objectivity requires not only apperceptual intending but apperceptual reflecting as well.

Sartre is correct in assuming that the totality *subject-object* is delivered as a totality to *presentational* consciousness only at the *next* ekstatic plateau; but he is assuredly wrong in supposing that a subject-object totality can in no way be presented on its own level. The prereflective perception of an object involves a prereflective apperception of (belief in) the subject. Sartre's 'prereflective *cogito*', the immediate, unthematic self-presence of consciousness, involves an unthematic belief in the self, a self-apperception. Understanding the term *horizon* to mean the totality of possibilities for the profiled intending of any given object, it becomes clear that

> the reflecting and the reflected on are each in the horizon of the other, the reflecting in the protentional horizon of the reflected on and the reflected on in the retentional horizon of the reflecting.[12]

Not only must we be able to retain the reflected on, we must be able to anticipate the reflecting as well. The empty 'I can reflect' must be capable of being filled by the actual achievement of a reflecting act. Prereflective experience is precisely *that-which-can-be-reflected-on*. But more profoundly, retention, as informing the lived present, is itself a seminal reflection capable of being brought to explicitness within a fully reflective consciousness. The germinal 'I can reflect', established by retention, is an act-possibility 'on the verge' of actualization. Protention involves the empty intending of this actualization. Retention is potential reflection.

Every lived experience is a *possibility-for-reflection*. And, inasmuch as the self-presence of prereflective experience is the immediate presence to consciousness of *what consciousness is*, prereflective self-presence is thereby the awareness of *being* a possibility-for-reflection. Lived experience involves an unthematic, apperceptive anticipation of being reflected on. Though prereflective, consciousness nonetheless *apperceives itself* as it *would* appear to a reflecting consciousness. Self-apperception thus fills in the gap, enabling prereflective object-consciousness to be appresented *as a totality* at the level of prereflective consciousness. And similarly for higher-order reflective totalities.

This, then, is no less true of the intersubjective ekstasis. The totality *I-Other* is never *presented* in its entirety. Yet, since the Other is precisely *that which can intend me from a source that I am not* (the one for whom I may myself serve as 'object'), my intending of the Other necessarily involves self-apperception. Intending the Other, I apperceive myself as I would appear to the Other. And thus, through the mutual cooperation of perceiving and apperceiving, the totality *I-Other* is present to me *in its entirety* in my intending of the Other.

In this way there remains room for the theist who may wish to assert the same with respect to the totality God-Intersubjectivity. Insofar as I, on behalf of the entire intersubjective community of finite minds, may legitimately and meaningfully employ the indexical 'we', I must apperceive this intersubjective totality as such. A divine mind may, then, be said to perceive what I thus apperceive. The totality *God-Intersubjectivity* is therefore, contrary to Sartre's contention, not 'detotalized' but present *as a totality* within the divine envisagement, in virtue of the presentation of intersubjectivity and the divine self-apperception.

IV

Any act of unqualified assertion presupposes the universal validity of the asserted. To *assert* is to claim that anyone who is in possession of the appropriate evidence, who 'stands where I am standing', must yield assent. And to *assert to* someone presupposes that it is incumbent upon that individual to yield assent, that the agent and recipient of the assertion are by right, if not in fact, 'of one mind'. A *de jure* 'we' thus emerges in the assertion that structurally mirrors a divine mind's envisionment of the intersubjective totality.

The factual incorrectness of an assertion is of course irrelevant to its claim to *de jure* universality. However, *de facto* universality of viewpoint cannot be achieved so long as the assertion is, in Husserl's sense, *precommunalized*.

> In general the world exists not only for isolated men but for the community of men; and this is due to the fact that even what is straightforwardly perceptual is communalized.
>
> In this communalization, too, there constantly occurs an alteration of validity through reciprocal correction. . . . If one attends to the distinction between things as "originally one's own" and as "em-

pathized" from others, in respect to the how of the manners of appearance, and if one attends to the possibility of discrepancies between one's own and empathized views, then what one actually experiences *originaliter* as a perceptual thing is transformed, for each of us, into a mere "representation of," "appearance of," the one objectively existing thing. . . . "The" thing itself is actually that which no one actually experiences as really seen, since it is always in motion.[13]

One might think, in this connection, of Wittgenstein's 'duck-rabbit'. *Prior* to communalization the agent of assertion claims *de jure* universality for, as it were, the 'duck-picture'. *After* communalization, *we* (agent and recipient) assent, as it were, to that which lies 'between' us—the *objective* 'duck-rabbit' of which the duck-picture is a *subjective* aspect. The result of communalization is not that of forcing us to renounce our original assertion but rather that of bringing us into a vantage point from which our unique, subjective contribution to what is objective (or better: intersubjective), as well as the contribution of the Other, are *both* thematized, brought to intuitive givenness *within a single comprehensive act of consciousness*. The result, then, of communalization is the establishment of a vantage point that all parties may share, the *de facto* coming into the unity of 'one mind', the establishment of unanimity, on the part of all communalizing individuals.

The above must not be taken to imply the 'Brahmanic absorption' of all individuality of consciousness into some homogeneous mass of mind. To be in a position to see that a given subject, S_1, believes one thing and that S_2 believes its contrary (a 'position' accessible, through communalization, to both S_1 *and* S_2) demands that S_1 and S_2 maintain their divergent viewpoints. Individual viewpoints are not sacrificed at the altar of communalization but are rather brought to 'communal givenness' through 'communal reflection'. The unity achieved through communalization is at least the thematization of individual diversity.

V

Every episode of communalization is an advance in the direction of what Husserl calls the "God-world" (*Gotteswelt*), understood as the *telos* of communalization, the ideal of maximal, apperceptive interpenetration of finite minds. The God-world may be pictured as a cleverly constructed hall of mirrors in which every mirror reflects within itself every other without thereby forfeiting its own unique angle, its 'position'. The 'chamber' itself comprises the universal standpoint upon all standpoints, the 'science' of the point of view. Each 'mirror' (consciousness) has access to the ideally communalized metastance from which each consciousness, in its intersubjective relationships with each other consciousness, may be viewed.

At every pre-*Gotteswelt* stage of communalization, 'we', uttered on behalf of the universal intersubjective community of finite minds, is merely *de jure*. The teleology of communalization is the order in virtue of which mere claims-to-universality, indicated by the candid, though precommunalized, employment of 'we' are adjusted in such a way that each claimant is enabled to see all claims (including the claimant's own) *as claims* with respect to an object that stands, as it were, in their midst. But to say as much is to indicate, on the part of the agent of a merely *de jure* employment of 'we', an apperception of the precommunalized community of finite minds *as a totality*. Communalization is an advance in the direction of establishing a *de facto* universal 'we', an intersubjective *ego*.

VI

The world may be understood as an ideal, a *telos*: the indefinitely approximable, but nonetheless unattainable, synthesis of all perspectives. Each individual finite mind comprises, as it were, a 'perspective' upon the world. And the primal belief-in-the-world, the General Thesis, is the belief that all such 'perspectives' (minds) may be recognized as comprising a *world*: a *Gotteswelt*. The *Urdoxa*, whose 'bracketing' is the fundamental necessary condition for assuming the stance of transcendental reflection, is, then, our primal belief in the possibility of relatively approximating the *Gotteswelt*, our belief in the *Gotteswelt* as the ideal-pole that orients the process of communalizing 'synthesis' or 'coalescence'.

Every intersubjective situation, understood as the totality of personal indexical referents, the totality of actual finite minds referred to by such indexicals as 'I', 'you', 'the Other', and so on, has as its ideal possibility the realization of a synthesis of the perspectives of all minds in question, a synoptic view ideally accessible, through apperception, to each such mind. The achievement of such a synthesis of perspectives on the part of all finite minds within a given intersubjective situation is, of course, communalization. But it is important to see that communalization presupposes the possibility of apperceptive access to this synthesis.

The world is the approximable synthesis of the 'depicted scenes' of all 'world pictures' (minds). And the synthesis of all 'world pictures' *as such*, the synthesis of all 'media of depiction', is the vision apperceptively accessible to each communalizing 'I', a vision in which

> I am not *an* ego, who still has his *you*, his *we*, his total community of cosubjects in natural validity. All of mankind, and the whole distinction and ordering of the personal pronouns, has become a phenomenon within my epoche.[14]

the 'world for all' is the correlate of "the functioning system of egopoles."[15] And the *intersubjectivity phenomenon*, accessible through communalization, serves as the *telos* of *transcendental intersubjectivity*. Each finite mind contains the intersubjectivity phenomenon *in semine*, as it were, through its apperceptual grasp of its total intersubjective situation. The intersubjectivity phenomenon is apperceptually 'implicit' in the intentional experience of every object appreciated *as objective*.

VII

Over the preceding several decades the course of research into Husserl's work has brought to light and further articulated numerous philosophically significant aspects of Husserl's thought. At the present writing, however, many of Husserl's private musings and unfinished reflections still lie buried within his astonishingly prodigious *Nachlass*. Effort has not been spared in making at least important portions of the *Nachlass* accessible to philosophical readers. And as the recovery of Husserl's philosophical vision proceeds, we are enabled, with ever greater accuracy, to set forth Husserl's theological ideas.

Not least among those glimpses of Husserl's theology to be discovered within the *Nachlass* is the view of God as both *telos* and *entelechy* of the world process. And this aspect of Husserl's theology has not been without its discussants. As the culmination of our development of a philosophy of the divine envisionment, I shall turn now to the sorely neglected theological theme found in Husserl's somewhat speculative identification of the intersubjectivity phenomenon with the divine envisionment.

Husserl clearly entertains the notion of God as an 'All-Consciousness' that views the world *through* the intersubjectivity phenomenon. The intersubjectivity phenomenon *is* the divine field of consciousness, the 'world picture', or, as it might appropriately be called, the 'omniprofile' that reveals the world to the divine Ego. The All-Consciousness is the 'picture' of all finite 'pictures', the mind that embraces within its envisionment all minds. This comes out nowhere so clearly as in the posthumous *Intersubjectivity* texts compiled by Iso Kern. There Husserl is explicit that "God would not have . . . *one* visual field but as many as there were consciousnesses."[16] Or more precisely, the visual field of the All-Consciousness is the synoptic envisionment of the visual fields of all finite minds. Indeed, "God . . . sees the thing from one side (with *my* consciousness) and 'at the same time' from the other side (with the consciousness of the *Other*)."[17] There is a single *field of fields*—a *single* divine envisionment, which embraces a plurality of finite minds. The 'internal negation', as Sartre would have it, between one mind and another is 'taken up' into the metalogical field of divine consciousness. Indeed, if (as Sartre believes) in reflection "we are in the presence of a synthesis of two consciousnesses, one of which is consciousness *of* the other,"[18] we may understand the relationship between the divine mind and the universal intersubjective community of finite minds as a peculiar case of 'reflection' in which the reflecting consciousness is, of course, the divine All-Consciousness and in which there is a plurality of reflected consciousnesses, that is, the plurality of finite minds. The All-Consciousness is the 'science' of perspectives, the 'All-of-Monads'. The Husserlian God is the 'Stream' of all 'streams', within which is represented the flowing life of each finite mind.

> When I make present to myself two *cogitations* together, I cannot do otherwise than imagine them as in one time consciousness. . . . And do I not suppose a time in which all consciousnesses are arranged? Therefore my acts and those of an other have relationships of contemporaneity or temporal succession. They are therefore imaginable in *one* consciousness, which envisages these relationships, which therefore as an All-Consciousness has everything mental in itself in the way each individual consciousness has its own individual acts in a single temporal flow.[19]

This understanding of God makes clear certain of Husserl's rather obscure intimations in the *Ideas*. Without the complementation provided by the All-Consciousness, we find in Husserl's writings a many-one schema involving a plurality of individual monads as subjects of a single world-pole. The 'world picture' of each monad is 'absolute' in the sense of being 'self-verifying' or 'self-evident'. Yet Husserl speaks of a divine Being 'beyond the world' that transcends the 'absolute' (finite) consciousness.[20]

> It would . . . be an "Absolute" *in a totally different sense from the Absolute of Consciousness*, as on the other hand it would be a *transcendent in a totally different sense* from the transcendent in the sense of the world.[21]

This 'Absolute' is the Absolute Consciousness of all finite consciousnesses. The finite subject is not its own foundation. 'Absolute' though it may be, it has its roots in that which is *absolute* in the most profound sense. The divine Absolute 'transcends' each finite consciousness both in the direction of immanence, as the Absolute Subject of all subjects, and in the direction of transcendence, as the infinitely remote, relatively approximable, *omni-telos*, the Goal of all Goals, Object of all Objects. The Husserlian God is Alpha and Omega, Source and Destination. In its subjective aspect the All-Consciousness functions as the unitary subject-pole of all actual world experience. Thus,

> after abandoning the natural world, we strike in our course another transcendence, which is not given like the pure Ego immediately united to consciousness in its reduced state, but comes to knowledge in highly mediated form, standing over against the transcendence of the world as if it were its polar opposite. We refer to the transcendence of God.[22]

The All-Consciousness is the synthesis of all constituting subjectivity and the synthesis of all constituted objectivity.

The all-consciousness views the plurality of finite 'world pictures' *as 'pictures'*. It cannot be 'taken in' by the 'pictured scenes' of finite minds, though its 'sophistication' cannot be such as to inhibit access to the 'world scenes' available through such 'world pictures'. Inasmuch as each finite mind apprehends the intersubjectivity phenomenon through its apperceptual grasp of its total intersubjective situation, the All-Consciousness views each finite mind as that mind would view itself were it to reflect upon itself, in an ideally explicit way, as 'world picture'. And the All-consciousness also views the universal intersubjective community of finite minds as a whole as that community would view itself were it, through communalization, to reflect upon itself, again in an ideally explicit way, as a coordinated 'gallery' of 'world pictures'.

Implicit within the intentional experience of any object is an apperception of possible, alternative perceptual views of that object, each, in turn, apperceived as the view of some possible viewer. The richness of our immediate apperceptual grasp of an object may be represented in an ideally explicit, synoptic consciousness of such apperceived views—a consciousness that serves as the *telos* of the original intentional act. Though we may never succeed in fully explicating the apperceptual richness of any intentional act, we may still, to some degree, relatively approximate the act-*telos*, thus establishing a *direction toward* that *telos*. The act-*telos* may remain indefinitely remote, but at least we know in what direction its realization lies. Likewise, although we remain indefinitely remote from the *Gotteswelt* as the ideally explicit synoptic consciousness of apperceived world-viewings implicit within any act of world-viewing, every such act necessarily involves an 'empty' intending of the *Gotteswelt*. Every presencing act occurs, as it were, within the 'space' created by this empty reference. This 'space', however, this *tabula rasa*, or contentually indeterminate horizon, has its own peculiar unity. It is a 'space' to be filled, if at all, only by the fully realized *Gotteswelt*, and every 'stroke' upon this 'blank canvas' is to be taken as an effort in this direction. The unity of the emptily intended *Gotteswelt* is that of a synoptic vision of 'world pictures'. Hence, finally, the apperceptual thread unraveled from any intentional act is seen as terminating in an apperception of the Viewer of this synoptic view. The Husserlian God thus unites all such apperceptual strands. Every intentional act can be 'apperceptually unraveled' in two directions. At one extremity the strands are joined in the Absolute Subject, and at the other extremity, in the Absolute Object. The dipolarity of the All-Consciousness is mediated by the intersubjective community. God sees the world *through* finite intersubjectivity.

Thus far, of course, we have considered Husserl's God only as the object of prethematized anticipations. Yet anticipations are notoriously falsifiable. Might it not, then, turn out that both view and Viewer are merely inactual possibilities; that, though it remains the case that *were* God to exist, God *would* see the world through finite intersubjectivity, nonetheless there is no God? Can phenomenology deliver the *existence* of God, or merely the *essence*?

It bears emphasizing that the General Thesis of the natural attitude, the underlying commitment-to-the-reality-of-the-world that Husserl regarded as the primal presupposition for the truth or falsity of any mundane belief, *is* a commitment to the relative approximability of the *Gotteswelt*. Even in phenomenological reflection the *Urdoxa* is not eliminated. Phenomenological reflection involves a reflective investigation of the *Urdoxa* and would undercut its own possibility were the *Urdoxa* to disappear under phenomenological scrutiny. As such, the *Urdoxa* is an adamant necessity of both the natural and reflective life of the mind. We cannot cease believing in the possibility of relatively approximating the *Gotteswelt*. Every intentional act involves a reference to the *Gotteswelt as absent*. And every act of presentation is a stage in the progressive fulfillment of this 'empty' reference. The *Gotteswelt* must, then, be grasped as progressively *presentable*. To understand the *Gotteswelt* is to understand it as *there-to-be-presented*. We thus have an 'ontological' (or more precisely, phenomenological) argument for the existence of a universal view of all views. Its existence (presentability) is implicit in our understanding of it. And, needless to say, having secured the existence of the view, the existence of the Viewer is no less necessary than the intuition that views are viewed.

Every episode of communalization on the part of the intersubjective community represents a phase in the fulfillment of the *Gotteswelt*. That constancy underlying the variety of possible fulfillment stages is *Reason*, the subject-form that makes possible the intending of any object whatsoever. The *Gotteswelt*, the object-form or intentional objectivity as such, is the highest genus of *esse apparens*. *Logos* is the subject-form of *telos*. Thus, writes Husserl,

> in the general process of idealization, which proceeds from philosophy, God is logicized, so to speak; indeed he becomes the bearer of the absolute *logos*.[23]

Reason and Truth are inseparable. The universal advance of consciousness in the direction of making explicit the structure implicit in every possible presentation of the world is an advance in the direction of the self-reflection of the All-Consciousness.

Notes

1. Edmund Husserl, conversation with Edith Stein, cited in R. Dumareau, "Un témoin de la lumière: Edith Stein," in Les Etudes philosophiques, nouvelle série, 2 (1955), 238–249, quoted in Henry Duméry, *Critique et Religion: Problèmes de méthode en philosophie de la religion* (Paris: Société d'Édition d'Enseignement Supérieur, 1957), 165.

2. Volume IX of *Analecta Husserliana* is rich in insights concerning Husserl's phenomenology of God. Of particular interest are contributions by Stephan Strasser, "History, Teleology, and God in the Philosophy of Husserl"; Angela Ales Bello, "Teleology as 'The Form of All Forms' and the Inexhaustibility of Research"; Mario Sancipriano, "Teleology and the Constitution of Spiritual Forms"; A. L. Kelkel, "History as Teleology and Eschatology: Husserl and Heidegger"; and Pierre Trotignon, "The End and Time."

3. Husserl explicitly declares that

God is not the universe of monads itself but rather the entelechy residing in the universe of monads as the idea of the infinite telos of development of the absolute.

Edmund Husserl, *Zur Phaenomenologie der Intersubjectivitaet: Texte Aus Dem Nachlass*, Pt. II, Iso Kern, ed. (The Hague: Martinus Nijhoff, 1973), 380. I am indebted to Professor James G. Hart for his translation of this and all subsequent passages cited from the *Intersubjectivity* texts. Toulemont's statement that "*la perfection absolue que visent tous les êtres à travers et par delà les réalisations relatives, c'est Dieu*" indicates how God may be conceived both as *entelechy* and as *telos*. As *entelechy*, God is that which 'aims' in all intentional 'aiming'; and as *telos*, God is the teleological 'target'. René Toulemont, *L'Essence de la société selon Husserl* (Paris: Presses Universitaires de France, 1962), 276.

4. Dorion Cairns, "An Approach to Phenomenology," in Marvin Farber, ed., *Philosophical Essays in Memory of Edmund Husserl* (New York: Greenwood Press, 1968), 3.

5. Duméry's reflections run in perfect alignment:

Philosophy always comes after life. Philosophy is a recovery of life, but it cannot be identified with life. . . . There exist . . . two planes that must never be confounded: the *speculative plane* and the *concrete plane*. They are distinct yet interdependent. Reflection lives on concrete life. For its part, the concrete would never become "reason" and system without a technically reflected ordering.

Henry Dumery, *The Problem of God in Philosophy of Religion*, translated by Charles Courtney (Evanston: Northwestern University Press, 1964), 5–6.

6. Edmund Husserl, *Drei Vorlesungen ueber Fichtes Menschheitsideal*, MS. F I 22, 25, quoted in Stephan Strasser, "History, Teleology, and God in the

Philosophy of Husserl," Tymieniecka, ed., *Analecta Husserliana*, vol. IX, 325–326.

7. Jean-Paul Sartre, *Being and Nothingness: An Essay in Phenomenological Ontology*, translated by Hazel E. Barnes (New York: Washington Square, 1971).

8. *Ibid.*, 396.

9. *Ibid.*, 396.

10. *Ibid.*, 314.

11. *Ibid.*, 400.

12. Thomas Prufer, "An Outline of some Husserlian Distinctions and Strategies, Especially in 'The Crisis,' " in *Phaenomenologische Forschungen* 1 (1975), 95.

13. Edmund Husserl, *The Crisis of European Sciences and Transcendental Phenomenology: An Introduction to Phenomenological Philosophy*, translated by David Carr (Evanston: Northwestern University Press, 1970), 163–164.

14. *Ibid.*, 184.

15. *Ibid.*, 186.

16. Husserl, *Intersubjectivity* I, 9.

17. *Ibid.*, 9.

18. Jean-Paul Sartre, *The Transcendence of the Ego: An Existentialist Theory of Consciousness*, translated by Forrest Williams and Robert Kirkpatrick (New York: The Noonday Press, 1972), 44.

19. Husserl, *Intersubjectivity* I, 18–19. The context of this text requires caution and reserve toward the conclusion that this is Husserl's definitive position.

20. Edmund Husserl, *Ideas: General Introduction to Pure Phenomenology*, translated by W. R. Boyce Gibson (London: Collier-Macmillan, 1969), 158.

21. *Ibid.*, 158.

22. *Ibid.*, 157.

23. Husserl, *Crisis*, 288.

JAMES BUCHANAN

9. The Rhetorics of Appropriation/Transgression: Postmodernity and Religious Discourse

This essay is an attempt to indicate some of the implications of Husserlian phenomenology for post-Husserlian philosophical and theological discourse. It will focus on the work of two who are arguably the most important of the post-Husserlian thinkers, Paul Ricoeur and Jacques Derrida. What makes them interesting for the present volume is that they both began their careers in conversation with Husserl and have pursued that conversation in radically different directions, both of which can be characterized as 'postmodern'. Given the impossibility of a rigorously argued presentation of the positions represented by Ricoeur and Derrida, the essay will attempt to sort out their positons at a rhetorical level. This strategy has been chosen for two reasons: first, it is, one hopes, an interesting and new way of approaching the subject at hand, and second, it is consistent with the positions of the two thinkers under examination, both of whom in very different ways have moved rhetorics to the forefront of their thinking. Given the emphasis of both thinkers upon the metaphorical nature of language, the essay should not be expected to address every philosophical conundrum that may arise or that has arisen in the extended dialogue between Ricoeur and Derrida or between each of them and Husserl. Rather the essay attempts to be 'true' to their intention by remaining metaphorical and rhetorically suggestive throughout.

I. From a Revelation of the Word to a Rhetoric of Words

I am not what I am (P. Ricoeur, "Negativity and Primary Affirmation,"
p. 311).
  The project is inserted into the future of the world which world
includes voids, the indeterminate, the nonresolved. . . . The world is
such that it can be the object of provision and of projects. (P. Ricoeur,
The Phenomenology of Will and Action, pp. 17–18).
  Word has the power to change our understanding of ourselves.
This power does not originally take the form of an imperative. . . .
Word addresses itself to our existence as effort and desire. (Ricoeur,
"Religion, Atheism and Faith," p. 454.)

Heidegger tells us that the history of being in the West is
dominated by ontotheological constructions that act as the
metaphysical guarantors of presence.[1] From Plato to Husserl the ideal
of presence has fascinated the human mind, a fascination that has
resulted in the construction of a wide variety of philosophical and
theological paths seeking its actualization. Among the most interesting, influential, and intricately constructed of these paths is the
transcendental phenomenology of Edmund Husserl. I want to address
briefly the theological dimension of transcendental phenomenology.[2]
  As is well known, presence for Husserl is egologically founded.
Transcendental phenomenology constructs an ontology in which being is equated with being-known.[3] It accomplishes this by defining
regions of being, which are hierarchized according to criteria of adequation. The process of adequation is one in which Husserl begins his
career with a theory of signs[4] and constructs a path of reductions into
a transcendental realm in which those signs might be fulfilled.[5] The
whole 'method' of transcendental phenomenology is based upon a
number of presuppositions that defy attempts at proof and that in fact
constitute the unquestioned background beliefs of the
phenomenological project.[6] Primary among these is absolute faith on
Husserl's part in a region of consciousness in which being is presence;
further, and more importantly, is his conviction that, given an adequate method, we might be able to bring this presence to expression.[7]
Transcendental phenomenology attempts to supply us with an ariad-
nean thread, which will lead us out of the density of history into that
realm in which there is a truth to be spoken, a language with which to
speak it, and a self that might speak. It is an act of will based upon a
faith, a faith powerful enough to justify the commitment to the 'infinite tasks' of phenomenology.[8]

Transcendental phenomenology extrapolates a region of general presences from a region of apperceptive presence. Inasmuch as apperceptive presence is the final criterion for critical consciousness, as a region it cannot be 'proved' but only 'experienced' as the unity of experience itself. This experience of unity is taken as more than the illusion of unity based upon the assumption that as a transcendental unity it is founded as presence. Thus as the unity of apperception this ego is necessarily a transcendental ego. The background of the unity of apperception and the transcendental ego as well as the implications of these for the possibility of transcendental community is a faith in presence.[9]

In this region of apperceptive unity the practice of radical reflection is abandoned to a moment of pure manifestation, a moment in which the possibility embodied in words is transformed into the saturating presence of the WORD.[10] It is a moment of identity worthy of a God or of that which bears within it the Image of a God. In this region that which began by an act of will and proceeded along a path of radical reflection is transformed into a purely participating revelation. It is revelatory because it guarantees that the Being of being-known is Being-itself and that the presence to/of self and to/of other is Presence-itself. It is a region in which words achieve their fullness and every word reveals itself as the WORD.[11]

The infinite tasks of transcendental phenomenology are onto-theological tasks, which set for themselves nothing short of the goal of revelatory presence in which our absolute participation and presence is guaranteed by the saturating presence of a Divine Envisionment.[12] In following Husserl's career, one cannot help but be struck by the manner in which he, the more his project is challenged by the contingencies of the historical subject, ever more tenaciously holds to his faith in the WORD.

But it is the 'infinity' of those tasks and the de facto situation (this side of infinity) that presence is deferred (we might say infinitely deferred) that interests us. Without the presence of an Absolute Consciousness, which necessarily speaks all words as the WORD, the project of phenomenology is left without *telos*, without hope. We can speak of this infinite deferral in terms of each of the three things necessary for the project of phenomenology to 'succeed', namely, a truth to be spoken, a self to speak it, and a language with which to speak it. Beginning with the latter two, what we see in the progress of Husserl's career as well as in the Heideggerian critique is that the density of human subjectivity increasingly destructs the project of transcendental phenomenology.[14] The method of reduction enters this density only to find that each attempt to clear away by bringing to light and bracketing results is yet another layer of historical entanglements, which must be encountered and bracketed.[15] The perspectival subject remains ever so in a historical density that affords no pure point from which to see or speak. Likewise, language itself takes on a historical density, which no amount of reductive purification can pierce.[16] Between infinitely deferred presence and the words desiring its achievement there is a gap that can only be filled by faith.[17] Faith then is not just a faith in presence; it is the only genuine presence that is possible, but now as an always already absent/presence that must face itself in the infinite gap. What is revealed in the present as faith is revealed in the infinite as presence. Husserl's ontotheology is so permeated by the presence of faith and hope that they form the unquestioned background of his project of radical reflection, constituting the ultimate horizon of the 'natural attitude' that phenomenology seeks to bring to light.[18]

A faith that must face itself in its own absent/presence suffers from a crisis of words, and a faith that would bind itself to reason becomes dependent upon these words-in-crisis. The necessity of binding faith to reason follows from Husserl's demand that we be able to proclaim the presence we come to see.[19] The project of transcendental phenomenology is built upon the faith and the hope of enabling humanity to witness and communicate the WORD in words. His faith is bound to reason because he would have the revelation it presences be intersubjective. For Husserl, presence must be communicable presence; he would have us be able to speak and understand the WORD.

In the end his project cannot but fall prey to those exigencies of the gap, those words-in-crisis full of desire yet always already infinitely deferred. This side of the WORD there are no words that adequately express presence, or should we say, there are nothing but words for it, endless, interconnecting webs of words, which lack the criteria that issue from a presence that for them is absent.

If we admit that presence is absent (as even Husserl does), the gap becomes an opening opened by/to the questioning that characterizes it.[20] The gap is infinitely opened, with no determinate presence save the absent/presence of faith-and-hope-in-question. Mediately (in the gap) the hierarchies of words are at best ambiguous. The ambiguity is so basic that the criteria of hierarchy suffer from that which they would claim to remedy. This ambiguity can take on a viciousness when we realize the awesome materiality of words in which hierarchies of words manifest institutionally and in which institutions become not the "fragments of freedom attempting to realize themselves"[21] but embodiments of the will-to-self-preservation, which mistake their own power for truth.

The crisis of words in the absence of the Presence of the WORD leads us from revelation to rhetorics. Life in the gap (and we do not say the abyss)[22] allows for no inherent hierarchies of words; rather, those hierarchies are worked out in complex webs of intersubjective exchange. Within the restricted economies available to words-in-crisis, axiological criteria are not determined by transcendental norms but by the system of exchange we call rhetorics.[23]

To enter the region where rhetoric reigns is to enter a region in which the potential for anarchy is as great as the potential for tyranny. It is a realm in which words mask their absence with varying degrees of seriousness and varying degrees of success. It is a realm in which words are actively purposeful, engaging in everything from conversation to coercion in order to be persuasive of exigencies that are determined by their own faith and hope for the absent/presence.[24] Such exigencies may be as divergent as is the will-to-truth from the will-to-power; the distinction between them too often collapses altogether. The realm of rhetorics is one in which the transcendentally signified is infinitely deferred, thus pitting signifier against signifier in infinite struggles of signification. It is a region in which the hierarchies that emerge from these struggles may well be the only stakes of the play. Rhetoric is the realm of the effective use of words for a purpose, even if the purpose or the criteria for validating the purpose are ultimately missing. It is words at their most self-referential, in that the *what* to which they refer is actually the exigency or the project for which they proclaim and of which they seek to persuade. An exigency for which they would claim a greater proximity to a revelation, which *de facto* is that *of which* they hope to be persuasive as well as the *de jure* source of their capacity to persuade, is in any case only an absent/presence.

II. The Metaphor of Voice and the Voice of Metaphor

The metaphor of the home is really 'a metaphor for metaphor: expropriation, being away from home, but still in a home but in someone's home, a place of self-recovery, self-recognition, self-mustering,

> self-resemblence: it is itself. Ths philosophical metaphor as a detour in (or in view of) the reappropriation, the second coming, the self-presence of the idea in its light. A metaphorical journey from the Platonic eidos to the Hegelian Idea. (Jacques Derrida, "the White Mythology," p. 55.)

The self, the truth, and God are buried in the density of words not yet become the WORD. Lacking the enlightenment of revelation or intuition, words can only feign referentiality, and then only within localized economies such as the text.[25] Words always find themselves on the way, in the nonstate of never having arrived, condemned to the incessant search for a way to proceed in their quest to become the presence of the WORD. They grope homeward in the darkness in catachrestic spasm of light which we call metaphor. Words figure and refigure the gap, giving it voice, in the hope that one day (the coming day) they will get it right and speak the cosmos as Self, Truth, and God. Catachresis[26] is the process of words, particularly those words searching for the WORD, words that hear the absent/presence as an acute and demanding voice. *De facto* all words, all language, is metaphorical, regardless of its *de jure* claim/desire for itself.[27] Thus metaphor is language recognizing its own need to proceed, language unsatisfied by its own event and drawn by the absent/presence of the event of revelation.

Rhetorically metaphor struggles against itself. First, it constantly forgets itself, a forgetfulness that allows the word to become its own myth.[28] Its mask is worthy of nothing less than the WORD, as desire and will veil its existence in the gap. Language that so forgets itself becomes moribund, its forgetfulness a suicide of sorts, rendering itself up for sacrifice in order to become the WORD of God by right of amnesia. Metaphor forgets its inherent metaphoricity by an act of will-to-truth—a double bind, which must forget itself in order to claim itself.[29] It must forget its own metaphoricity, the truth of the truth*less*ness of the gap, in order to claim itself as the truth of presence.

Second, metaphor constantly runs the risk that, due to embodiment within rhetorical economies, it will mistake its exchange value within those economies for proximity to the Presence of Revelation.[30] Thus in an act of forgetfulness, identification is mistaken for identity, and persuasion is mistaken for Presence. As metaphors institute themselves, they often fall prey to a will-to-self-preservation. But metaphor, in acknowledging its own metaphoricity, understands itself as but a moment of language in process, a moment that lives only as a catachrestic event. Institutionalized forgetfulness leads not only to the mythologies of sight but also to the political technologies that empower those mythologies, just as the mythologies of sight legitimate the political technologies.

III. Transgression/Appropriation: the Rhetorics of the Word

> The virgin remains ungraspable, dying without murder, swooning, withdrawing into her future beyond every possibility promised to anticipation. Alongside of the night as anonymous rustling of the *there is* extends the night of the erotic, behind the night of insomnia the night of the hidden, the clandestine, the mysterious, land of the virgin—simultaneously uncovered by *Eros* and refusing *Eros*. (Levinas, *Totality and Infinity*, p. 258.)

The question that remains concerns the exigencies from which and for which words rhetorically muster themselves within discourses that we call religious. Shy of the revelation of the WORD, we live the life of the gap, rhetorically forging and foraging, wagering words based upon mere glimpses of the Divine Face. Such glimpses we may trust or not, as we trust ourselves or not, and as we trust our words or not. The questioning, which must be faced in the gap, concerns the exigencies of the glimpse and of one's responsibility to those exigencies, given that that to which we seek response is an absent/presence. It first demands our acknowledgement that responsibility itself can only manifest as a questioning. The nature of the glimpse is that it opens a space of possibility which always manifests as an interrogative knowing—a knowing that knows the openness of the situation above any knowing of what might adequately fill that openness.[31] It is a question nevertheless *presenting* itself as an exigency which must be addressed by a wager. Into the gap we must wager a project in response to the demand made upon us by that glimpse of the absent/presence of the WORD.

The contemporary scene offers us two bold wagers in response to the exigencies of the WORD and two powerful voices, which in turn make demands upon those of us less gifted with sight or voice. Paul Ricoeur and Jacques Derrida both began their careers in deep conversation with Husserl and emerged as philosophers of infinite tasks in their own right, but adrift in a manner quite different from Husserl's.[32] For these are dwellers of the gap, and the voices they present are in-response to the exigencies of that dwelling. There is surprisingly little disagreement between them as to the *fact* of that dwelling; their differences concern, rather, what they believe to be the exigencies of that fact and thus the responsibility demanded.

Rhetorically they give voice to a polarity that is basic to religious discourse, a polarity that is important *as* polarity. Thus, my argument will be that it is not necessary to choose between them but that we need to learn to dwell dialectically between the extremes to which they give voice.[33]

I would first characterize the two voices in which they speak as *theoretical* and *practical*, although, as we shall see, even this characterization breaks down. From the beginning of his career, Ricoeur's concern has been with philosophies of praxis. By this concentration upon the problem of the will, both early and late in his corpus, he has focused his work upon the problem of human action. For Ricoeur, freedom is a doing done within the limitations of life in the gap. The point of words is not their status as words (the crisis of the gap), but the discursive contexts within which they *do*, in which projects reach presentation. His interest is not in the theoretical quandary, which he admits, nor is his concern with the famed speaking/writing debate.[34] For Ricoeur words exist discursively. This shifts the problem of language beyond theoretical distinctions into a practical realm, which must confront the problems of communication and the enabling of language to *do* something. Ricoeur's confrontation with the WORD demands of him that he discursively present himself within a hermeneutics of hope, which is founded within the possibility of *communitas*. This hope is in turn based upon a faith, not far removed from that of Husserl. It is a hope for a universal history of humankind, not as a metaphysical problem but as a practical one. Ricoeur does not seek to overcome the ambiguity and contingency of the historical but to search for the possibilities within that situation. While Husserl's voice always issues from the transcendental standpoint, urging us toward self-responsibility, transcendental community, and a revelation of the WORD that can be spoken, Ricoeur's voice issues from the gap; thus his hope is a thoroughly historical hope, which does not seek ways to speak the WORD but rather ways discursively to manifest the fragmented glimpses we receive of it. The decentering of the cosmos and the self is confronted in terms of the practical ramifications. The *Other* for Ricoeur is always the *Practical Other*.

Ricoeur's rhetoric urges us toward appropriation. Whereas the text as context of discourse[35] is the objectification of participation, appropriation is the subjectification of participation.[36] It demands of us that we *act as if* we were the subject, the virginal home that our situation never allows. It demands of us the commitment to projects that hold within them the possibility of light in the face of darkness, the possibility of meaningful action in the face of meaninglessness. To appropriate is to *do* what is appropriate. It is to commit to horizons of action, which extend as far as I can see and which are critically polarized by what I cannot see, that of which I may only receive a glimpse—the always already absent/presence.

Derrida has little concern for the practical. This does not mean that there are no implications for praxis in his work, for in a sense his theoretical concerns are a form of praxis.[37] But the power of his rhetoric remains at a theoretical level and its importance to our dialectic must be approached at this level. Derrida figures the gap transgressively speaking in a voice that has no faith in, or even hope for, glimpses of the WORD. For Derrida the glimpse is just enough to blind us and never enough to guide us. The only possible insight is into our blindness.[38] Such an insight transforms the gap into a abyss, a projectless falling in endless free play, a falling that dances with the darkness rather than attempting to enlighten it. It is the voice that issues from the hopelessness of any wager made in the abyss to manifest even a remnant of presence. It is the voice of *theoria* speaking, with a detachment that only *theoria* can afford.[39] Derrida'a voice is the voice within voice; it is the silence that nevertheless always speaks and has always already spoken. It is the infinity of the gap inscribing, iterating, irritating.[40] Rhetorically it demands that our every attempt to come to voice listen to the infinite cacophony of voice and silence that plays this side of the WORD. If Ricoeur is the voice of the absent/PRESENCE, Derrida is the voice of the ABSENT/presence. Whereas we might hear the voice of Ricoeur calling us to the possibility of cosmos, Derrida calls with the voice of chaos. He would argue that we cannot act from where we stand, that we cannot appropriate, inasmuch as we and where we stand are always already missing-in-action.

The death of the God of the ontotheological tradition marks also the death of language and of the self. It is a death accomplished by the ongoing act of decentering. Human being, language, in fact all of what we term reality, is left without, centerless. From the nonperspective of decentered reality, all is *Other* (including the self). Our relationship with the Other is that which is manifest in the projects that we wager. The breadth of this relationship may reach from terror to love. For Derrida the Other is irreducibly Other and is thus but a point in the endless free play of possibilities, all of which are equally impossibilities. The Other is for him a theoretical exigency that only secondarily exists within a sphere of practicality and action. The radical activity of Derridian reflection is autoerotic in that his relationship to the Other occurs only in a radically decentered intertextuality, which manifests as a deconstructed autodiscourse. *Theoria* is self-contained activity, even if the self in question is always in question. For Derrida the exigency is not to learn from the tradition so much as to show its failings, to indicate from the inside out the inadequacy that it has too often denied— a denial that has as often had dire consequences.[41] Tradition, *sensus communis*, in fact any court of appeal of the practical sphere, fall before the blade of Derrida's mighty, theoretical scythe. He would no more submit his voice to the consensus of community than he would appeal to standards such as reason, truth, and so on. He is not merely a peripheral voice seeking the center but a voice that issues vocationally from the periphery, standing just outside all attempts at truth, reasonableness, and meaning, bearing witness to the double bind, the penetration, the invagination inherent to all such attempts. Following his many reversals of traditional hierarchies, Derrida opts for the supplement of the autoerotic life of *theoria* without feeling the need to reemerge into *communitas*.

For Ricoeur, community is the locus of the hopeful, faithful speculations,[42] which he would grant make no theoretical difference at all but which might make practical differences. Even his moments of suspicion never attain the radicality of the Derridian voice. Ricoeur sees no freedom in free play; rather, he would have us search for freedom as a *doing* within the limits of human communities and human praxis. The pure life of *theoria* is for him no purer than the life of *praxis*, and he would claim that the distinction is in fact a false one. The danger of the deconstructionist position (and note that I am giving it the ideological status of an ism) is that its oblivion becomes so seductive that it can lead to a social catatonia that sees no point in responding to the practical problems which face us. If Derrida is autoerotic in his deconstructive praxis, Ricoeur practices an *eros* of *communitas*, trusting consensus where possible and searching for new possibilities for action where suspicion demands.

In conclusion, let me sketch some of the implications of the rhetorics of transgression/appropriation for theology. First, the tendency to choose between the approaches of Ricoeur and Derrida as if they were 'systems' of thought forgets the fundamental situation out of which both voices issue. Ontological difference, regardless of the radicality or exigencies of its constitution, marks the end of all systematic theology in the traditional sense.[43] Thus to appropriate the work of either Ricoeur or Derrida for a new systematics is contrary to the projects of either. Revelation, which issues as the WORD, hypostasizes into the concealment of an endless interplay of words, which no systemic cement can recollect. The rhetoric of both Ricoeur and Derrida herald the end of systematic theology, the varieties of which have typified the ontotheological tradition. Systematic theology is exposed as the body of myths legitimating institutional sites of power, little more than an extremely sophisticated manifestation of the will-to-power.[44] This realization of the linguistic nature of theology further obscures the boundaries between truth and fiction, science and art. Following the same line of thinking, it is apparent that the theologies of the Word that typify 'proclamation' traditions must now seek the balance of a 'manifestation' orientation.[45] The assumed superiority of the western tradition must now look beyond its old borders in new ways, ways that listen seriously to voices old and new from other traditions.[46] The ontological exigency demands that new practical theologies become the locus of speculation replacing the metaphysical speculations of the past.[47] Finally, the retorics of transgression demand of theology a new 'atheology'.[48] Atheology is not a new voice but a voice that issues from the margins and from the heart of what the tradition has considered to be theology. It is thus a theology caught in a double bind—seeking to preserve the integrity of traditions whose fundamental ambiguities have been revealed; it is a theology that, along with the rest of the dwellers of the gap, must struggle for self-identity while acknowledging that it can never again totally trust whatever sense of identity emerges from that struggle.[49]

The new situation heralded by the rhetorical turn demands that the new theology change in both style and substance. As we have seen, the new modality can be characterized as fundamentally disruptive to the tradition. It is a disruption that issues from three sources, each of which has previously been without voice in the tradition and has now come to voice with truly threatening and truly promising relevance. The first, and perhaps most unsettling, is the internal disruption to the ontotheological tradition that is inherent to the

nature of the world, to the self, and to language. Theology is unraveled from within and must find a way in which to address its own
deconstruction. Second, theology is disrupted by the voice of the
cross-cultural other. To ignore or reduce this other is no longer a
tolerable response. Third, a disruption is issuing from the 'underside
of history', from those nonpersons of history who have irrupted on
the scene with demands that speak in a compelling new voice.[50] This
disruption has found expression in the political and liberation
theologies, which demand that the tradition be reinterpreted and
relocated in the face of such radically negating historical events as the
Holocaust and the suffering of the poor.[51] The demand of the rhetorics
of transgression for theology is that it somehow find the resources to
speak the margins and allow the margins to speak themselves. The
challenge to theology is that it find new possibilities for appropriation
within this disruption, that it face its future in the gap rather than in
some divine altitude above it.

The voices of both Ricoeur and Derrida issue from moments of
being to which we need be responsible. Both are moments of being
that religious discourse has always attempted to address.[52] Religious
discourse rhetorically calls us to an Other that is beyond possibility,
beyond good and evil, beyond all meaning—but it also calls upon us
to engage in 'possibilizing' activity, to wager meaning and the Good. It
is that Otherness that demands of us not to mytholigize our institutions just because we must institutionalize our mythologies. While the
life of *theoria* in the Derridean sense cannot provide the guideposts
that would show us the way, it serves to rupture the boundaries that
surely keep us from its dynamic manifestation. While the life of praxis
is a wager from poverty at best, it forces us into face-to-face confronta-
tions with the only transcendence *assuredly* available to us—the concrete other. It is in the tension represented by the rhetorics of trans-
gression/appropriation that we religiously dwell—each is at once
anathema and necessary to the other. An appropriation that ceases to
respond to the demands of the rhetorics of transgression becomes
stagnant and repressive in its institutional willfullness. It fails to
acknowledge that, even in the light of hope, we always dance with the
darkness. Transgression that ceases to respond to the demands of appropriation becomes detached and self-absorbed, thus failing to be
responsible to the demands of its own concretion. It fails to
acknowledge that even in the abyss we must manifest a will-to-risk,
which wagers in the light of hope. Religiously we are strung on the

tensions of the voices of appropriation/transgression, always already playing and being played, dancing with the darkness in the light of hope.

Notes

1. See Martin Heidegger, *The End of Philosophy* (New York, 1973); *An Introduction to Metaphysics*, trans. by Ralph Manheim, Harper & Row, (New York: Doubleday/Anchor Books, 1961.)

2. The suggestion of taking a theological perspective on Husserl's work originates with Steven Laycock and James Hart. See *Foundations for a Phenomenological Theology* by Steven Laycock (forthcoming).

3. This is one way of stating the basic idealist position. Husserl stands at the end of the idealist tradition marking its culmination as well as its demise. See for example: P. Ricoeur, *Husserl: An analysis of his Phenomenology*, trans. by Edward Ballard and Lester Embree (Evanston: Northwestern University Press, 1967); M. Heidegger, *The Basic Problems of Phenomenology*, trans. by Albert Hofstadter (Bloomington: Indiana University Press, 1982); V. Descombes, *Modern French Philosophy*, trans by L. Scott Fox and J. M. Harding (Cambridge: Cambridge University Press, 1980).

4. See E. Husserl, *Logical Investigation I*, trans by J. N. Findlay (New York: Humanities Press, 1970); J. Derrida, *Speech and Phenomena,* trans by David B. Allison (Evanston: Northwestern University Press, 1973); E. Husserl, *The Origin of Geometry* (New York: Nicholas Hays, 1977).

5. E. Husserl, *Ideas I*, trans. by W. R. Boyce-Gibson (New York: Humanities Press, 1972) and most of the subsequent work. Also see Derrida, *Speech and Phenomena*.

6. See P. Ricoeur, *Husserl*; Derrida, *Speech and Phenomena* and his introduction to *The Origins of Geometry* trans. by John P. Leary (New York: Nicholas-Hays 1977).

7. Husserl often spoke in terms of 'infinite tasks' and of the phenomenologist as an eternal 'beginner'. It is the infinity of these tasks that results in *de jure/de facto* contradictions in Husserl's work. The project rests ultimately upon the *telos*, which is infinitely deferred. It is this deferral that Husserl is admitting when he speaks of 'infinite tasks', a deferral that is in the end bridgable only by faith.

8. The precise nature of presence in Husserl is debatable. My own claim is that *de jure* presence, which can be brought to expression, plays a central and motivating role in Husserl's rhetoric.

9. See, for example, René Toulemont, *L'Essence de la Société selon Husserl* (Paris: Gallimard, 1962). See also Laycock, *Foundations*.

10. My use of WORD refers to the pure revelatory presence of subject and object mediated by words. The reason words become the WORD is that, like the WORD of God, they become the transcendental signifiers/signifieds that 'manifest' presence.

11. For a better idea of the perspective that I have adopted on so-called 'theologies of the Word' see David Tracy, *The Analogical Imagination: Christian Theology and the Culture of Pluralism* (New York: Crossroads, 1981) 202–231, 286ff., 386–393. Theologians such as Karl Barth and Rudolf Bultmann and the many thinkers in their traditions also represent theologies of the Word.

12. "Divine envisagement" is drawn from the work of Steven Laycock. In his forthcoming work, he describes divine envisionment as "the 'field' of consciousness mediating divine intentional access to the world-pole" arguing that "the intersubjective totality of finite minds is precisely identical with the divine envisagement." I cannot recapitulate Laycock's argument except to point out that his operative notions concern the internal relatedness of finite minds and thus the possibility of Presence in the form of "the intersubjective community *as a whole*". When I speak of the 'glance' that is available to the dwellers of the gap, I am referring to something like Laycock's notion of the 'divine envisagement' and trying to explore the ramifications of that glance both hermeneutically and deconstructively.

13. Edmund Husserl, *The Crisis of European Sciences and Transcendental Phenomenology*, trans. by David Carr (Evanston: Northwestern University Press, 1970). What we see in the progressive stages of Husserl's development is an increasing density of the constituting subject such that growing numbers of reductions are needed to achieve the pure transcendental ego. As David Carr has shown in *Phenomenology and the Problem of History* (Evanston: Northwestern University Press, 1974). Husserl adds a 'historical reduction' in *Crisis* in response to the challenges of the position of Heidegger and others. The point is that he never abandons his faith in transcendental phenomenology.

14. The term 'density' as applied to subjectivity is taken from Michel Foucault, *The Order of Things* (New York: Random House, 1970), 322ff. Also see Jacques Derrida, *Speech and Phenomenon* (Evanston, 1973), in which an analysis of Husserl's theory of signs in *The Logical Investigation* is criticized based upon a constituting subjectivity that is unable to reduce its historical density. This is also the point of Derrida's analysis in the introduction to *The Origins of Geometry*.

15. This is the point of Merleau-Ponty's oft-repeated phrase that "the most important lesson which the (transcendental) reduction teaches us is the impossibility of a complete reduction" in *The Phenomenology of Perception*, trans. by Colin Smith (London: Routledge & Kegan Paul, 1962), xiv.

16. J. Derrida's *Speech and Phenomenon* is the most direct example of this as applied to Husserl, but his entire corpus is built around this insight.

17. Husserl himself does occasionally use faith language, but my argument does not depend upon its overt presence in the texts. Rhetorically his work has a 'poetic prefiguration' that is founded in faith. For an idea of 'poetic prefiguration' see Hayden White, *Metahistory: The Historical Imagination in Nineteenth Century Europe* (Baltimore: John Hopkins University Press, 1973). It is obviously impossible to enter into the necessary discussion concerning the nature of faith. To speak in general terms we might say that faith is transformative by means of its ability to be transformative. It is faith that has the power to transform the absence of the gap into presence.

18. My point is that the naive faith in the world, which phenomenology is constructed to overcome, is replaced by yet a deeper faith in the possibility of bringing it to light.

19. Even if Husserl only held this as a *de jure* possibility, we must be aware of the history of effects of this belief.

20. The idea of the 'question of being' as the key to human being is of course Heidegger's. See also Ricoeur's "Heidegger and the Question of the Subject" in *Conflicts in Interpretation* (Evanston: Northwestern University Press, 1974).

21. The phrase is one that I have heard Paul Ricoeur use on a number of occasions. For examples see "La philosophie et la politique devant la question de la liberté," in *La Liberté et l'order social* (Genève: Recontres Internationales de Genève, 1969) and "The Problem of the Foundation of Moral Philosphy," in *Philosophy today* 22, 1978, 175–192.

22. 'Abyss' is Derrida's term. I do not accept it for reasons that will be made clear by this article. I have chosen to use the term 'gap' in order to relieve myself of the burdens of the history already attached to the term.

23. Rhetorical analysis has become important in many areas. In philosophy the debate between Ricoeur and Derrida not only concerns the nature of rhetorics but, as this article attempts to argue, can best be sorted out rhetorically. For the central writings of this discussion see in particular Derrida's "The White Mythology" in *Margins,* trans. by Alan Bass (Chicago: University of Chicago Press, 1982) and Ricoeur's *The Rule of Metaphor* Toronto, University of Toronto Press, 1977), pp. 257–315, the whole of which can be seen as a proposal against the deconstructionist position which he describes as "more seductive than earth-shaking", 291. Derrida's response can be found in "The Retrait of Metaphor" in *Enclitic* 2, 1978, 5–33. Ricoeur responded to this in two lectures delivered in a course entitled "Speaking and Writing" at the University of Chicago in the winter of 1984. For the most part the conversation is a nonconversation. My own explanation for this is that the exigencies to which they feel compelled to respond are (as this article argues) so diametrically at odds that they are unable to find a common subject matter. Other important writers in the field of rhetorics are Kenneth Burke, *A Grammar of Motives and a Rhetoric of Motives* (New York: Meridien Books, 1962), *The Philosophy of Literary Form* (New York: Vintage, 1957), and *The Rhetoric of Religion* (Boston: Beacon Press, 1961); Wayne Booth, *The Rhetoric of Fic-*

tion (Chicago: University of Chicago Press, 1983) and *Critical Understanding* (Chicago: University of Chicago Press, 1979); Chaim Perelman and L. Olbrechts-Tyteca, *The New Rhetoric* (Notre Dame: University of Notre Dame Press, 1969), and Perelman's *The Realm of Rhetoric* (Notre Dame: Notre Dame Press, 1982); Christopher Norris, *The Deconstructive Turn: Essays in the Rhetoric of Philosophy*. (London: Methuen, 1983). Also of interest are Frank Lentricchia, *After the New Criticism* (Chicago: University of Chicago Press, 1980) and *Criticism and Social Change* (Chicago: University of Chicago Press, 1983); Fred Dallmayr, *Language and Politics* (Notre Dame: University of Notre Dame Press, 1984); Jonathan Culler, *The Pursuit of Signs* (Ithaca: Cornell University Press, 1981); Paul De Man, *Blindness and Insight: Essays in the Rhetoric of Contemporary Criticism* (New York: Oxford Press, 1971); and *Allegories of Reading: figural Language of Rouseau, Nietzsche, Rilke and Proust* (New Haven: Yale University Press, 1979).

24. My focus throughout will be upon the rhetorics of religious discourse; thus I tie the rhetorics in question to the faith and hope out of which such discourse issues.

25. While denying ostensive reference, Ricoeur does allow for a limited referentiality within the text itself. See *The Rule of Metaphor*, "Metaphor and Reference," 216ff. The referentiality here is within the 'world of the text', which is hermeneutically constituted by a three-tiered process that Ricoeur describes in terms of understanding-explanation-understanding. Ricoeur is interested in contexts of action and meaning; he maintains throughout his writings that meaning and, more importantly, meaningful action are both possible.

26. Both Derrida and Ricoeur tie words to their contexts (and intertexts) and continue by showing how contexts are subject to polysemic flux. "Polysemy attests to the quality of openness in the texture of the word: a word is that which has several meanings and can acquire more" (*The Rule of Metaphor*, 117). Metaphors operate catachrestically because they attempt to express that which has not been previously expressed. To the degree that all language is metaphorical, all language is likewise catachrestic. My own claim is that this is acutely the case for religious discourse inasmuch as that which it attempts to express is always radically 'other'.

27. This is one of the possible implications not only of the work of Ricoeur and Derrida but of other philosophical writings. If one moves to the level of rhetorical analysis, the question at the heart of this discussion is both the possibility and nature of the referentiality of language. Derrida speaks, for example, of the absence of a transcendental signifier/signified. Ricoeur will allow for a modified notion of referentiality within the contextualized world of the text. I would argue that for both language is essentially metaphorical. This of course avoids the lengthy and interesting debate concerning natural languages and natural kinds. See, for example, Saul Kripke *Naming Necessity and Natural Kinds,* (Cambridge: Harvard University Press, 1979).

28. This is Derrida's point in "The White Mythology." Here 'myth' has double meaning: on the one hand it expresses the "really real" (Eliade's formulation), but on the other, it is the myth of the real in the sense that Horkheimer and Adorno use the term in *The Dialectics of Enlightenment* (New York: Herder & Herder, 1972). Inasmuch as Derrida is denying the presence of the really real, he sees the mythologization as a process of the reification in which the metaphor forgets its own dynamism, that is, forgets its own metaphorcity.

29. "Double bind" is Derrida's phrase. The classic examples of what is meant here are found in such well-known paradoxes as: All Cretans are liars and I am a Cretan. Derrida and De Man have shown that all texts suffer from the same confusion and thus must be read against themselves. The double bind can be used to describe the metaphorical process as well. We may speak of the bind of the tenor/vehicle with the new meaning that issues from the process that is neither yet both.

30. The best analyses of rhetorical economies have been produced by Michel Foucault. His method, which archaeologically locates the discursive figures then genealogically analyzes them in terms of 'institutional sites of power', can be looked at as an economy of ideas. He draws our attention to the relationship existing between knowledge and power such that they collapse into knowledge/power complexes, which do not allow for an analysis of one without the other. Knowledge and power exist in a mutually constitutive relation that de facto constitutes truth according to the rules of exchange. This entails that even revelation is constituted within those rules but *de jure* legitimates the rules of exchange by the Presence of revelation.

31. The term *interrogative-knowing* is taken from Merleau-Ponty. See *The Visible and the Invisible*, trans. by Alphonso Lingis (Evanston: Northwestern University Press, 1964).

32. I have already mentioned the major works to which I refer. Ricoeur's *Husserl*, Derrida's *Speech and Phenomena* and *The Origins of Geometry*. There are also numerous articles by both writers on Husserl or Husserlian themes. The other figure with whom I am not dealing here is Emmanuel Levinas. In many ways he represents a mediating position between Ricoeur and Derrida. See his *The Theory of Intuition in Husserl's Phenomenology*, trans. by Andre Orianne (Evanston: Northwestern University Press, 1973); *Totality and Infinity* (Pittsburg, 1969); *Otherwise Than Being or Beyond Essence*, trans. by Alphonso Lingis (The Hague: Nijhoff, 1978).

33. The term *dialectically* is an uneasy one, inasmuch as it implies that some form of synthesis is possible between these positions or apositions. My thanks to Mark C. Taylor for pointing out that my use of the term is not consistent with its tradition.

34. The articles and books out of which this debate has been drawn have already been cited in footnote 21. As stated in that footnote, I do not feel that

genuine conversation between the two has taken place, due to the extreme differences in their positions. One way of understanding the distinction between speaking and writing is to look at the metaphors that play central roles within an overall rhetoric of each. They are as fundamentally different as the rhetorics of each man. Writing for Derrida is the event of language characterized as infinitely deferred meaning (presence), due to the inherent intertextuality of all language. Speaking, or more properly discourse, for Ricoeur is the event of language that seeks to accomplish something within a specific context. For both, the transcendentally signified is absent but the exigencies issuing from that absence are radically different.

35. Ricoeur's theory of discourse is a rich one and is in many ways the key to his philosophy. Rejecting Saussurian structuralism, he develops a theory of discourse based in part of Benveniste's writings. For Ricoeur, as for Benveniste, the basic unit of language is not the sign but the sentence. Unlike the sign, which obtains meaning only through difference, the sentence is a synthetic unit that integrates the smaller components into a domain in which things are communicated between people. In the discourse there is a dialectic of event and meaning in which language is actualized. With discourse the event aspect does not pass into oblivion but may become something more enduring. What endures is meaning. In Ricoeur's phrase, "discourse occurs as event but is understood as meaning." It is the sublation of event to meaning that is the key to discourse and it is the need and fact of human communication that is the key to discourse. It is crucial here to understand that Ricoeur has not suddenly abandoned his project of practical philosophy for an intramural inquiry into language. Rather, discourse ultimately emerges as the praxis of language. Language is the mediating event by means of which we do things. It is within the context of discourse that Ricoeur will retrieve the subject—not the theoretical subject, which has plagued modern philosophy, but the practical subject, the subject who must act in the world. For Ricoeur the retrieval of the subject within the text is best found in authorial style. What is interesting is that Ricoeur will parallel what goes on in the text (narrativity etc.) with the textuality of the practical life in which the style of one's lived narrative is of utmost importance. This is borne out by his recent concern with narrativity. See the first two volumes of a proposed three-volume work, *Time and Narrative*, trans. by Kathleen McLoughlin and David Pellauer (Chicago: University of Chicago Press, 1984).

36. This formulation is drawn from John W. Van Den Hengel's excellent study of Ricoeur entitled *The Home of Meaning* (Washington: University Press of America, 1982), 187 ff.

37. The implications of the deconstructive turn are a kind of negative praxis, which exposes the internal inconsistencies of any constructed position, philosophical or otherwise. One is drawn towards comparisons to Theodore Adorno's *Negative Dialectics* (New York: Seabury, 1979), although Derrida's critique is more fundamental. Also see Michael Ryan's *Marxism and Deconstruction: A Critical Articulation* (Baltimore: Johns Hopkins University Press, 1982).

38. See Paul De Man, *Blindness and Insight*.

39. Derrida's deconstruction is *theoria* in the best and the worst sense of the term. Aristotle tells us that *theoria* is an activity done at leisure. As such *theoria* is not beset by the practical concerns of daily living but is the essence of the contemplative life (see particularly Book X of the *Nicomachean Ethics*). Thus detachment is not a pejorative but a necessary dimension of human being, which acts as a corrective to the blindness of practical living. It is interesting to turn back to the Frankfurt School for comparisons here. In books such as *Theory and Practice*, trans. by John Vievtel (Boston: Beacon Press, 1968) and *Knowledge and Human Interests*, trans. by Verony J. Shapiro (Boston: Beacon Press, 1971), and continuing on to his most recent works on communicative action, Jurgen Habermas has insisted upon the importance of critical theory as a corrective for human praxis. Derrida's *theoria* is even more radical, inasmuch as it deconstructs any and every attempt to construct a critical theory. It is an unconstructed theory, or atheory. As such it may well be as pure a form of *theoria* as we can imagine. Deconstruction as contemplation functions as a corrective by means of a *via negativa*, which destructs all constructs from within. The *via negativa* is a dialectic of negativity much as we find in Ch'an and Madyamaka Buddhism. For an interesting comparison of Derrida's *differance* and Nagarjuna's *sunyata*, see Robert Magliola's *Derrida on the Mend* (West Lafayette: Purdue University Press, 1984).

40. These and other terms like them occur constantly in Derrida's writing. They refer to the double bind of all language inasmuch as it desires to 'get it right'. We endlessly inscribe and reinscribe, iterate and reiterate, to no avail. Words lead inevitably to more words with no progress ever being made towards the final word.

41. Again it is Faucault who has done the best job of pointing to the nature of some of these consequences. For both Derrida and Foucault, it is the recognition of the *de facto* situation over and above all *de jure* claims of legitimation. It would indeed be interesting to employ Faucault's insights in a theological reassessment of the tradition. One of the implications of the Heideggerian critique of metaphysics is that all philosophers and theologians must now turn their attention to the history of being (for Heidegger) or the history of difference (for Derrida).

42. One can even see this in the form of Ricoeur's writings. Ricoeur is possibly the finest example we have ever seen of the scholar-philosopher. The complaint most often made against his work is that he attempts to bring everyone into the conversation. He is in fact a bridge-builder who seeks to form communities of inquiry between disparate groups and scholars. *The Rule of Metaphor* is a prime example of this. In that work one is overwhelmed by the number of positions with which he deals. Derrida, on the other hand, is extremely nonconversational with the texts with which he deals. He 'teaches' the text about its inherent intertextuality rather than learning from it. For Ricoeur, community is the only chance we have; it is the locus of hope. For Derrida, community does not represent a locus of hope; rather, he would deconstruct the very meaning around which communities constitute themselves.

43. Let me point to a few attempts at such asystematic systematics. David Tracy's *Analogical Imagination: Christian Theology and the Age of Pluralism* (New York: Crossroads, 1981) is his so-called 'systematic' volume. Even a cursory reading will make evident its very unsystematic nature. Tracy's hermeneutic pluralism is heavily influenced by Ricoeur and, for him at least, marks the end of theologies that build systems.

44. Let me point out one more time the importance of the work of Michel Foucault as a resource not only for theology but for religious studies in general.

45. The terms are drawn from an article by Ricoeur entitled "Manifestation and Proclamation" (*Journal of the Blaisdell Institute*, Winter, 1978, 13–35). For a more complete idea of the importance of these distinctions for religious discourse, see Tracy's *Analogical Imagination*, pp. 193–229; also my own article entitled "Creation and Cosmos: The Symbolics of Proclamation and Participation" in *Cosmology and Theology*, edited by David Tracy and Nicholas Lash (New York: Winston Press, 1983).

46. The literature beginning to confront the 'other religions' is growing. Many see it as *the* great theological issue of the future.

47. This can be seen not only by the increasing number of practical theologies on the scene but by the type of theologian who is turning to praxis. These latter include people who have been previously concerned with the more theoretical aspects of theology such as David Tracy and John Cobb. In addition, it is heralded by the growing importance of both political and liberation theology.

48. The term atheology is drawn from Mark C. Taylor's *Erring: A Postmodern a/theology* (Chicago: University of Chicago Press, 1984). See also his *Deconstructing Theology* (Chicago: Scholars Press, 1982), and a collection of essays by Thomas Altizer, Max Myers, Carl Raschke, Robert Scharlemann, Mark C. Taylor, and Charles Winquist entitled *Deconstruction and Theology* (New York: Crossroads, 1982).

49. It is this moment of negation that is inherent to the approaching of theology as part of the event of history within which it is constituted. Theology in the postmodern reality is a decentered theology. For an example of this, see D. G. Leahy, *Novitas Mundi* (New York: New York University Press, 1980).

50. Here I am referring to the political and liberation theologies that rhetorically function to disrupt all theological and institutional formulations issuing from the centers of culture. I can point to the work of Johannes Baptiste Metz, Gustavo Gutierrez, Juan Luis Segundo, Mathew Lamb, Charles Davis, and Rebecca Chopp, to name but a few who are contributing to this important body of theological literature.

51. Here I would also like to point out the work of the Jewish Holocaust writers such as Emile Fackenheim, Elie Wiesel, Arthur Cohen, and Susan Shapiro as important and disruptive voices for contemporary theology. They raise the issues of theodicy and the presence of God in a radically new voice, which is crucial for Christian and Jew alike.

52. I have not addressed the religious contexts out of which Ricoeur and Derrida work. Ricoeur's Calvinist background is clearly reflected in his rhetoric, as is the post-Holocaust Jewish background for Derrida.

Index

DATE DUE

OC 25 '92			